Europe in a Wider World, 1350–1650

Europe in a Wider World

1350–1650

Robin W. Winks
Yale University

Lee Palmer Wandel
University of Wisconsin–Madison

New York   Oxford
OXFORD UNIVERSITY PRESS
2003

Oxford University Press

Oxford   New York
Auckland   Bangkok   Buenos Aires   Cape Town   Chennai
Dar es Salaam   Delhi   Hong Kong   Istanbul   Karachi   Kolkata
Kuala Lumpur   Madrid   Melbourne   Mexico City   Mumbai
Nairobi   São Paulo   Shanghai   Taipei   Tokyo   Toronto

Published by Oxford University Press, Inc.
198 Madison Avenue, New York, New York, 10016
http://www.oup-usa.org

Oxford is a registered trademark of Oxford University Press

Library of Congress Cataloging-in-Publication Data
Winks, Robin W.
   Europe in a wider world, 1350–1650/Robin W. Winks, Lee Palmer Wandel.
   p. cm.
   Includes bibliographical references.
   ISBN 978-0-19-515447-4; 978-0-19-515448-1 (pbk.)
   1. Europe—Church history—600-1500. 2. Crusades. 3. Civilization, Medieval. 4.
Europe—History—1492-1648. 5. Renaissance. 6. Discoveries in geography. 7.
Reformation. 8. Russia—History—To 1533. I. Wandel, Lee Palmer. II. Title.

D116.W56 2003
940.2—dc21   2002034633

Printed in the United States of America
on acid-free paper

Contents

Maps

Preface

The Value of History

History is a series of arguments to be debated, not a body of data to be recorded or a set of facts to be memorized. Thus controversy in historical interpretation—over what an event actually means, over what really happened at an occurrence called "an event," over how best to generalize about the event—is at the heart of its value. Of course history teaches us about ourselves. Of course it teaches us to understand and to entertain a proper respect for our collective past. Of course it transmits to us specific skills—how to ask questions, how to seek out answers, how to think logically, cogently, lucidly, purposefully. Of course it is, or ought to be, a pleasure. But we also discover something fundamental about a people in what they choose to argue over in their past. When a society suppresses portions of its past record, that society (or its leadership) tells us something about itself. When a society seeks to alter how the record is presented, well-proven facts notwithstanding, we learn how history can be distorted to political ends.

Who controls history, and how it is written, controls the past, and who controls the past controls the present. Those who would close off historical controversy with the argument either that we know all that we need to know about a subject, or that what we know is so irrefutably correct that anyone who attacks the conventional wisdom about the subject must have destructive purposes in mind, are in the end intent upon destroying the very value of history itself—that value being that history teaches us to argue productively with each other.

Obviously, then, history is a social necessity. It gives us our identity. It helps us to find our bearings in an ever more complex present, providing us with a navigator's chart by which we may to some degree orient ourselves. When we ask who we are, and how it is that we are so, we learn skepticism and acquire the beginnings of critical judgment. Along with a sense of narrative, history also provides us with tools for explanation and analysis. It helps us to find the particular example, to see the uniqueness in a past age or past event, while also helping us to see how the particular and the unique contribute to the general. History thus shows us humanity at work and play, in society, changing through time. By letting us experience other lifestyles, history shows us the values of both subjectivity and objectivity—those twin conditions of our individual view of the world in which we live, conditions between which we constantly, and usually almost without knowing it, move. Thus, history is both a form of truth and a matter of opinion, and the close study of history should help us to distinguish between the two. It is important to make such distinctions, for as Sir Walter Raleigh wrote, "It is not truth but opinion that can travel the world without a passport." Far too often what we read, see, and hear and believe to be the truth—in our newspapers, on our television sets, from our friends—is opinion, not fact.

History is an activity. That activity asks specific questions as a means of arriving at general questions. A textbook such as this is concerned overwhelmingly with general questions, even though at times it must ask specific questions or present specific facts as a means of stalking the general. The great philosopher Karl Jaspers once remarked, "Who I am and where I belong, I first learned to know from the mirror of history." It is this mirror that any honest book must reflect.

To speak of "civilization" (of which this book is a history) is at once to plunge into controversy, so that our very first words illustrate why some people are so fearful of the study of history. To speak of "Western civilization" is even more restrictive, too limited in the eyes of some historians. Yet if we are to understand history as a process, we must approach it through a sense of place: our continuity, our standards, our process. Still, we must recognize an inherent bias in such a term as "Western civilization," indeed two inherent biases: first, that we know what it means to be "civilized"and have attained that stature; and second, that the West as a whole is a single unitary civilization. This second bias is made plain when we recognize that most scholars and virtually all college courses refer not to "Eastern civilization" but to "the civilizations of the East"—a terminology that suggests that while the West is a unity, the East is not. These are conventional phrases, buried in Western perception of reality, just as our common geographical references show a Western bias. The Near East or the Far East are, after all, "near" or "far" only in reference to a geographical location focused on western Europe. The Japanese do not refer to London as being in the far West, or Los Angeles as being in the far East, although both references would be correct if they saw the world as though they stood at its center. Although this text will accept these conventional phrases, precisely because they are traditionally embedded in our Western languages, one of the uses of history—and of the writing of a book such as this one—is to alert us to the biases buried in our language, even when necessity requires that we continue to use its conventional forms of shorthand.

But if we are to speak of civilization, we must have, at the outset, some definition of what we mean by "being civilized." Hundreds of books have been written on this subject. The average person often means only that others, the "noncivilized," speak a different language and practice alien customs. The Chinese customarily referred to all foreigners as barbarians, and the ancient Greeks spoke of those who could not communicate in Greek as *bar-bar*—those who do not speak our tongue. Yet today the ability to communicate in more than one language is one hallmark of a "civilized" person. Thus definitions of civilization, at least as used by those who think little about the meaning of their words, obviously change.

For our purposes, however, we must have a somewhat more exacting definition of the term, since it guides and shapes any book that attempts to cover the entire sweep of Western history. Anthropologists, sociologists, historians, and others may reasonably differ as to whether, for example, there is a separate American civilization that stands apart from, say, a British or Italian civilization, or whether these civilizations are simply particular variants on one larger entity, with only that larger entity—the West—entitled to be called "a civilization." Such an argument is of no major importance here, although it is instructive that it should occur. Rather, what is needed is a definition sufficiently clear to be used throughout the narrative and analysis to follow. This working definition, therefore, will hold that "civilization" involves the presence of several (although not necessarily all) of the following conditions within a society or group of interdependent societies:

1. There will be some form of government by which people administer to their political needs and responsibilities.
2. There will be some development of urban society, that is, of city life, so that the culture is not nomadic, dispersed, and thus unable to leave significant and surviving physical remnants of its presence.
3. Human beings will have become toolmakers, able through the use of metals to transform, however modestly, their physical environment, and thus their social and economic environment as well.
4. Some degree of specialization of function will have begun, usually at the workplace, so that pride, place, and purpose work together as cohesive elements in the society.
5. Social classes will have emerged, whether antagonistic to or sustaining of one another.
6. A form of literacy will have developed, so that group may communicate with group and, more important, generation with generation in writing.
7. There will be a concept of leisure time—that life is not solely for the workplace, or for the assigned class function or specialization—so that, for example, art may develop beyond (although not excluding) mere decoration and sports beyond mere competition.
8. There will be a concept of a higher being, although not necessarily through organized religion, by which a people may take themselves outside themselves to explain events and find purpose.
9. There will be a concept of time, by which the society links itself to a past and to the presumption of a future.
10. There will have developed a faculty for criticism. This faculty need not be the rationalism of the West, or intuition, or any specific religious or political mechanism, but it must exist, so that the society may contemplate change from within, rather than awaiting attack (and possible destruction) from without.

A common Western bias is to measure "progress" through technological change and to suggest that societies that show (at least until quite recently in historical time) little dramatic technological change are not civilized. In truth, neither a written record nor dramatic technological changes are essential to being civilized, although both are no doubt present in societies we would call civilized. Perhaps, as we study history, we ought to remember all three of the elements inherent in historical action as recorded by the English critic John Ruskin: "Great nations write their autobiographies in three manuscripts, the book of their deeds, the book of their words, and the book of their art."

The issue here is not whether we "learn from the past." Most often we do not, at least at the simple-minded level; we do not, as a nation, decide upon a course of action in diplomacy, for example, simply because a somewhat similar course in the past worked. We are wise enough to know that circumstances alter cases and that new knowledge brings new duties. Of course individuals "learn from the past"; the victim of a mugging takes precautions in the future. To dignify such an experience as "a lesson of history," however, is to turn mere individual growth from child into adult into history when, at most, such growth is a personal experience in biography.

We also sometimes learn the "wrong lessons" from history. Virtually anyone who wishes to argue passionately for a specific course of future action can find a lesson from the past that will convince the gullible that history repeats itself and therefore that the past is a map to the future. No serious historian argues this, however. General patterns may, and sometimes do, repeat themselves, but specific chains of events do not. Unlike those subjects that operate at the very highest level of generalization (political science, theology, science), history simply does not believe in ironclad laws. But history is not solely a series of unrelated events. There are general patterns, clusters of causes, intermediate levels of generalization that prove true. Thus, history works at a level uncomfortable to many: above the specific, below the absolute.

If complex problems never present themselves twice in the same or even in recognizably similar form—if, to borrow a frequent image from the military world, generals always prepare for the last war instead of the next one—then does the study of history offer society any help in solving its problems? The answer surely is yes—but only in a limited way. History offers a rich collection of clinical reports on human behavior in various situations—individual and collective, political, economic, military, social, cultural—that tell us in detail how the human race has conducted its affairs and that suggest ways of handling similar problems in the present. President Harry S. Truman's secretary of state, a former chief of staff, General George Marshall, once remarked that nobody could think about the problems of the 1950s who had not reflected upon the fall of Athens in the fifth century B.C. He was referring to the extraordinary history of the war between Athens and Sparta written just after it was over by Thucydides, an Athenian who fought in the war. There were no nuclear weapons, no telecommunications, no guns or gunpowder in the fifth century B.C., and the logistics of war were altogether primitive, yet twenty-three hundred years later one of the most distinguished leaders of

American military and political affairs found Thucydides indispensable to his thinking.

History, then, can only approximate the range of human behavior, with some indication of its extremes and averages. It can, although not perfectly, show how and within what limits human behavior changes. This last point is especially important for the social scientist, the economist, the sociologist, the executive, the journalist, or the diplomat. History provides materials that even an inspiring leader—a prophet, a reformer, a politician—would do well to master before seeking to lead us into new ways. For it can tell us something about what human material can and cannot stand, just as science and technology can tell engineers what stresses metals can tolerate. History can provide an awareness of the depth of time and space that should check the optimism and the overconfidence of the reformer. For example, we may wish to protect the environment in which we live—to eliminate acid rain, to cleanse our rivers, to protect our wildlife, to preserve our majestic natural scenery. History may show us that most peoples have failed to do so and may provide us with some guidance on how to avoid the mistakes of the past. But history will also show that there are substantial differences of public and private opinion over how best to protect our environment, that there are many people who do not believe such protection is necessary, or that there are people who accept the need for protection but are equally convinced that lower levels of protection must be traded off for higher levels of productivity from our natural resources. History can provide the setting by which we may understand differing opinions, but recourse to history will not get the legislation passed, make the angry happy, or make the future clean and safe. History will not define river pollution, although it can provide us with statistics from the past for comparative measurement. The definition will arise from the politics of today and our judgments about tomorrow. History is for the long and at times for the intermediate run, but seldom for the short run.

So if we are willing to accept a "relevance" that is more difficult to see at first than the immediate applicability of science and more remote than direct action, we will have to admit that history is "relevant." It may not actually build the highway or clear the slum, but it can give enormous help to those who wish to do so. And failure to take it into account may lead to failure in the sphere of action.

But history is also fun, at least for those who enjoy giving their curiosity free reign. Whether it is historical gossip we prefer (how many lovers did Catherine the Great of Russia actually take in a given year, and how much political influence did their activity in the imperial bedroom give them?), the details of historical investigation (how does it happen that the actual treasures found in a buried Viking ship correspond to those described in an Anglo-Saxon poetic account of a ship-burial?), more complex questions of cause-and-effect (how influential have the writings of revolutionary intellectuals been upon the course of actual revolutions?), the relationships between politics and economics (how far does the rise and decline of Spanish power in modern times depend upon the supply of gold and silver from New World colonies?), or cultural problems (why did western Europe choose to revive classical Greek and Roman art and literature instead of turning to some altogether new experiment?), those who enjoy history will read almost greedily to discover what they want to know. Having discovered it, they may want to know how we know what we have learned and may want to turn to those sources closest in time to the persons and questions concerned—to the original words of the participants. To read about Socrates, Columbus, or Churchill is fun; to read their own words, to visit with them as it were, is even more so. To see them in context is important; to see how we have taken their thoughts and woven them to purposes of our own is at least equally important. Readers will find the path across the mine-studded fields of history helped just a little by extracts from these voices—voices of the past but also of the present. They can also be helped by chronologies, bibliographies, pictures, maps—devices through which historians share their sense of fun and immediacy with a reader.

In the end, to know the past is to know ourselves—not entirely, not enough, but a little better. History can help us to achieve some grace and elegance of action, some cogency and completion of thought, some harmony and tolerance in human relationships. Most of all, history can give us a sense of excitement, a personal zest for watching and perhaps participating in the events around us that will, one day, be history too.

History is a narrative, a story; history is concerned foremost with major themes, even as it recognizes the significance of many fascinating digressions. Because history is largely about how and why people behave as they do, it is also about patterns of thought and belief. Ultimately, history is about what people believe to be true. To this extent, virtually all history is intellectual history, for the perceived meaning of a specific treaty, battle, or scientific discovery lies in what those involved in it and those who came after thought was most significant about it. History makes it clear that we may die, as we may live, as a result of what someone believed to be quite true in the relatively remote past.

We cannot each be our own historian. In everyday life we may reconstruct our personal past, acting as detectives for our motivations and attitudes. But formal history is a much more rigorous study. History may give us some very small capacity to predict the future. More certainly, it should help us arrange the causes for given events into meaningful patterns. History also should help us to be tolerant of the historical views of others, even as it helps to shape our own convictions. History must help us sort out the important from the less important, the relevant from the irrelevant, so that we do not fall prey to those who propose simple-minded solutions to vastly complex human problems. We must not yield to the temptation to blame one group or individual for our problems, and yet we must not fail to defend our convictions with vigor.

To recognize, indeed to celebrate, the value of all civilizations is essential to the civilized life itself. To understand that we see all civilizations through the prism of our specific historical past—for which we feel affection, in which we may feel comfortable and secure, and by which we interpret all else that we encounter—is simply to recognize that we too are the products of history. That is why we must study history and ask our own questions in our own way. For if we ask no questions of our past, there may be no questions to ask of our future.

Robin W. Winks

ONE

The Late Middle Ages in Eastern Europe

Introduction

"History" does not exist apart from us—in the telling of it, we reveal our own sensibilities, orientations, concerns, questions. In part, we simply do not have the sources to recover "as it really was," in its detail, its specificity, or its complexity. Historians of necessity work from fragments of information—we never have "complete" or exhaustive data—and the further one goes into the past, the less data there are. Wars, fires, and theft have depleted collections. Far more important, however, the questions we ask of the past are very much anchored in our present lives, our own experiences. Those collections were never designed to provide all the information we might seek to have about a past society or culture. Neither the librarians nor the original authors and compilers knew what questions we would be asking. Thus, when historians turn to the past with questions such as "What was the role of women?" we may encounter individual women, such as Marguerite de Navarre, decrying their gendered definition of place in society, but Marguerite's contemporaries did not organize their knowledge according to that question. The relationship between our sources and our curiosities is a dialogue with silences, not a fulsome conversation: We may ask and they do not answer, or we may fail to hear the nuances in their answers.

Perhaps no period better demonstrates how vulnerable to the present the past can be than does 1350–1650. In the nineteenth century, different European national cultures looked to different aspects of the period for their own "origins": "the Italian Renaissance," "the French Renaissance," "the German Reformation," "the English Renaissance." Each saw it as a period of dramatic change, in which a common medieval culture, of feudalism and universal Christendom, was left behind as something "modern" emerged. Nineteenth-century European historians looked to "Renaissance monarchs" for the beginnings of a bureaucratically rationalized "state," such as they themselves experienced, with centralized administrations and abstract notions of "power" and "legitimacy." In a time of dynasties and personal rule, they searched for bureaucracies and bureaucrats. The French and English monarchs were viewed as "successful," even as the Habsburgs in Spain and the Empire became "failures." So, too, European Lutherans, such as Leopold von Ranke and Max Weber, situated the "origins" of "Protestantism" not in the early church, but in the sixteenth century, precisely at Martin Luther's call for reform. In keeping with this particular conception of Protestantism, as originating in the sixteenth century, many historians treated Catholicism as a timeless religion, existing from the earliest church into the nineteenth century. Protestantism, then, became the "modern" form of Christianity, according to Max Weber, the forerunner of nineteenth-century liberalism and capitalism, while Catholicism was labeled "traditional" and "conservative."

The very notion of "origins" is itself a particular construct, largely of the nineteenth century, a time when Darwin posited the "origin" of the species, with its linear conception of time and its particular linkages of diverse flora and fauna. That conceptualization of history seeks in a more "primitive" form something that is known in the present. Equally troubling, it tends to ignore all that cannot be found in the present. States have sought to locate their own "origins" in the activities of monarchs who could not have imagined the modern nation-state, so alien from their own resources and notions of "power" and "law" as it is. Modern American churches have sought their "origins" in Europe, most often England, in a time and place utterly remote from them and their conceptualizations of "individual rights" and "justice." Both views come to the past with modern orientations, modern values, modern concerns.

So, too, different groups have been drawn to different dimensions of the period 1350–1650. The study of the Italian Renaissance received an extraordinary boost in the 1930s when European scholars, fleeing Nazism, brought with them to the United States a lifelong devotion to the "Renaissance." In their study of the period, they focused on "humanists" and found in them the beginnings of a "secularism" that would lead to a cosmopolitan and learned toleration they sought in their own world. That sense of the Renaissance, as a time of secularism and humanism, resonated with particular power in a country defining its own "civilization" in college curricula and high school requirements. Seventy years later, it continues to shape the curriculum of hundreds of American universities, in which the "the Renaissance" is taught separately from "the Reformation," even as particular figures such as Lorenzo Valla and Erasmus figure in both courses.

The search for "origins" has separated men who were in correspondence with one another, severing delicate linkages of influence and conversation. So, too, it effectively silences affinities, shared orientations, that confound our modern perceptions of individual thinkers, for example, the resonances between Galileo's and Calvin's discussions of nature. Politically, it treats separately those Italian city-states from the single most powerful ruler in sixteenth-century Europe, who did indeed exert his power over them, forcing out regimes and plundering their wealth. The Medici were very much aware of the Habsburg Holy Roman Emperor Charles V: In 1530, he appointed Alessandro de' Medici hereditary rule.

At least "Renaissance" and "Reformation," as terms, have their origins in fourteenth-, fifteenth-, and sixteenth-century European self-perceptions. The most recent term adopted by American universities and now spreading to European universities, "early modern Europe," is entirely a construct of the modern age. What is "modern"? For a fifteenth-century Hollander, "modern" would have been something quite different, technically referring to a particular group of Christians who were known as "the Modern Devotion," or, in the Latin, the language of all learned Europeans, the "devotio moderna." "Modern" for twenty-first-century university students comprises a technology unimaginable even in 1650, a global economy sixteenth-century Europeans were seeking to realize, and a sense of the world so fundamentally shaped by the totalitarianisms of the twentieth century that even the nineteenth century can be called "the world we have lost."

In its chapter divisions, this volume acknowledges how deeply those divisions—Renaissance, Reformation, Seventeenth Century—have shaped how the history of the period 1350–1650 is taught. The volume also seeks, however, to mitigate those divisions. First, it seeks to restore interconnections, for example, of biblical scholarship between "Renaissance humanists" and "Reformation theologians," or between classical philology and science—interconnections, in other words, of time and place that these constructions sever. Second, it views the political landscape not of one or another single state, but of *Europe*, as a geographic entity, with the many different diplomatic and military exchanges. Most importantly, perhaps, this volume seeks to redress one imbalance in particular also generated by those searches for "origins." Those earlier constructions, so much driven by nineteenth-century nationalism, all tended to treat Europe in isolation from the world it so dramatically encountered in precisely this period. This volume, therefore, opens not with "the Renaissance," in keeping with traditional constructions, but with the world that made possible the "Renaissance," that of the Crusades and the Turks. The Crusades shaped European self-perceptions for three hundred years: The *hidalgos* in Spain saw themselves as carrying out a Cruzada, or Crusade, first against the Muslims and Jews within the Iberian peninsula, then against the Aztec and Incan empires. The "Renaissance" would not have been possible without the Ottoman Turks, whose conquest of Constantinople drove scholars of classical Greek to flee westward with their libraries, bringing Plato and Aristotle's complete works to the Latin West. The Turks, moreover, far more than the Americas, preoccupied Luther and Charles V.

To open a volume on the period 1350–1650 with the Crusader states and the Ottoman Turks is to shift the perspective from a Europe looking out at the world to a Europe situated within a world it did not yet dominate. The Muslims or "Moors" in Crusader romances, Arabs, and Turks each terrorized "Europe" in turn. Islam expanded at lightning speed in the seventh and eighth centuries, conquering Europe to the Pyrenees. Those Muslims spoke Arabic, carrying with them into the Iberian peninsula the riches of Arab medicine, mathematics, and philosophy. The Muslims who captured Constan-

The Written Record

POPE URBAN AT CLERMONT

Pope Urban proclaimed the First Crusade with these words:

The Turks, a race of Persians, who have penetrated within the boundaries of Romania even to the Mediterranean to that point which they call the Arm of Saint George, in occupying more and more of the lands of the Christians, have overcome them, have overthrown churches, and have laid waste God's kingdom. If you permit this supinely for very long, God's faithful ones will be still further subjected. . . .

I speak to those present, I send word to those not here; moreover, Christ commands it. Remission of sins will be granted for those going thither, if they end a shackled life either on land or in crossing the sea, or in struggling against the heathen. I, being vested with that gift from God, grant this to those who go.

O what a shame, if a people, so despised, degenerate, and enslaved by demons would thus overcome a people endowed with the trust of almighty God, and shining in the name of Christ! O how many evils will be imputed to you by the Lord Himself, if you do not help those who, like you, profess Christianity!

Let those who are accustomed to wage private wars wastefully even against Believers, go forth against the Infidels in a battle worthy to be undertaken now and to be finished in victory. Now, let those, who until recently existed as plunderers, be soldiers in Christ; now, let those, who formerly contended against brothers and relations, rightly fight barbarians; now, let those, who recently were hired for a few pieces of silver, win their eternal reward.

"The Chronicles of Fulcher of Chartres" trans. Martha E. McGinty, from *The First Crusade: The Chronicle of Fulcher of Chartres and Other Source Material*, ed. Edward Peters (Philadelphia: University of Philadelphia Press), pp. 30–33.

tinople in the fourteenth century and laid siege to Vienna in the sixteenth were Turkish. In the sixteenth century, the seemingly unstoppable advance of the Ottoman Turks would recall that earlier European experience of vulnerability and inferiority of military force. Throughout the period, from the seventh century to the seventeenth, Europe lived in the shadow of an expansionist Islamic Mediterranean.

The Crusades

In 1095, Pope Urban II called for a "Crusade," a military campaign to recover the Holy Land from the Infidels, the Muslims, whose expansion had already taken major sites of Christian history. In 1097, European knights and their retinues crossed Asia Minor, defeated the Turks in a battle at Dorylaeum, captured the Seljuk sultan's treasure, and opened the road to further advance. The Norman noble Baldwin left the main army and marched to Edessa. Here, after negotiations with the local Armenian rulers, he became count of Edessa—the lord of the first crusader state to be established (1098). After some seven months of siege, in 1098 the European crusaders conquered by treachery the great fortress city Antioch. Antioch became the second crusader state under the Norman Bohemond. The other crusaders then took Jerusalem by assault in July 1099. Godfrey of Bouillon was chosen "defender of the Holy Sepulcher." The third crusader state had been founded.

Venetian, Genoese, and Pisan fleets now assisted in the gradual conquest of the coastal cities. In 1109 the son of Raymond of Toulouse founded the fourth and last of the crusader states, centering around the seaport of Tripoli. The king of Jerusalem was the theoretical overlord of the other three states but was often unable to enforce his authority. The Byzantine emperors never relinquished the rights that had been secured to them by the oath that the crusaders had made to Alexius.

The holdings of the Westerners lay within a long narrow coastal strip extending from the Euphrates River to the borders of Egypt, more than five hundred miles long and seldom as much as fifty miles wide. Danger constantly threatened. The Westerners failed to take obvious measures for the common defense. The great lords built superb castles at strategic places but often fought with one another, sometimes in alliance with neighboring Muslims.

The Assizes of Jerusalem record the governmental practices of the crusader states. The great officers of the realm were the officers of the king's household: seneschal, constable, marshal, and the like. The high court of barons not only settled disputes but also acted as council of state for the king's business. The lords had rights of justice on their own fiefs. Police and civil cases were under the direction of *viscounts*, royal officers in the towns, and there were special commercial and maritime courts. Revenues were raised by customs dues, by monopolies on tanning and similar industries, by a poll tax on Muslims and Jews, and by a land tax on the native population. Yet money was scarce, and the kings raided Muslim caravans or married rich wives in an effort to bolster their shaky finances. Ecclesiastical organization was complex: The two Latin patriarchs of Jerusalem and Antioch each had a hierarchy of Roman Catholic archbishops and bishops subject to them, but Greek, Syrian, and Armenian churches continued to exist, each with its own clergy, in addition to the Muslim and Jewish faiths.

The Military Orders, 1119–1798

Early in their occupation of the eastern Mediterranean, the Westerners founded the military orders of knighthood. The first of these were the Templars, started about 1119 by a Burgundian knight who sympathized with the hardships of the Christian pilgrims. These knights took vows of poverty, chastity, and obedience and were given headquarters near the ruins of the

A fourteenth-century miniature illustrating a French account written in 1337 of the crusader assault on Jerusalem in 1099. Leading the assault is Godfrey of Bouillon; to the far left is Peter the Hermit.   (The Granger Collection)

Temple of Solomon—hence the name Templars. St. Bernard himself inspired their rule, based on the rules for his own Cistercians. A second order was attached to the ancient Hospital of St. John of Jerusalem and was therefore called the Hospitalers. Made up of knights, chaplains, and serving brothers under the command of a grand master, the two orders were the most effective fighting forces in the Holy Land. Each had a special uniform; the Templars wore red crosses on white, the Hospitalers white crosses on black. Later a third, purely German group became the order of the Teutonic Knights with headquarters at Acre; they wore black crosses on white.

The orders had fortresses and churches of their own in the Holy Land and villages from which they obtained produce. Moreover, Western monarchs endowed them richly with lands in Europe. They often allied themselves with Muslims and so completely forgot their original vows of poverty that they engaged in banking and large-scale financial operations. In the early fourteenth century the Templars were destroyed by Philip IV of France for political reasons. The Teutonic Knights transmitted some of their lands and much of their outlook to the modern state of Prussia. The Hospitalers moved first to Cyprus and then to Rhodes in the early fourteenth century; they were driven to Malta by the Turks in 1522 and continued there until Napoleon's seizure of the island in 1798.

The Muslim Reconquest and the Later Crusades, 1144–1291

It is a wonder that the crusader states lasted so long. It was not the castles or the military orders that preserved them as much as the disunion of their Muslim enemies. When the Muslims did achieve unity under a single powerful leader, the Christians suffered grave losses. Beginning in the late 1120s, Zangi, governor of Mosul on the Tigris, succeeded in unifying the local Muslim rulers of the region. In 1144 he took Edessa, first of the crusader cities to fall.

As an answer to the loss of Edessa, St. Bernard himself preached the so-called Second Crusade in Europe. He aroused enormous enthusiasm, and for the first time Western monarchs—King Louis VII of France and King Conrad III of Germany—came to the East. But the Second Crusade proved a shattering failure. As the German and French armies passed through Constantinople, relations with the Byzantines were worse than ever. It is quite likely that the emperor, Manuel I Comnenus (r. 1143–1180), mixed chalk with the flour that he sold them before he managed to get them across the Straits.

The Western armies were almost wiped out in Asia Minor. When the remnants reached the Holy Land, they found themselves in hopeless conflict with the local lords, who feared that the newcomers would take over the kingdom. The crusaders' failure to take Damascus in 1149 brought its own punishment. In 1154 Zangi's son, Nureddin, took it, and Muslim Syria was united against the Latins.

The next act of the Muslim reconquest was carried out in Egypt by a general of Nureddin's who was sent to assist one of the quarreling factions in Cairo. This general became vizier of Egypt and died in 1169, leaving his office to his nephew Saladin, who became the greatest Muslim leader of the Crusade period. A vigorous and successful general, Saladin brought the Muslim cities of Syria and Mesopotamia under his control and distributed them to faithful members of his own family. By 1183 his brother ruled Egypt, his sons ruled Damascus and Aleppo, and close relatives ruled all the other important centers. Internal decay in the kingdom of Jerusalem and a squabble over the throne gave Saladin his chance, and a violation of a truce by an unruly crusader lord gave him his excuse. In 1187 Jerusalem fell, and soon there was nothing of the kingdom left to the Christians except the port of Tyre and a few castles.

These events elicited the Third Crusade (1189–1192). The Holy Roman emperor, Frederick Barbarossa, led a German force through Byzantium, only to be drowned in Asia Minor (1190). Some of his troops, however, continued to Palestine. There they were joined by Philip Augustus of France and Richard I, the Lionhearted, of England, each at least as interested in thwarting the other as he was in furthering any common cause. The main operation of the Third Crusade was a long siege of the seaport of Acre, which was finally captured in 1191. Jerusalem itself could not be taken, but Saladin signed a treaty with Richard allowing Christians to visit the city freely.

When Saladin died in 1193, the Christians obtained a respite. Reinforcements from the West, however, had dwindled away to a small trickle. The failures in the East were partly balanced by successes in Spain, where, by the end of the thirteenth century, the Christians had restricted the Muslims to the kingdom of Granada in the southeastern corner of the peninsula; far to the northeast, the pagan Lithuanians and Slavs received the attention of the Teutonic Knights in the Baltic region.

Innocent III came to the papal throne in 1198 and called for a new Crusade, the Fourth. Several powerful lords responded. The Venetians agreed to furnish transportation and food and also to contribute fifty armed warships on condition that they would share equally in all future conquests. The doge (duke) of Venice, Enrico Dandolo (c. 1108–1205) agreed to forgive the debt temporarily if the crusaders would help him reconquer Zara, a town on the eastern side of the Adriatic that had revolted against Venetian domination. So the Fourth Crusade began with the sack and destruction of a Roman Catholic town in 1202. Angrily, the pope excommunicated the crusaders, who settled down to pass the winter in Zara before pressing on. Their primary worry was finance; the leaders had badly overestimated the number who would join the crusade and had committed themselves to a larger contract to which the Venetians intended to hold them.

During the winter the crusaders turned their attention to a new goal: Constantinople. The German king, Philip of Swabia, proposed that the massed army escort Alexius, a young prince with a strong claim to the Byzantine throne, to Constantinople and enthrone him in the place of a usurper. If successful, Alexius would finance the subsequent expedition. The idea had much to recommend it, for it would serve to pay off the debt, would restore the unity of Christendom by bringing Byzantium under its rightful and friendly heir, and would most likely vastly expand Venice's power. Most of the knights agreed to this plan.

In the spring of 1203 a greatly augmented crusader fleet, with enthusiastic Venetian support, attacked Constantinople. In the initial onslaught the attackers won a resounding naval victory, although the city held. A second attack on land and sea broke through the defenses, and Alexius III fled the city. The young Alexius was then crowned as Alexius IV. While he was away pursuing Alexius III, the city was badly damaged by the worst fire in its history, probably begun when a group of Franks set fire to a mosque in the Saracen quarter. Angry, Alexius IV declined to make the promised payment. Certain that he could neither bring peace with the increasingly impatient crusaders nor defeat them in battle, a group of senators, clergy, and the populace deposed Alexius IV.

In March 1204 the crusaders and Venetians agreed to seize the city a second time, to elect a Latin emperor who would receive a quarter of the empire and its booty, and to divide the other three quarters equally between Venetians and non-Venetians. The second siege ended in a second capture and a systematic three-day sack of Constantinople.

The pope himself criticized the outrages committed by the crusaders. What was destroyed in the libraries of the capital is untold. Despite general destruction, the Venetians salvaged much of great value and beauty, shipping it all back to their city. The booty included the four great bronze horses that had been a symbol of the city since Constantine, a host of sacred relics the Greek emperors had been collecting, and hundreds of works of Byzantine art. The crusaders now paid their debt in full to the Venetians.

The zeal that had driven men toward the Holy Land was thoroughly tainted by the Fourth Crusade. Perhaps most of all, it was diluted by the struggle between the papacy and its European opponents: first, the Albigensian heretics of southern France between 1208 and 1240; and second, the emperor Frederick II between 1220 and 1250. In these affairs the popes were offering those who would fight against a European and nominally Christian enemy the same indulgence they offered those who fought Muslims. All these developments brought disillusionment when combined with the spectacle of repeated military failure.

Perhaps the culmination of tragic futility was the so-called Children's Crusade in 1212, when throngs of French and German children went down to the Mediterranean, expecting that its waters would divide before them and open a path to the Holy Land along which they could march to a bloodless victory. When this failed to happen, several thousand pushed on to Marseilles and other seaports. There many were sold into slavery.

The rest was a history of short-term victory measured against long-term defeats. In the Fifth Crusade (1218–1221) the Christians attempted the conquest of Egypt and failed. Emperor Frederick II personally led the Sixth Crusade (1228–1229). No fighting was involved, partly because Frederick was too sophisticated to fight when he could get what he wanted by diplomacy. Speaking Arabic and long familiar with the Muslims from his experience in Sicily, he secured more for the Christians by negotiation than any military commander since the First Crusade had secured by war. In 1229 he signed a treaty with Saladin's nephew that restored Jerusalem to the Latins. Bethlehem and Nazareth were also handed over, and a ten-year truce was agreed upon. But the Egyptian ruler now took into his service several thousand Turks from central Asia who took Jerusalem in 1244. Jerusalem remained in Muslim hands until 1917.

Now St. Louis, king of France, launched the first of his two Crusades, sometimes called the Seventh (1248–1254), aimed at Egypt. Louis himself was taken prisoner and had to pay a very heavy ransom. In 1250 the household troops of the Egyptian sultan (called Mamluks, or slaves) took power into their own hands in Egypt. Soon after, the Mongols, fresh from their victories in Asia, invaded Syria and were defeated in battle by the Mamluk general

Baibars, who immediately made himself sultan. Baibars reduced the number of strongholds remaining to the crusaders, taking Antioch in 1268. He delayed his advance in fear of a new Crusade (the Eighth) by St. Louis in 1270, then resumed it when the king landed in Tunis and died there. The Muslims took Tripoli in 1289 and Acre in 1291.

The century-long, partly secular sequel to the first hundred years of more pious crusading fervor was now over, and the Christian settlements were wiped out. They were not deeply mourned even in western Europe, from which so much blood and treasure had flowed for their establishment and defense. They had proved divisive, had distracted attention from the building of states in Europe, and had produced little of spiritual value.

There would be a final burst of crusading. Between 1305 and 1378, the Roman Catholic Church sought not so much to recover Palestine as to protect its lands against non-Christian peoples. Crusaders fought from Alexandria to the Canary Islands, from Livonia to Greece, in defense of the Faith, while the papacy devoted enormous effort to planning, taxing, and campaigning, especially through naval warfare. The Church also used economic sanctions against those who threatened it. Still, except for the capture of Smyrna and, for a time, Alexandria, these last crusades achieved little.

The Impact of the Crusades on the West

The number of crusaders and pilgrims who went to the East and returned home was large. From Marseilles alone the ships of the Hospitalers and the Templars carried six thousand pilgrims a year. Ideas flowed back and forth with the people. Arabic words in Western languages testify to the concepts and products borrowed by the Westerners in commerce: *bazaar, tariff,* the French *douane* and the Italian *dogana* (a customs house, from the Arabic *diwan,* the sofa on which the officials sat); in foods; *sugar, saffron, rice, lemon, apricot, shallot, scallion, melon,* and *pistachio;* in manufactured goods: *cotton, muslin, damask* (from Damascus), and many others.

The new products stimulated the growing commercial life of the West. Venice and Genoa, the ports from which much of the produce of the East was funneled into Europe, prospered exceedingly. So did the cities of Flanders, whose own manufacture of woolen goods was stimulated by the availability of Eastern luxuries for trade. Letters of credit and bills of exchange became a necessity in an ever more complex commercial and financial system. Italian banking houses sprang up with offices in the Holy Land.

Thus the Crusades contributed to the introduction of new products and helped create the conditions that led to modern methods of finance. They probably also stimulated the movement of population from the country to the towns, which in turn permitted the smaller rural population to live better on their lands and perhaps to improve their methods of agriculture.

Some believe that the Crusades helped to weaken and impoverish the feudal nobility and therefore benefited the monarchies. Certainly, kings could tax directly for the first time as a result of the need to raise money for expe-

---

The Written Record

THE SACK OF CONSTANTINOPLE

A contemporary Greek historian who was an eyewitness to the sack of Constantinople in 1204 described atrocities of which he had thought human beings incapable:

How shall I begin to tell of the deeds done by these wicked men? They trampled the images underfoot instead of adoring them. They threw the relics of the martyrs into filth. They spilt the body and blood of Christ on the ground, and threw it about. . . .

They broke into bits the sacred altar of Santa Sophia, and distributed it among the soldiers. When the sacred vessels and the silver and gold ornaments were to be carried off, they brought up mules and saddle horses inside the church itself and up to the sanctuary. When some of these slipped on the marble pavement and fell, they stabbed them where they lay and polluted the sacred pavement with blood and ordure. A harlot sat in the Patriarch's seat, singing an obscene song and dancing lewdly. They drew their daggers against anyone who opposed them at all. In the alleys and streets, in the temple, one could hear the weeping and lamentations, the groans of men and the shrieks of women, wounds, rape, captivity, separation of families. Nobles wandered about in shame, the aged in tears, the rich in poverty.

Nicetas Choniates, *Historia*, ed. Immanuel Bekker (Bonn, 1835), pp. 757 ff. Condensed; our translation.

---

ditions to the Holy Land. The papacy was strengthened by sponsoring so vast an international movement. Yet this short-term gain may have been outweighed by a long-term loss. The religious motive was diluted more and more by worldly considerations. The spectacle of churchmen behaving like laymen, the misuse of the crusading indulgences, and the cumulative effect of failure and incompetence contributed to a disillusionment with the original concept of the Crusades. Moreover, the discovery that all Muslims were not savage beasts, that profit lay in trade with them, and that coexistence was possible must have broadened the outlook of those who made the discovery.

The Fall of Byzantium, 1081–1453

During its last 372 years, the fate of the Byzantine Empire increasingly depended upon western Europe. The flood of crusaders first made the Byzantines uneasy and ultimately destroyed them. From 1204 to 1261, while the Byzantine government was in exile from its own capital, its chief aim was to drive out the hated Latins. But even after the Byzantine leaders had recaptured Constantinople in 1261, they still could not shake off the West.

The Western attitude is revealed in the crisp words of the great fourteenth-century Italian poet Petrarch:

> I do not know whether it is worse to have lost Jerusalem or to possess Byzantium. In the former Christ is not recognized; in the latter he is neglected while being worshipped. The Turks are enemies but the schismatic Greeks are worse than enemies. The Turks openly attack our Empire [the Empire of the West]; the Greeks say that the Roman Church is their mother, to whom they are devoted sons; but they do not receive the commands of the Roman pontiff. The Turks hate us because they fear us less. The Greeks both hate and fear us deep in their bellies.*

The Greek attitude is revealed by a fifteenth-century Greek churchman who said that he would rather see the turban of the Turk in Constantinople than the red hat of a cardinal. Those who shared this opinion got their wish in 1453. One of the great ironies of history is that the fate of Eastern Christendom was settled by Western Christendom, and that the Muslim rule that the Latin West had sought to roll back was vastly extended by Western Christians.

Byzantine Decline, 1081–1204

The drama of Byzantium's last centuries was played out to the accompaniment of internal decay. Alexius I Comnenus had captured the throne in 1081. Thereafter the imperial accumulation of land seems to have gone unchecked. With the weakening of the central government and the emergence of the local magnates, a form of feudalism became the characteristic way of life, as free peasants increasingly were forced by economic decline to sell their lands to the great landowners and sink into serfdom. Severe depopulation of the countryside followed, while in the cities imperial police officials or local garrison commanders acted as virtually independent rulers.

Economic ruin and social misery mounted steadily in the twelfth century. The tax collectors demanded food and lodging, presents and bribes. They would seize cattle on the pretext that they were needed for work on state projects, and then sell them back to the owners and keep the money for themselves. Irregular taxes for defense gave further chances to oppress the population. With the decline of the navy, piracy became a major problem. The coasts of Greece and the Aegean islands became nests of raiders, preying not only on merchant shipping but upon the population on shore.

In 1171 Emperor Manuel I Comnenus made a desperate effort to rid the capital of Venetian merchants by suddenly arresting all he could lay his hands on in one day; more than ten thousand were imprisoned. But the economic hold of Venice was too strong, and the emperor was soon forced to restore its privileges. In 1182 a passionate wave of anti-Latin feeling led to a savage massacre of thousands of Westerners living in Constantinople. In 1185

---

*From H. A. Gibbons, *Foundation of the Ottoman Empire* (New York: Century, 1916), p. 133.

the Normans of Sicily avenged the Latins by sacking Thessalonica. The last of the Comnenian dynasty, Andronicus I (r. 1182–1185), was tortured to death by the frantic citizens of Constantinople as the Norman forces approached the city walls. The weak dynasty of the Angeloi succeeded, and in 1204 Constantinople fell to the West.

The Latin Empire, 1204–1261

After the sack of Constantinople, the Latins elected Baldwin of Flanders as the first Latin emperor (1204–1205), and the title continued in his family during the fifty-seven years of Latin occupation. The Venetians chose the first Latin patriarch and kept a monopoly on that rich office. The territories of the Empire were divided on paper, since most of them had not yet been conquered. The Venetians secured the long sea route from Venice by claiming the best coastal towns and strategic islands. A hybrid state was created in which the emperor's council consisted half of his own barons and half of Venetian merchants. Although in theory the Latin emperors were the successors of Constantine and Justinian, in practice they never commanded the loyalty of the Greek population and could not make important decisions without the counsel of their barons.

In Asia Minor Greek refugees from Constantinople set up a state in Nicaea and constantly threatened to recapture Constantinople. Outnumbered, incompetent as diplomats, miserably poor after the treasures of Byzantium had been wasted, the Westerners could not maintain their empire. When the popes became deeply involved in their quarrel with the Western emperor Frederick II, the Latin Empire was doomed. In 1261 the Greeks of Nicaea seized Constantinople and reestablished the Byzantine Empire.

Meanwhile, however, the Latins had fanned out from Constantinople. Greece was divided into a series of feudal principalities. The Peloponnesus became the principality of Achaia, with twelve feudal baronies and many minor lordships. Thessalonica became the capital of a new kingdom, which, however, fell to the Greeks in 1224. In the Aegean a Venetian adventurer established the duchy of Naxos, and other barons, mostly Italian, founded their own tiny lordships among the islands. The Venetians held Crete. These feudal states lasted for varying periods, but most of them were wiped out during the Turkish conquest in the fifteenth century.

Despite its decline, Byzantium in the eleventh and twelfth centuries retained much vitality. Economic activity appears to have increased as government controls were relaxed. Literature, law, and scholarship flourished. Vernacular literature was popularized; heresy grew, and alien cultures were viewed with less suspicion. A class of professional intellectuals emerged, as did a new aristocracy. Such social changes did not enable Byzantium to retain its earlier sense of pride, however. Unlike the West, where provincial towns became centers of importance, Byzantine towns did not develop beyond an artisanal level. International trade was left to foreigners. Byzantium was clearly advancing far less rapidly, culturally and economically, than the West.

Byzantium after 1261

When the Greeks of Nicaea under Michael VIII Palaeologus (r. 1259–1282) recaptured Constantinople, they found it depopulated and badly damaged and the old territory of the Empire mostly in Latin hands. It was impossible for Michael to reconquer all of Greece or the islands, to push the frontier in Asia Minor east of the Seljuk capital of Konia, or to deal effectively with the Serbians in the Balkans. However, he staved off the threat posed to his Empire by Charles of Anjou, younger brother of St. Louis. Just as a new and powerful force seemed headed for Byzantium in 1282, a revolt known as the Sicilian Vespers forestalled invasion and Charles of Anjou's plans had to be abandoned.

So incompetent and frivolous were most of the successors of Michael VIII that they contributed materially to the decline of their own beleaguered Empire. Wars among rival claimants for the throne tore the Empire apart internally. Social unrest reappeared as Thessalonica was torn by civil strife. The value of the currency was allowed to decline. New controversy divided the clergy, already tormented by the choice between uniting with Rome or, it appeared, perishing.

From about 1330 a new movement was reviving monasticism throughout the whole of eastern Europe, a revival associated with *Hesychasm* (Greek *hesychia*, "quietude"). In the tenth century, monks of the Orthodox Eastern Church had founded at Mount Athos in northern Greece a remarkable monastery from which females, human or animal, were banned. Responsible directly to the patriarch of Constantinople, these monks preserved their independence, governing themselves and devoting their energies to self-sufficiency and to scholarship. From Mount Athos many monks founded other movements. One of these monks, St. Gregory of Sinai, set up a monastery in southeastern Bulgaria that emphasized the Hesychast goal: a mystical state of recollection and inner silence that would be achieved after man's victory over his passions. Only contemplative prayer could lead to God, though bodily exercises meant to aid spiritual concentration were also important.

In the early fourteenth century monastic churches within the walls of Constantinople were restored under the patronage of wealthy men. Byzantine churchmen took a renewed interest in scholarship, in the maintenance of libraries, and in the Greek heritage, preserving for future generations the knowledge of the past. Byzantine society recognized both the life of the world and the life of the spirit. Some monks emphasized Greek literature and philosophy, known as the "outer" wisdom, which prepared one for the truth; others, often illiterate, emphasized the "inner" knowledge that came from the "divine light" that illuminated the soul. Humans were sanctified through this divine light, through a direct experience that involved the body and the soul. Obviously such teachings posed grave problems for the traditional views of the Orthodox Church, and many commentators ridiculed the Hesychast movement. Nonetheless, the mystical movement initiated a renaissance of learning and spirituality in fourteenth-century Byzantium.

The Advance of the Ottoman Turks, 1354–1453

By the fourteenth century the Ottoman Turks had begun to press against the borders of Byzantine Asia Minor. Economic and political unrest led the discontented population of this region to prefer the Ottomans to the harsh and ineffectual Byzantine officials. Farmers willingly paid tribute to the Turks, and as time went on many of them were converted to Islam to avoid payment. They learned Turkish and taught the nomadic Turkish conquerors the arts of a settled agricultural life.

Having absorbed the Byzantine territories in Asia Minor, the Turks built a fleet and began raiding in the Sea of Marmora and the Aegean. In 1354 one of the rivals for the Byzantine throne allowed them to establish themselves in Europe. Soon they had occupied much of Thrace. In 1363 they moved their capital to Adrianople, well beyond the European side of the Straits. Constantinople was now surrounded by Turkish territory and could be reached from the West only by sea. To survive it all, the later emperors had to make humiliating arrangements with the Turkish rulers.

Although the Byzantine Empire lasted to 1453, its survival was no longer in its own hands. The Turks chose to attack much of the Balkan region first, conquering the Bulgarian and Serbian states in the 1370s and 1380s. A French and German "crusade" against the Turks was wiped out at Nicopolis on the Danube in 1396.

But further Turkish conquests were delayed for half a century when a new wave of Mongols under Timur the Lame (celebrated in literature as Tamerlane, c. 1336–1405) emerged from central Asia in 1402 and defeated the Ottoman armies at Ankara. Like most Mongol military efforts, this proved temporary, and the Ottoman armies and state recovered. In the 1420s and 1430s the Turks moved into Greece. The West, now thoroughly alarmed at the spread of Turkish power in Europe, tried to bolster the Byzantine defenses by proposing a union of the Eastern and Western churches in 1439 and by dispatching another "crusade," this time to Bulgaria in 1444. Both efforts proved futile.

With the accession of Muhammad II (also called Mehmed the Conqueror) to the Ottoman throne in 1451 (r. to 1481), the doom of Constantinople was sealed. New Turkish castles on the Bosporus prevented ships from delivering supplies to the city. In 1453 strong forces of troops and artillery were drawn up in siege array, and the Turks even dragged a fleet of small boats uphill on runners and slid them down the other side into the Golden Horn itself. The last emperor, Constantine XI (r. from 1448), died bravely defending the walls against the Turkish attack.

On May 29, 1453, with the walls breached and the emperor dead, the Turks took the city. Muhammad II gave thanks to Allah in Hagia Sophia; thenceforth, it was to be a mosque. Shortly thereafter, he installed a new Greek patriarch and proclaimed himself protector of the Christian Church. On the whole, during the centuries that followed the Orthodox Church accepted the sultans as the secular successors to the Byzantine emperors.

The Ottoman Empire, 1453–1699

Part of the Ottomans' inheritance no doubt came from their far-distant past in central Asia, when they had almost surely come under the influence of China and had lived like other nomads of the region. Their language, their capacity for war, and their rigid adherence to custom may go back to this early period. From the Persians and the Byzantines, the Turks seem to have derived their exaltation of the ruler, their tolerance of religious groups outside the state religion, and their practice of encouraging such groups to form independent, separate communities inside their state. From Islam, the Turks took the sacred law, the Arabic alphabet, and the Arabic vocabulary of religious, philosophical, and other abstract terms.

The Ottoman System

Until the sixteenth century, the Ottomans showed tolerance to their infidel subjects, permitting Christians and Jews to serve the state and allowing the patriarch of Constantinople and the Grand Rabbi to act as leaders of their own religious communities, or *millets.* The religious leader not only represented his people in their dealings with the Ottoman state but also had civil authority over them in matters that affected them alone. Non-Muslims paid a head tax and lived in comparative peace.

From 1280 to 1566 ten able sultans ruled the Ottomans. In theory, the sultan possessed the entire wealth of his dominions, and his object was to exploit it to the full. To do so he maintained an elaborate system of administrators whose lives and property belonged absolutely to him. To belong to the ruling class, a man had to be loyal to the sultan, a Muslim, and a true Ottoman—that is, he had to master the "Ottoman way" of speaking and behaving. Anyone who lacked one or more of these attributes was not a member of the ruling class but a subject (*raya*). Any raya could become an Ottoman by acquiring the necessary attributes. Beyond collecting, spending, and increasing the imperial revenues and defending and adding to the imperial possessions, the Ottomans had no duties.

The Ottoman ruling class included four subdivisions: the men of the emperor, the men of the sword, the men of the pen, and the sages. The first comprised an inner service, embracing the sultan himself and his wives, sons, servants, private purse, and palace attendants, including the entire harem. In addition, there was an outer service, including the grand viziers and the other highest officers of the state, those who directed all the other branches of the service. A grand vizier presided over the council of state, and if the sultan trusted him might exercise great influence; but the sultan, too, could depose or kill him.

In the early days of the Ottoman Empire, the Turkish princely families from Anatolia virtually monopolized both the inner and the outer services of this imperial class. But by the fourteenth century the sultans had learned to balance their influence by recruiting new talent from among their Christian subjects. Some entered the system as prisoners of war; some the sultan bought or received as presents. But most he obtained through the regular levying of a tribute of male children between the ages of ten and twenty that took place every four years. The recruits had to accept Islam, and so these recruits, all originally Christian, competed with the older Turkish aristocratic families for the honor of staffing the imperial class.

The men of the sword included all those connected with the Ottoman armies. Besides the usual irregular troops and garrison forces, these were the cavalrymen who predominated in early Ottoman history. They received fiefs of land in exchange for service and could administer these fiefs as they wished, collecting taxes from their tenants and keeping order and justice among them. With the introduction of gunpowder and the development of artillery and rifles, the Ottomans founded a special new corps to use these weapons, the *janissaries*. Most of the janissaries came from the recruits who were not selected for training for the imperial class. The janissaries lived in special barracks in the capital and enjoyed special privileges. They were both a source of strength and a constant potential danger to the state.

The men of the pen performed the other duties of government, striving to see that all land was tilled and that all trade was carried on as profitably as possible, so that the sultan might obtain his share in taxes. Once the money came in, these officials spent it on the necessary expenses of state, including salaries for troops and other employees. To keep an official honest and zealous, the Ottoman system often rewarded him by giving him in place of a salary a portion of the sultan's property as a kind of fief to exploit for himself. In the country every farm and village, in town every business and trade, in government every job thus became a kind of fief.

The sages (*ulema*) included all those connected with religion: the judges who applied Muslim law in the courts, the teachers in the schools, and the scholars of the Koran and the holy law (*Shariya*), the *muftis*. The muftis answered questions that arose from lawsuits. They applied the sacred law of Islam and usually gave short replies without explanation. The grand mufti in Istanbul whom the sultan himself consulted was known as *Sheikh-ul-Islam*, the ancient or elder of Islam, and outranked everyone except the grand vizier. Since he could speak the final word on the sacred law, he exercised a kind of check on the absolute power of the sultan himself. He alone could proclaim the beginning of war or denounce a sultan for transgressing the sacred law.

Ottoman Expansion and Retraction, to 1699

By the end of the 1460s most of the Balkan peninsula was under Turkish rule. Thus the core of the new Ottoman state was Asia Minor and the Balkans. From this core, before the death of Muhammad II in 1481, the Turks expanded across the Danube into modern Romania and seized the Genoese outposts in the Crimea. They also fought the Venetians and landed forces in Italy. The limits of their expansion were marked by the great Hungarian fortress of Belgrade and the island fortress of Rhodes in the Aegean, stronghold of the Hospitalers.

Sultan Muhammad II of Turkey, painted by Gentile Bellini (1429–1507). Muhammad ruled from 1451 to 1481; he is seen here shortly before his death. Most famous for painting Venetian ceremonial occasions with exceptional detail, Bellini lived in Constantinople from 1476 until 1481.   (National Gallery, London)

Sultan Selim I, the Grim (1512–1520), nearly doubled the territories of the Empire in Asia at the expense of the Persians and in Africa at the expense of Egypt, which was annexed in 1517. The sultan inherited the duty of protecting the Muslim holy cities of Mecca and Medina. He also assumed the title of Caliph. It is doubtful whether this alone greatly enhanced his prestige, since the title had for centuries been much abused. At one moment in his reign,

Selim contemplated a general massacre of all his Christian subjects; only the refusal of the Sheikh-ul-Islam to grant consent saved the Christians. This episode vividly illustrates the insecurity of Christian life under the Turks.

Suleiman I, the Magnificent (r. 1520–1566), resumed the advance into Europe. The Ottoman Empire thus became deeply involved in western European affairs. It participated in the wars between the Habsburgs and France and affected the Protestant Reformation in Germany by the threat of military invasion from the southeast. Suleiman took Belgrade in 1521 and Rhodes in 1522, thus removing the two chief obstacles to westward advance. In 1526 at Mohács in Hungary, he defeated the Christian armies, and the Turks entered Buda, the Hungarian capital on the middle Danube. In September 1529 Suleiman besieged Vienna but had to abandon the siege after two weeks. In the years that followed, Suleiman acquired Algeria, which remained an Ottoman vassal state. In Asia he defeated the Persians, annexed modern Iraq, including Baghdad, and secured an outlet on the Persian Gulf from which he fought naval wars against the Portuguese.

In 1536 a formal treaty was concluded between France and the Ottoman Empire. It permitted the French to buy and sell throughout the Turkish dominions on the same basis as any Turk. In Turkish territory, the French were to enjoy complete religious liberty and were also granted a protectorate over the Holy Places, the old aim of the Crusades. These "capitulations" contributed to the wealth and prestige of France and gave it a better position in the Ottoman Empire than that of any other European power. They also brought the Turks into the diplomatic world of western Europe.

After Suleiman the Ottoman system, already manifesting signs of weakness, deteriorated despite occasional successes. The Ottoman capture of Cyprus was preceded by the formation of a Western Holy League headed by the pope against the Turks. In 1571 the League won a great naval battle (Lepanto) off the Greek coast, destroying the Ottoman fleet. However, the Spanish and Venetians failed to follow up the victory, and the Turks rebuilt their fleet.

In 1606 the Turks signed a peace treaty with the Habsburgs. Previously all treaties with western states had been cast in the form of a truce granted as a divine favor from the sultan to a lesser potentate and had required the other party to pay tribute to the sultan. This time the Turks had to negotiate as equals; they gave the Habsburg emperor his proper title and were unable to demand tribute. Had western Europe not been preoccupied by the Thirty Years' War, the Ottoman Empire might have suffered even more severely in the first half of the seventeenth century than it did. As it was, internal anarchy disturbed the state; janissaries rebelled, troops rioted, and several sultans were deposed within a few years. The Persians recaptured Baghdad, and rebellion raged in the provinces.

A firm sultan, Murad IV (r. 1623–1640), temporarily restored order through brutal means. He reduced the janissaries, initiated a new military system, reorganized military fiefs, and abolished tribute in Christian children. Despite renewed revolts after Murad's death, the revival continued under a

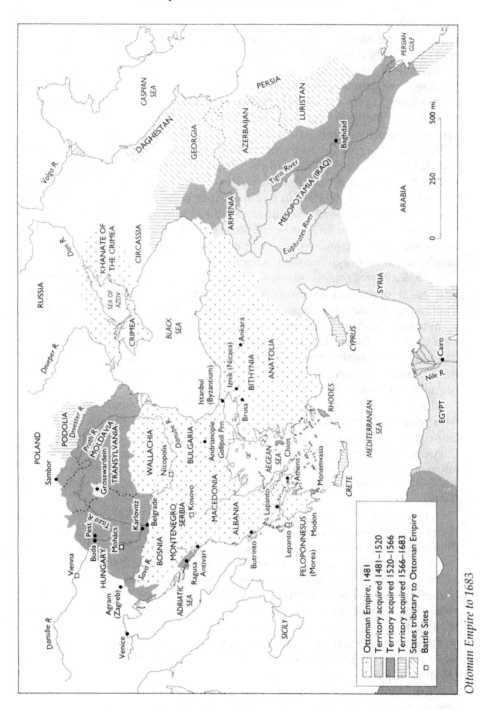

Ottoman Empire to 1683

family of viziers, the Köprülü of Albania. The first Köprülü executed thirty-six thousand people in five years (1656–1661), rebuilt the army and navy, and suppressed revolt. Between 1661 and 1676 the second Köprülü took Crete from Venice and temporarily won large areas of the Ukraine from the Russians and Poles. In 1683 the Turks again penetrated the heart of Europe and besieged Vienna. All Europe anxiously awaited the outcome. But for the second time in two centuries the Turkish wave was broken, this time by a German and Polish army, and Europe began a great counteroffensive.

The Habsburgs drove the Turks out of Hungary, the Venetians seized the Peloponnesus, and the Russians appeared on the shores of the Sea of Azov, which opens into the Black Sea. In 1699 most of the gains of the European counteroffensive were recognized by the Turks. The western European powers could stop worrying about the Ottoman menace, which had preoccupied them since the fourteenth century.

Russia from the Thirteenth to the End of the Seventeenth Centuries

Scholars refer to "the Russian question" as a means in invoking several historical concerns. What forces were at work to generate a Russian expansionism and consolidation of outlying territories? For how long would an enlarged or enlarging Russia remain stable? Would individual nationalities and languages reassert themselves despite Russian conquest? What role would Russia, a society of both the West and the East, play in European affairs, or in Near or Middle Eastern? Although these questions have been the focus of an enormous literature in the last two centuries, their origins lay in the fifteenth century.

Western and Northern Lands, 1386–1478

The collapse of Kievan Russia about the year 1200 led to the formation of a series of virtually independent petty principalities. These states were too weak and disunited to resist the constant pressure from Poland and Lithuania. By the early fourteenth century, the grand duke of Lithuania, with his capital at Vilna, ruled nominally over most of western Russia. The Lithuanians, still mostly pagan, gradually took over the language and manners of their Russian vassals. But in 1386 the grand duke married the heiress to the Polish throne and became king of Poland. As a result, the Polish Roman Catholic Church and the Polish nobility came to the fore in Lithuania.

Had it not been for the antagonism between Orthodox Russians and Catholic Poles and for the conflicting interests of the nobles of different religions and languages, the original Lithuanian-Russian combination might have proved to be the center around which Russia could reunite. Yet even before the connection with Poland, this region had become so feudal that its potential ability to unify Russia is doubtful. Even under the grand duke of Lithuania, most of the lands nominally affiliated with his duchy were ruled without interference by local nobles who were bound to him only by an oath of fealty and by their obligations to render military service. An assembly of nobles also limited the political authority of the grand duke. As in the West, the economic basis of society in western Russia was manorial, and restrictions were placed on the freedoms of the peasant farmer quite early.

In the north the town commonwealth of Novgorod came to rule over the vast, empty, infertile regions that were explored by armed merchants and pioneers in search of furs and other products. The town council, or *veche*, became very strong. Internally, Novgorod had a rigid class system. The representatives of the richer merchants came to control the veche, and a few powerful families concentrated the city's wealth in their hands and vied for political power. The gap between rich and poor grew wide. A man who could not pay his debts would be made a slave, and slaves frequently revolted and became brigands. Because the surrounding countryside had little good soil, the city depended upon the region to the southeast, around Moscow, for its grain. In 1478 the ruler of Moscow conquered Novgorod and deported the upper classes to central Russia.

The Tatars, 1223–1400

By the early thirteenth century Genghis Khan had consolidated under his command the Mongolian nomads of central Asia—Huns, Avars, and Polovtsky—who had repeatedly erupted into Europe. Having conquered northern China and Asia from Manchuria to the Caspian Sea, Genghis Khan led his Tatars across the Caucasus Mountains and into the steppes of southern Russia, defeating the Russians and dissident Polovtsky together near the Sea of Azov in 1223. He then retreated to Asia, where he died in 1227. Batu Khan (d. 1255) brought the Tatars back again in the 1230s, sacked Moscow in 1237 and Kiev in 1240, and moved into the western Russian regions and into Poland, Hungary, and Bohemia.

Tatar success seems to have been due largely to excellent military organization: unified command, general staff, clever intelligence service, and deceptive battle tactics. Although Batu defeated the Poles and the Germans in 1241, political affairs in Asia drew him eastward, and the Tatars never again appeared so far to the west. Batu retreated across Europe, and at Sarai, near the great bend of the Volga, he founded the capital of a new state—the Golden Horde—which accepted the overlordship of the far-off central government of the Mongols in Peking.

Other Mongol leaders ended the Abbasid caliphate in 1258 and were defeated by the Mamluks in 1260. The enmity between Mongols and Muslims led the leaders of western Europe to hope that they could convert the Mongol rulers to Christianity and ally with them against the Muslims. Several embassies were sent to Mongolia and China during the thirteenth and fourteenth centuries with this end in view. Nothing came of it except a great increase in geographical knowledge derived from the accounts of the European ambassadors.

The most lasting effect of the Tatar invasions was in Russia. Here the Tatars' main purpose was the efficient collection of tribute. Although they ravaged Russia while they were conquering it, after the conquest they shifted to a policy of exploitation. They took a survey of available resources and assessed tribute at the limit of what the traffic would bear. They did not disturb economic life as long as their authority was recognized. They did draft Russian recruits for their armies, but they made the local Russian princes responsible for the delivery of manpower and money, and they stayed out of Russian territory except to take censuses, survey property, and punish rebels. Each tributary Russian prince traveled to Sarai or to China on his election to do homage.

Toward the end of the fourteenth century the Russians grew bolder. The first Russian victories over the Tatars, scored by a prince of Moscow in 1378 and 1380, were fiercely avenged. Yet they showed that the Tatars could be defeated. The Golden Horde did not disintegrate until the early fifteenth century, and even then the Tatars did not disappear from Russian life. Three separate *khanates*, or Tatar states, were formed: one at Kazan on the middle Volga, one at Astrakhan at the mouth of the Volga on the Caspian, and one in the Crimea.

There was no inherent reason why Russia in the late twelfth century should not have developed as a European state with characteristics of its own. After two centuries of Tatar domination, however, it had not advanced, as measured against the material progress of western Europe. Contemporaries felt that the Tatar yoke was a calamity, and historians have yet to prove otherwise. When the Tatar power was finally shattered in the fifteenth century, Russian civilization was far less complex than that of the West.

The Development of the Muscovite State

Moscow lay near the great watershed from which the Russian rivers flow north into the Baltic or south into the Black Sea. It was richer than the north, could provide enough food for its people, and had flourishing forest industries. Thus, when the Tatar grip relaxed and trade could begin again, Moscow was advantageously located. Moreover, Moscow was blessed with a line of remarkably able princes. They married into powerful families, acquired land by purchase and by foreclosing mortgages, and inherited it through wills. They scored the first victories over the Tatars and could truthfully claim to be the champions of Russia. Finally, the princes of Moscow secured the support of the Russian Church. In the early fourteenth century the metropolitan archbishop made Moscow the ecclesiastical capital of Russia.

By the middle of the fifteenth century, Moscow was a self-conscious Russian national state that could undertake successful wars against both the Polish-Lithuanian kingdom and the Tatars. Ivan III (r. 1462–1505) put himself forward as the heir to the princes of Kiev and declared that he intended to regain the ancient Russian lands that had been lost to Poles and Tatars. Many nobles living in the western lands came over to him with their estates and

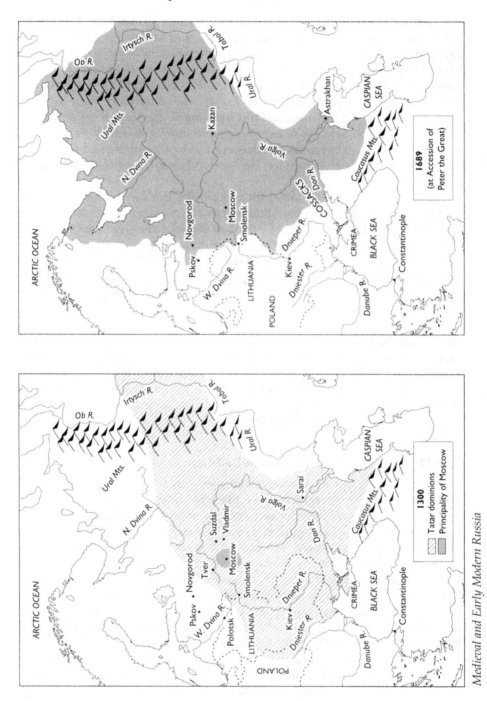

Medieval and Early Modern Russia

renounced their loyalties to the Lithuanian-Polish state. In 1492 the prince of Lithuania was forced to recognize Ivan III as sovereign of "all the Russians."

In 1472 Ivan had married Zoe, niece of the last Byzantine emperor, Constantine XI, who had been killed fighting against the Turks in Constantinople in 1453. Ivan adopted the Byzantine title of Autocrat and began to behave like a Byzantine emperor. He sometimes used the title *Czar* (Caesar) and no longer consulted his nobles. Italian architects built him an enormous palace, the Kremlin (or fortress). When the Holy Roman emperor in the 1480s decided to make an alliance with Ivan III and to arrange for a dynastic marriage, Ivan responded that he already had unlimited power derived directly from God.

When a rebellious noble fled Russia under the reign of Czar Ivan IV, the Terrible (1533–1584), he wrote the czar from abroad, denouncing him for failing to consult his nobles on important questions. Ivan replied that he was free to bestow favors on his slaves or inflict punishment on them as he chose. The first formally to take the title of czar, Ivan broke the power of the Tatars, conquered Kazan, Astrakhan, and Siberia, and systematically and brutally suppressed the most powerful nobles to establish a thoroughly autocratic government.

Part of the explanation for this rapid growth of autocratic theory is that Russia lived in a constant state of war or preparation for war. Perhaps more significant is that in Moscow, feudalism had not developed a united class of nobles who would fight against the rising monarchy for their privileges, as it had in the West. Instead of uniting against the pretensions of the monarch, the Muscovite nobility produced various factions with which the monarch could deal individually.

But most important of all was the ideology supplied by the Church. In the West, the Church itself was a part of feudal society and jealous of its prerogatives. In Russia it became the ally of the monarchy and something like a department of state. Russian churchmen were entirely familiar with Rome's claim to world empire and to Constantinople's centuries-long position as "new Rome." With the fall of Constantinople to the Turks, they elaborated a theory that Moscow was the successor to the two former world capitals.

Russian churchmen spread the story that Rurik, the first political organizer of Russia, was descended from the brother of Augustus. They claimed that the Russian czars had inherited certain insignia and regalia not only from the Byzantines but even from the Babylonians. All the czars down to the last, Nicholas II (r. 1894–1917), were crowned with a cap and clothed with a jacket that were of Byzantine manufacture. Thus the Church supplied the state with justification for its acts. Imperial absolutism became one of the chief political features of modern Russia.

Nobles and Serfs

Between the accessions of Ivan III in 1462 and Peter the Great in 1689, the autocracy overcame the opposition of the old nobility. The estates of the old nobility, which had always been hereditary, became service estates. By the end of the period the two types of nobles and the two types of estates had by a gradual process become almost identical: the hereditary nobles often owed service; the military service nobles often had hereditary land.

This important social process was accompanied by the growth of serfdom. Economic factors and political unrest in Russia had forced more and more peasants to ask large landowners for protection. The peasants would accept contracts that required payment of rent in produce and performance of service on the landlord's own land, in return for a money loan that had to be repaid over a period of years with interest or with extra services. By the early seventeenth century the peasant could not leave his plot until he paid off his debt; but since the debt was often too great for him to repay, he could in fact never leave.

The process was speeded up when the czars gave estates to the new military service gentry. An estate was not much good unless there was farm labor to work it. In the bitter agrarian and political crises of the sixteenth and seventeenth centuries, the government helped the service gentry to keep their farmers where they were. And since the peasants paid most of the taxes, it was easier for the government to collect its own revenues if it kept the peasants where they were. Gradually it was made harder for a tenant to leave his landlord, until by 1649 the avenues of escape were closed, and the serf was fixed to the soil. The status of serf became hereditary; children of serfs were enrolled on the estate's census books as serfs like their fathers.

The Reign of Ivan the Terrible, 1533–1584

Many of the disorders that characterized Russian history in the sixteenth and seventeenth centuries began in the long reign of Ivan IV, the Terrible. Pathologically unbalanced, Ivan succeeded to the throne as a small child. In 1547 he threw off the tutelage of the nobles and embarked upon a period of sound government and institutional reform. He regulated the greediness of the imperial administrators in the provinces, who had oppressed the population. He convoked the first *zemski sobor* (land assembly), a consultative body consisting of nobles, clerics, and representatives from the towns, to assist with imperial business, particularly with important questions of war and peace.

When Ivan fell ill in 1553, the nobles refused to take an oath of allegiance to his son. This refusal apparently reawakened his anger. Upon his recovery he created a new institution—the *oprichnina*, or "separate realm"—to belong to him personally, while the rest of Russia continued to be administered as before. The men Ivan appointed to run the oprichnina (called *oprichniks*), dressed grimly in black and, riding black horses, bore on their saddlebows a dog's head (for vigilance) and a broom (symbolizing a clean sweep). They were the forerunners of the secret police forces that have long characterized Russian society. They waged a fierce, relentless war on the nobles, confiscating their estates, exiling them, killing them. By Ivan's death, many of the oprichniks themselves had been murdered at his orders, and Russian administration was close to chaos. Yet Ivan had extended Russian authority far to the east against the Kazan and Astrakhan Tatars, thus for the first time opening the whole Volga waterway to Russian commerce.

The Time of Troubles, 1598–1613

Although the territory was wide and the imperial rule absolute, ignorance, illiteracy, and inefficiency weakened Russian society. Although the old nobility had been weakened, the new gentry was not firmly in control of the machinery of government. Ivan's son and heir, Fëauedor (r. 1584–1598), was an imbecile, and with his death the Moscow dynasty, descended from the rulers of Kiev, died out. Cliques of rival nobles intrigued for power. Fëauedor's brother-in-law, Boris Godunov (r. 1598–1605), emerged as the dominant figure.

Godunov could not overcome Ivan's legacy of disorder, the intrigues of the nobility, and a famine and plague that began in 1601. Bandits roamed the countryside, and when in 1603 a pretender arose under the protection of the king of Poland and falsely declared that he was a son of Ivan the Terrible, he won the support of many of the discontented. Russia was launched on the period known as the "Time of Troubles" (1598–1613).

After Godunov's death, the pretender ruled briefly as czar. But within a year he was murdered and was succeeded by a representative of the ancient aristocracy. New pretenders arose, the mobs of peasants and bandits were rallied once again, civil war continued, and Polish forces took Moscow. It soon appeared that the king of Poland intended to reign in Russia himself. It was this specter of foreign and Catholic domination that aroused the national sentiments of the Russians. In answer to a summons from the patriarch, there assembled a kind of national militia, drawn largely from prosperous free farmers of the middle Volga region. They were organized by a butcher named Kuzma Minin and led by a nobleman named Dmitri Pozharski. Under their command the militia won the support of other rebellious elements and drove the Poles from Moscow in 1612–1613.

The Role of the Zemski Sobor, 1613–1653

The zemski sobor now elected as czar Michael Romanov, grand-nephew of Ivan IV. Michael succeeded with no limitations placed upon his power by the zemski sobor or by any other body; he was an elected autocrat. For the first ten years of his reign, the zemski sobor stayed in continual session. It assisted the uncertain new dynasty to get underway by endorsing the policies of the czar and his advisers, thus lending them the semblance of popular support. But after 1623 the zemski sobor was summoned only to help declare war or make peace, to approve new taxation, and to sanction important new legislation. It endorsed the accession of Michael's son Alexis (r. 1645–1676), and in 1649 confirmed the issuance of a new law code. After 1653 Alexis did not summon it again, nor did his son and successor, Fëauedor III (r. 1676–1682). Autocratic czardom was taken for granted.

The Role of the Church

The Church remained the partner of the autocracy. The czar controlled the election of the patriarch of Moscow, a rank to which the archbishop was elevated in 1589. In the seventeenth century there were two striking instances when a patriarch actually shared power with the czar. In 1619 the father of Czar Michael Romanov, Filaret, who had become a monk, became patriarch and was granted the additional title of "Great Sovereign." He assisted his son in all the affairs of state. In the next generation Czar Alexis appointed a cleric named Nikon to the patriarchal throne and gave him the same title and duties. Nikon proved so arrogant that he aroused protests from clergy as well as laity, especially when he revised Russian Church ritual to bring it into line with Greek practice.

Nikon also argued that the authority of the patriarch in spiritual affairs exceeded that of the czar and that, since the spiritual realm was superior to the temporal, the patriarch was actually superior to the czar. In 1666 a church council deposed Nikon, who died a mere monk. Thereafter, the Church accepted that it depended upon the state.

The Church inspired the literature and art of the Muscovite period. History was written by monks in the form of chronicles. Travel literature took the form of accounts of pilgrimages to the Holy Land. Theological tracts attacked the Catholics and later also the Protestants. This literature is limited, and it was still dominated by the Church several centuries after the West had begun to produce secular writing. Almost all of it was written in Old Church Slavonic, the language of the liturgy. Although stately and impressive, Old Church Slavonic was not an appropriate vehicle for innovation. There was almost no secular learning, no science, no flowering of vernacular literature, no philosophical debate.

The Expansion of Russia, to 1682

The sixteenth and seventeenth centuries saw tremendous expansion of the Russian domain. Russian pioneers, in search of furs to sell and new land to settle, led the way, and the government followed. Frontiersmen in Russia were known as Cossacks. Cossack communities gradually became more settled, and two Cossack republics, one on the Dnieper River, the other on the Don, were set up. As time passed, more Cossack groups formed along the Volga River, in the Ural Mountains and elsewhere.

The frontier movement took the Russians eastward into the Urals and on across Siberia. Far more slowly, because of Tatar, Turkish, and Polish opposition, the Russians also moved southeast toward the Caucasus and south toward the Black Sea. Repeated wars were fought with Poland over the Ukraine. Sometimes the Cossacks favored the Poles and sometimes the Russians. By 1682 the Poles were weakening and were soon to yield. On the European frontiers it was the Swedes, still controlling the Baltic coast, against whom Russia's future wars would be fought. There were also constant struggles with the Tatars of the Crimea. The Ottoman Turks, overlords of the

St. Basil's Cathedral in Red Square, Moscow, built 1555–1560. (*Photograph by William C. Brumfield*)

Tatars, held the key fort of Azov and controlled the Black Sea. But in 1681 they abandoned most of their holdings in the Ukraine to the czars.

Russia and the West

A final development of these two centuries was to prove of the utmost importance for the future Russia. This was the slow and gradual penetration of foreigners and foreign ideas, a process welcomed with mixed feelings by those who prized the technical and mechanical learning they could derive from the West while fearing Western influence on society and manners. This ambivalent attitude toward Westerners and Western ideas became characteristic of later Russians.

The first foreigners to come were the Italians, who helped build the Kremlin at the end of the fifteenth century. But they were not encouraged to teach the Russians their knowledge, and they failed to influence even the court of Ivan III in any significant way. The English, who arrived in the mid-sixteenth century as traders to the White Sea, were welcomed by Ivan the Terrible. He gave the English valuable privileges and encouraged them to trade their woolen cloth for Russian timber and rope, pitch, and other naval supplies. The English were the first foreigners to teach Russians Western industrial techniques. Toward the middle of the seventeenth century the Dutch were able to displace the English as the most important foreign group engaged in commerce and manufacturing, opening their own glass, paper, and textile plants in Russia.

After the accession of Michael Romanov in 1613, the foreign quarter of Moscow, always called "the German suburb," grew rapidly. Foreign technicians received enormous salaries from the state. Foreign merchants sold their goods; foreign physicians and druggists became fashionable. By the end of the seventeenth century Western influence was fully apparent in the life of the court. A few nobles began to buy books and form libraries, to learn Latin, French, and German. The people, meanwhile, distrusted and hated the foreigners, looted their houses when they dared, and jeered at them in the streets.

Suspicion of foreign influences had divided the Russian church, cut the people off from sources of change, smothered the development of even modest representative institutions, assured the continuation of serfdom, and, together with the impact of the Ottoman Empire, kept the East under medieval conditions to the end of the seventeenth century. The Middle Ages came to have quite different dates in East and West, reflecting the different pace of change.

SUMMARY

By the late eleventh century, instability in the Muslim and Byzantine empires and the expansion of the Seljuk Turks had made pilgrimages to Palestine unsafe for Christians. When Byzantine envoys asked Pope Urban II for military aid against the Seljuks, the pope responded by calling for a Crusade. Crusades, or holy wars supported by the papacy against the infidel, had been waged in Spain since the Muslim invasions of the eighth century.

People responded to the pope's call for both religious and secular motives. During the First Crusade, feudal lords established four crusader states: Edessa, Antioch, Jerusalem, and Tripoli. The Templars, Hospitalers, and Teutonic Knights, orders of military knights, were established to protect pilgrims traveling to Palestine, but as the orders grew in wealth and power, they were diverted from their original purpose.

During the Second and Third Crusades, monarchs of France, Germany, and England tried to repel Muslim advances in the East. The Fourth Crusade, which resulted in the sack of Constantinople, and other later Crusades showed how far the crusaders had strayed from the original crusading spirit.

Increased trade and travel during the Crusades resulted in the introduction of new products, ideas, and methods of finance. The Crusades also helped foster the explorations of the fourteenth and fifteenth centuries. The failure of the Crusades, however, meant the closing of the eastern Mediterranean to western Europe.

The Byzantine Empire had been in decline even before crusaders looted its palaces and churches in 1204. Official corruption had contributed to economic and social decay. Under the Latin emperors, the Byzantine Empire was divided into feudal states, but in 1261, the Greeks of Nicaea ousted the Latin emperors from Constantinople.

Rival claims to the throne, social unrest, and religious controversy led to further decay in the Empire. Thus weakened, the Byzantine Empire could not withstand the advance of the Ottoman Turks in the fourteenth century. In 1453, even the supposedly impregnable city of Constantinople fell to the invaders and was renamed Istanbul.

Ottoman rulers were generally tolerant of other religions, including Christianity. They organized their state based on a strong ruling class that included men of the emperor, men of the sword, men of the pen, and the sages. The Turks expanded their empire into Africa, Persia, and Europe. Twice, Ottoman armies besieged Vienna, but each time, they were turned back. By the seventeenth century, however, the Ottoman Empire entered a long decline.

In the thirteenth century, Genghis Khan and his successors invaded Russia. For two hundred years, Tatars collected tribute from the Russians although they allowed Russian princes to rule themselves. In the fourteenth and fifteenth centuries the princes of Moscow challenged Tatar rule and eventually, with the support of the Church, established an absolute autocratic state.

Historians have debated the impact of Tatar rule on Russia, which resulted in Russia's falling behind the West. Not until the seventeenth century, after the accession of Michael Romanov, was Russia exposed to Western ideas and learning. During this period Russia expanded eastward to the Urals and into Siberia, south toward the Caucasus and Black Sea, north toward the Baltic Sea, and westward into territory ruled by Poland.

TWO

The Rise of the Nation

In eastern Europe medieval institutions continued to flourish long after the Turks captured Byzantium in 1453. Indeed, in Russia the Middle Ages ended comparatively recently, with the emancipation of serfs in 1861. In western Europe, by contrast, the Middle Ages ended about five centuries ago. No one year or event can be singled out; rather, a series of crucial developments took place over half a century in the late 1400s and early 1500s: the consolidation of royal authority in France, England, and Spain; the "discovery" of America; the virtual disappearance of serfdom in the West; and the international revolt against the medieval church.

A World Turned Upside Down

During the fourteenth and fifteenth centuries old forms and attitudes persisted in Western politics but became less flexible and less creative. The Holy Roman emperor Henry VII in the early 1300s sought to straighten out the affairs of Italy in the old Ghibelline tradition, even though he had few of the resources that had been at the command of Frederick Barbarossa. The nobles of France and England, exploiting the confusion of the Hundred Years' War, built private armies and great castles and attempted to transfer power back from the monarch to themselves. Their movement has been called *bastard feudalism,* for service in these neofeudal armies hinged upon money, not personal loyalty, mutual respect, and guarantees.

Manifestations like these have been interpreted as symptoms of senility, but they may also be viewed as experiments in the adjustment of old institutions to new demands. The nobles who practiced bastard feudalism were also putting soldiers in the field when neither French nor English monarchies could sustain a military effort. The importance of the monetary factor was characteristic of the passage from medieval to modern.

By the close of the fifteenth century, it was evident that the future lay not with neofeudal lords but with the so-called new monarchs, who were committed to power politics. Although politics and power had always gone hand in hand, the "new" monarchs did not hide their pursuit of power behind the church, and they were served by better instruments of government, better-equipped and better-trained soldiers, diplomats, and bureaucrats. Outstanding representatives of the new professionalism were Louis XI of France, Henry VII of England, and Ferdinand and Isabella of Spain. The princes of the various German states and the despots of the Italian city-states also often exemplified the new businesslike political behavior.

Meanwhile, the economy and society of western Europe had been undergoing even more strain and upheaval. In the countryside the traditional patterns of manorialism, serfdom, and payment in kind coexisted with a free peasantry producing for a cash market and paying rents and taxes in cash. The economy and society showed some of the same symptoms of senility affecting political life. Former serfs, who thought they were legally free peasants, often found that a lord could still oblige them to use his oven or flour mill or wine press and pay a stiff fee for the privilege. But they also found that they could no longer turn to a lord for protection in time of trouble. The uncertainty and insecurity of fluctuating climates both natural and political underlay the numerous outbreaks of rural violence. Crises also convulsed urban life. Civil war broke out in the prosperous woolen-manufacturing towns of Flanders, and chronic strife developed between the wealthy and poorer classes in Florence.

Life for the peasant—man or woman—was circumscribed, harsh, and, on the whole, short. Rural life showed a bewildering variety, however, particularly in England, and broad generalization is difficult, beyond noting a slow increase in the value of labor in western Europe and a slow descent into serfdom in eastern Europe.

High infant mortality rates intimate not only the limits of medical knowledge but also the sheer harshness of life itself: Illness, undernourishment, and climate each took human lives. Many women bore children throughout their child-bearing years; we have accounts of eight, twelve, or more children born to a single mother, of whom none might survive to adulthood. Without any of the protections offered by modern medicine, many women died in childbirth.

All but the most powerful were vulnerable to poverty: years of drought and flood could reduce a prosperous peasant family to destitution and insurmountable economic dependency within one generation. For most Europeans, "poverty" was not an abstract idea, but ever present at the edges of their lives. In times of famine, peasants starved while lords were still feasting—the tensions between "rich" and "poor" were not between two small minorities, but between perhaps at most 10 percent of the population and upwards of 60 to 70 percent.

Towns, which were growing in size and in complexity of economic life in the thirteenth and fourteenth centuries, provided opportunities to the landless. In the beginning, towns did not draw the great landed nobility, who remained in their castles, towers, and manors on the land, or prosperous peasants. The most stable form of wealth in this time remained land and agricultural production. Towns, however, particularly in Italy, were becoming distinctive centers of culture, economy, and politics.

In one way in particular, late medieval Europe seems brighter than the following centuries. The roles open to women were greater than they would be after the crises of the sixteenth century. Noblewomen might enter a convent, effectively a community of women, governed internally by an abbess; many nuns deplored the loss of self-determination that the closing of convents in the sixteenth century ultimately meant in particular for noble women. Peasant women often worked in the fields next to their husbands, fathers, and brothers. Domestic work, such as candle-making, carding, spinning, weaving, and clothes-making, in late medieval peasant households could have been feminine labor. Only with the development of the putting-out system would these domestic productions become predominantly masculine productions. So, too, in towns women might become masters of a workshop at the death of their husbands. Some married journeymen of the workshop in order to preserve their own governance.

Those of property, whether peasant or noble, had arranged marriages, in order for the family to preserve its patrimony and protect the integrity of its property. Younger sons and the daughters of those who could not afford dowries frequently could not marry. These children might enter a religious house or enter service in a household of a family of greater wealth. While most marriages were not arranged for love, scholars no longer argue that marriages were therefore loveless. Memoirs and letters suggest tenderness, trust, and intimacy. Among merchant families, the wife might well be the trusted advisor to her husband. Those same memoirs give a glimpse of the grief of parents at the death of perhaps more than half their children before adulthood.

Prayerbooks commissioned by wealthy women and account books provide some evidence for our understanding of late medieval women. Prayerbooks, of which there are hundreds, suggest that noblewomen and some wealthy wives of merchants practiced privately their own devotions, perhaps reading to themselves. Account books suggest not only literacy but also numeracy among some of the wives of townsmen. They also offer glimpses of both domestic and public economies and the diverse roles of women within them. A wide variety of sources intimate that women could become informal partners in their husbands' businesses.

Criminal women offer us other insights into late medieval conceptions of gender. While prescriptive definitions of "woman" might speak of "the weaker" sex, courts tried women for murder, not only through witchcraft, but also through physical violence; for infanticide; not only for prostitution, but also for procurement—the management of prostitutes; and even for illegal economic practices. The courts provide a different kind of evidence, that of women engaged in many kinds of actions ideally presented as "masculine." Women's roles were shaped by moral precept, but not absolutely determined. Even divorce, which the church formally forbade, was practiced: Some women simply ran away from abusive or unsatisfactory husbands, but a number of others sought the formal dissolution of their marriages through the loophole of "nonconsummated marriage." Certain central roles were universally denied to women: citizenship, the priesthood. But many others proved within the reach of the determined.

There were many private contracts of marriage, made in secret and without the blessings of the clergy. These often led to disputes about property and the marriage agreement, which eventually had to be adjudicated by an ecclesiastical court.

Two social traumas particularly undermined the morale and resiliency of fourteenth-century Europe. The first was the great famine of 1315–1317. Harvests failed in 1322 and 1329 and thereafter remained insufficient, so that populations were chronically undernourished. With Europe unable to grow enough grain, outright starvation was widespread. The second and greater trauma was the Black Death of 1347–1351, which is estimated to have killed one third to one half of an already weakened European population. This ghastly epidemic apparently marked the first appearance in Europe of bubonic plague, introduced by caravans coming from China to the Crimea and then by ship to Sicily. Propagated by flea bites, prevalent wherever there were rats, and also carried in the air by sneezing and coughing, the plague wiped out entire communities. Recurring in the 1360s and 1370s, the plague altered the socioeconomic pyramid and initiated a steady decline in population that lasted to about 1480. A major social consequence of the plague was a severe shortage of labor, which emboldened the peasants and workers who had survived the epidemic to press for greater rights, usually with transient success.

The Black Death transformed European imaginations. No one could remember such a cataclysmic event; indeed, one had to go back to Roman times to find a natural disaster of such proportions. Not until the early twentieth century did scientists finally determine what caused the disease, and therefore how to treat it; how it spread, and therefore how to quarantine it. It eluded all medieval and early modern efforts at cure or containment, striking seemingly randomly, killing one healthy adult, leaving untouched another more fragile person. Death seemed to so many Europeans to walk the streets, to tap random strangers on the shoulder, to seize them. No one—not noble, not wealthy merchant, not beautiful, not deformed, not innocent, not criminal, not sturdy worker, not recluse—no one was immune from Death's touch. Death from bubonic plague was particularly horrific, with excruciatingly painful boils beginning in the groin, armpit, or on the neck, followed by bleeding under the skin and the spitting of blood, the loss of bowel control, heavy sweating, and blackened urine, concluding, usually in roughly three days from the first symptoms, in death. Corpses piled up in towns as the healthy fled disease, the only way they thought they could survive; the stench of decay, the moans of the dying penetrated every human community, household, village, town, castle. By the end of the fourteenth century, a "Cult of Death" had emerged, as poets and artists sought with words, ink, and paint to grapple with the randomness of death. Among the most famous of those efforts was Hans Holbein's "Dance of Death," a book of prints depicting persons from all walks of life touched by the skeletal figure of Death.

One thing was clear to all Europeans. In enclosed places, the death of one person meant the likely death of all. In a society in which so many different people lived in enclosed communities—monasteries and convents, households of manors and villages—entire communities were wiped out. Efforts to isolate the disease failed, as it traveled seemingly invisibly. People offered all sorts of explanations—demons, witchcraft, the wrath of God, the Apocalypse—but no one explanation was embraced by all. People also sought to keep their distance from anything Asian; rumor had arrived that the plague had so severely struck India as to depopulate it entirely.

The Black Death confounded medieval medical practices. When the plague began its sweep across Europe, medical theory still depended upon the classical conception of the body articulated by Galen. According to Galen, the body had four "humors": blood, phlegm, yellow bile, and black bile. Each was the expression of one organ: phlegm from the brain, blood from the heart. Good health meant that the humors were in balance for a particular person. Illness required the physician to restore the balance of humors, through bloodletting or herbs directed at one of the biles. Well into the seventeenth century, medicine remained more theoretical than clinical, more a philosophy than an empirical science.

Contributing to the general sense of despair throughout Europe, the response of those charged with the physical health of human communities was utterly ineffectual. None of the hundreds of medical treatises on the plague correctly identified its cause. Almost no one saw any causal relation between the outbreak of plague in a place and the piles of dead rodents found immediately before the outbreak. As to causes, most commentators favored either the astral or the environmental theory. The astral theory held that a conjunction of three higher planets—Mars, Jupiter, and Saturn—in the sign of Aquarius corrupted the air, bringing poisonous material to the heart and lungs. The environmental theory held that a series of earthquakes between 1345 and 1347 had released poisonous fumes from the center of the earth. Others ascribed the plague to southerly winds and warmer weather.

Whatever the posited explanation, it was clear to all that physicians literally could not heal themselves, as the plague took the learned as well as the ignorant. In the medieval hierarchy of medicine, "physicians" were university-trained, often with substantial learning in theology, and were superior to and worked quite apart from "surgeons," who were closer to artisans in social status. (The barber's pole, traditionally red and white, is a reminder of the time when such surgeons hung out bloodied rags to dry.) Apothecaries, the pharmacists of their day stood next, but because they possessed almost magical knowledge of the properties of different drugs and herbs, the lay public held them in esteem. Apothecaries were also merchants, for they traded in spices, and as such they might well stand high in the social scale because of their relative wealth. Below all were the nonprofessionals, who charged little and worked by trial and error. Found primarily in the countryside, they were likely to know of "country remedies," which from experience might work, but they were also likely to depend on outdated knowledge. Up

*In the late Middle Ages herbalists and others with an interest in medicines established phar-
macies, stores to which individuals could go to obtain drugs. Pharmacists compounded and
studied drugs. At the end of the thirteenth century Arnald of Villanova, an alchemist with
an interest in medicine, worked on the qualitative effects of compounded medicines, and by
drawing upon the work of a ninth-century Arabian philosopher, Alkindi, was the first to link
a geometric increase in quantity of drug to an arithmetical increase in the sensed effect.*
(Scala/Art Resource, NY)

to 20 percent of this group were women who served as midwives, herbalists, and comforters of the sick.

The crisis of the plague and consequent search for remedies led to the professional evolution of medicine. As the older medical leaders perished in the plague, other physicians took their place. Surgeons displaced traditional physicians; in 1390 the medical faculty at the University of Paris invited surgeons to join the faculty as equals. The lay public also began to demand that medical writing be in vernacular tongues so that the patient might attempt to understand his or her own problems. The function of hospitals slowly changed over the next three centuries. They had largely served as charitable institutions for the sick poor, whose households could not care for them, either for want of resources or for want of persons free to attend to them. The persons in hospitals, therefore, were not there primarily because of the nature of their illness—even the most desperately ill were cared for at home until well into the nineteenth century—but because of the situation of their kin. Increasingly, however, these hospitals came to have the predecessors of staff physicians, local physicians and healers who were paid a salary to attend to the sick. Perhaps most importantly, people sought to separate those who were sick from plague or some other invisible ailment from those whose infirmity was visible, such as a broken bone or other injury.

From the middle of the fourteenth century to the end of the fifteenth, no one could know, from day to day, whether he or she would live or die. Recurrent cycles of plague taught a lesson about human helplessness in the face of nature, influencing religious belief, social organization, and the movement toward experimental science. Those who survived the plague may have been better off—there were fewer people, wages rose as labor was scarce, and many restrictive remnants of feudalism fell into disuse—but, as a poem at the time put it, for most people the world was truly "turned upside down."

The fourteenth century was particularly frightening, for even the climate turned against the rural population. In the midst of one of the earth's great climatic swings from an earlier time when wheat was grown in Sweden and there were vineyards in Newfoundland, Europe passed through a long succession of wet years when crops rotted, and panic, famine, and death were common in the countryside. Hygiene was generally lacking, even at court; disease was the normal state of things, even when there was no plague, for antisepsis was unknown, and simple injuries easily led to death. Even the presumed innocence of childhood was no joy, for while the children of the well-to-do certainly had toys, most were seen simply as small adults and were expected to behave as adults long before they were into their teens.

No action in history is without its reaction, and few disasters do not also lead to beneficial change, as in the rise of medical knowledge after the Black Death. One group benefited: middle-class women, particularly in England, who experienced what some scholars have called a "golden age" between about 1370 and 1470. In part the more secure position of women in society arose from depopulation, so that women were more valued for their work, knowledge, and property, and in part from other changes in society. Prior to this time women were legally viewed as "one flesh" with their husbands, but widows were able to break free from this phrase. They were able to make wills and testaments; in London especially they could continue their husband's business and occupy the family house (whereas elsewhere and earlier widows had to vacate their dead husband's home in forty days), and they were able to join in the social and economic life of guilds, companies, and fraternities, although they were denied the political activities of such groups. Some women—the widows of tanners, for example—had to struggle to keep a position in their craft and were seldom admitted to the guilds, but by and large the "custom of London" allowed growing participation.

In London, and in many other places, widows had full legal right to their dowry, the property they had brought with them at marriage. The widow's right to real estate differed from place to place; some had by law a right to a portion of their husband's landed property, others had no rights to the land a husband brought to the marriage. She also shared in the husband's goods and chattels by the custom of *legitim*, which meant that she kept half (or a third if there were surviving children) of the husband's movable goods.

Dower in land reverted to the husband's heirs at the widow's death, but the dower in chattels was hers to sell or use as she wished, and this made it possible for widows to enter business for themselves. Upper-class women also acquired property, and some, such as Elizabeth de Burgh, Lady of Clare (1295–1360), maintained large estates, engaged in significant public benefactions, and were the center of social gatherings.

Not all widows did inherit, however, for it was not uncommon to remarry, to enter a convent, or to assign an inheritance to someone else. Convents also offered education to girls who were not destined to be nuns, and women who did not enter a convent nonetheless could take a public vow of chastity, forestalling an arranged marriage or being seen to dishonor their deceased husband. In some jurisdictions, a fatherless child was considered an orphan, reflecting at least in part assumptions about economic roles and the ability of widows to support families without the help of their families. In some jurisdictions in the Empire, however, widows were seen as equally financially responsible for their children, suggesting that the government, at least, believed them capable of employment to support children. Policies on fatherless children may have also played a role in which widows chose to remarry, as we have clear evidence of women seeking a range of means to preserve their families, in particular, their children, together under one roof. Widows also were generally exempt from taxation by order of Henry III, unless they were widows of rich merchants, and remarriage might lead to taxation, so that the majority either remained widows or were widowed again following a second or third marriage. There were more women than men in England, and far more widows than widowers, since women tended to marry at a younger age. Noble widows might choose to follow the example of a number of female saints, from Elizabeth of Hungary onward, and enter a life of celibacy, often entering a convent. The widows of peasants were under greater pressure to remarry, in order to maintain the same level of agricultural production. Widows of poorer artisans rarely could afford to support a household on their own, while widows of masters might seek to keep control over the workshop themselves. Widows of merchants and entrepreneurs were in a singular position in many ways, their wealth not landed and often generated through forms of business they might have learned informally in partnership with their husbands. We know that some chose not to remarry, even as some were not able to remarry. Increasingly, these women were literate and were capable of their own correspondence, as well as of forming intimate circles of devotion among women and a range of communities of support for women for whom society had ambivalent value.

To the average person, then, these late Middle Ages must have seemed a time of incredible calamity and hardship. The Black Death ravaged the streets and the countryside. The Hundred Years' War brought political and social collapse to much of western Europe, sweeping aside old ways. Soldiers experienced an unprecedented death rate, as gunpowder and heavy artillery came into widespread use for the first time. The great schisms within the church forced Christians to take sides in a complex dispute that involved competing popes. The Turks were on the march, threatening the gates of Europe, as the powerful armies of the West fought one another. And yet, although the time may have seemed one of exceptional decline and instability, it also presaged rebirth. The crisis of the late Middle Ages ushered in what we conventionally call *modern history*.

The Emerging National Monarchies

At the death of Philip the Fair in 1314, the Capetian monarchy of France seemed to be evolving into a new professional institution staffed by efficient and loyal bureaucrats. Philip Augustus, Louis IX, and Philip the Fair had all consolidated royal power at the expense of their feudal vassals, who included the kings of England. Soon, however, France became embroiled in a long conflict with England—the so-called Hundred Years' War of 1337–1453—that crippled the monarchy for well over a century.

The Outbreak of the Hundred Years' War, 1337

The nominal cause of the war was a dispute over the succession to the French throne. For more than three hundred years son had followed father as king of France. This remarkable succession ended with the three sons of Philip the Fair, none of whom fathered a son who survived infancy. The crown then passed to Philip of Valois, Philip VI (1328–1350), a nephew of Philip the Fair. But the king of England, Edward III (r. 1327–1377), claimed that as the nephew of the last Capetian king he had a better right to succeed than Philip of Valois. To settle the question, French lawyers went back to the Frankish Salic law of the sixth century, which said that a woman could not inherit land. Although the Salic law had not been applied in France for centuries, the lawyers now interpreted it to mean that a woman could not transmit the inheritance to the kingdom. This legal quibble was to serve Edward III as the pretext for beginning the Hundred Years' War. English diplomats insisted that Edward's claim was legitimate, while the French saw him as a rebellious vassal. Rivals for the rich commerce of the Low Countries, the English and French were looking for an excuse for war.

England's continued possession of the rich duchy of Aquitaine, with its lucrative vineyards and its prosperous wine-shipping port of Bordeaux, was a glaring exception to an increasingly unified France. As suzerains over Aquitaine, the kings of France encroached upon the feudal rights of the kings of England. The English, for their part, wished to keep what they had and to regain Normandy and the other territories they had lost to Philip Augustus.

The most pressing issue arose farther north, in Flanders. This small but wealthy area, which today straddles the frontier between Belgium and France, was ruled by the count of Flanders, a vassal of the king of France. The thriving Flemish cloth manufacturers bought most of their wool from England and sold much of their finished cloth there; the English Crown collected taxes both on the exported wool and on the imported woolens. Inside Flanders the artisans and tradespeople of the towns were in almost constant conflict with the rich commercial ruling class. The rich sought the backing of the count of Flanders, and he in turn sought that of his overlord, the king of France; the workers got the help of the English, who feared the disruption of their lucrative trade. Warlike incidents multiplied during the early fourteenth century, culminating in a victorious invasion of Flanders by French armies. Edward III thereupon allied himself with a Flemish merchant of Ghent, Jacob van Artevelde, who expelled both the ruling Flemish oligarchy and the French and organized his own government of Flanders. It was in response to pressure from these Flemish allies that Edward III put forth his claim as king of France and started a war in 1337.

The first major operation of the war was an English naval victory at Sluys in 1340. When their Flemish ally, van Artevelde, was killed in 1345, the English invaded northern France and gained a great victory at Crécy in 1346. Despite inferior numbers, the English profited by incompetent French generalship and by relying upon large numbers of infantrymen armed with the longbow. From higher ground English archers poured arrows down on a confused crowd of mounted French knights and mercenaries armed with the crossbow, a cumbersome weapon rather like a giant slingshot. Next the English took Calais. When open warfare was resumed after the Black Death, the English not only defeated the French again, at Poitiers in western France (1356), but also captured the French king, John II (r. 1350–1364). John's teenage son, Charles, the future King Charles V, the Wise, became regent for his father in France.

In 1360 the Hundred Years' War paused when Edward III virtually renounced his claim to the French crown by treaty in exchange for all southwestern France and lands bordering the Channel near Calais. When the war was resumed in 1369, the French made impressive gains under Charles the Wise and his capable advisers. By his death in 1380 they had driven the English from French soil except for a string of seaports, including Bordeaux and Calais. The French fleet now could sail freely in the Channel and raid the English coasts.

The Valois kings were far less effective rulers than the Capetians had been. The English won the main battles and gained much French territory by treaty. France was racked by the Black Death and swept by social crisis and civil war. Yet the English were overextended, and the French ultimately drove them out and completed the unification of their country under a strong national monarchy. Necessity obliged the Valois kings to develop a standing army, finance it by direct taxation, and enlist the support of the middle classes, on whose assistance the whole accomplishment depended.

The Estates General

In these years the French monarchy faced increasingly hostile criticism at home. When summoned in 1355 to consent to a tax, the Estates General insisted on determining its form—a general levy on sales and a special levy on salt—and demanded also that their representatives rather than those of the Crown act as collectors. After the defeat at Poitiers, they demanded that the regent, Charles, dismiss and punish the royal advisers and substitute for them twenty-eight delegates chosen from the Estates. When Charles hesitated, the leader of the Estates, the Paris merchant Etienne Marcel, led a general strike and revolution in the capital and forced the regent to consent. But Marcel made two cardinal mistakes. He allied himself with a rival claimant to the throne, and he assisted a violent peasant revolt, the *Jacquerie*.

Already harrowed by the Black Death, the peasants endured fresh suffering from demands for more taxes and money to ransom nobles taken prisoner with King John. The peasantry felt harassed by the Estates General, which required them to repair the war-torn properties of the nobility. In several regions they rose up in 1358, murdering nobles and burning châteaux. The royal forces put down and massacred the peasants; the death toll has been estimated at twenty thousand. The outcome of the Jacquerie showed that, put to the test, the country failed to support either the more radical Parisians or the mobs in the countryside. In the final flare-up, Marcel was murdered, and Charles repressed the revolt.

Although the Estates had in effect run France for two years, they had imposed no principle of constitutional limitation upon the king. With the country in chronic danger of invasion, even rebels wished to strengthen rather than weaken the monarchy. Moreover, the critics of the Crown— clergy, nobles, townsmen—mistrusted one another because of conflicting class interests. Even members of a single estate were divided by the differing interests of the provinces from which they came. Charles the Wise was quick to exploit the advantages that these class and local antagonisms gave the Crown.

Burgundians and Armagnacs, 1380–1467

The new king, Charles VI (1380–1422), was intermittently insane. During his reign the monarchy was threatened by the disastrous results of the earlier royal policy of assigning provinces called *apanages* to the male members of the royal family. Such a relative might himself be loyal, but within a generation or two his heirs would be remote enough from the royal family to become its rivals. In 1363 King John II made Burgundy the apanage of his youngest son, Philip. Charles the Wise gave Orléans as an apanage to his younger son, Louis.

During the reign of Charles VI, the dukes of Burgundy and Orléans engaged in a bitter rivalry for influence and power, which was continued by their successors. In 1407 John, who followed his father, Philip, as duke of Burgundy, arranged the assassination of Louis, duke of Orléans. All France was now torn by the factional struggle between the Burgundians and the Orléanists, who were called Armagnacs after their leader, Count Bernard of Armagnác. The Armagnacs commanded the loyalty of much of southern and southwestern France, while the Burgundians controlled the north and east. The Burgundians were pro-English and had the support of the upper bourgeoisie in the towns. The careful king of England, Henry V (1413–1422), reopened the war and in 1415 won the battle of Agincourt, where the heavily armored French knights were mired in the mud. The Burgundians took over in Paris, killing partisans of the Armagnacs, whose factions fled south of the Loire River to set up a rival regime. The English took Rouen, the capital of Normandy, in 1419; the Burgundians tried to patch up a truce with the Armagnacs, but John, the duke of Burgundy, was assassinated, ostensibly to avenge the murder of the duke of Orléans a dozen years earlier.

Next, the unstable Charles VI declared his own son, the dauphin, to be illegitimate. (The title of dauphin and the right to hold the province of Dauphiné in southeastern France were reserved for the eldest son of the king.) By the Treaty of Troyes (1420), Charles adopted Henry V of England as his heir and made him his regent during his lifetime. Henry married Charles's daughter and was allowed to retain the conquests he had made north of the Loire until he should inherit all of France on the death of Charles. Had Henry V lived, it is possible that the entire future of France might have been changed. But in 1422 both Charles VI and Henry V died.

In France the dauphin, excluded from Paris by the Burgundians, ruled at Bourges as King Charles VII (r. 1422–1461) with Armagnac support. When the regent for Henry VI of England prepared to move south against Charles, the mystic Joan of Arc (c. 1412–1431) saved France. The demoralized forces of Charles VII were inspired by the visionary peasant girl from Lorraine who reflected the deep patriotism of the French at a moment when all seemed lost. Joan told the pitiful dauphin how saints and angels had told her that she must bring him to be crowned at Rheims, traditional coronation place for the kings of France. She was then armed and given a small detachment that drove the English out of Orléans. The king was crowned in 1429, but the next year Joan was taken prisoner by the Burgundians, sold to the English, turned over to the French Inquisition, and burned at the stake for witchcraft and heresy in Rouen in 1431.

Against heavy odds, the French monarchy managed to sustain the impetus provided by the martyred Joan. In 1435 Charles VII and Burgundy concluded a separate peace. Although Charles recovered Paris, for ten years the countryside was ravaged by bands of soldiers; moreover, leagues of nobles, supported by the new dauphin, the future Louis XI, revolted in 1440. Fortunately for the Crown, the Estates General in 1439 granted the king the permanent right to keep a standing army and to levy the *taille*, a direct tax collected by royal agents.

With these instruments available to him and with loans from the wealthy merchant Jacques Coeur, Charles VII reformed his inadequate military forces. Twenty companies of specialized cavalry were organized under commanders of the king's personal choice; these companies were assigned to garrison the towns. Professionals supervised the introduction of artillery. The new French force drove the English out of Normandy and Aquitaine (1449–1451), so that only Calais remained in English hands when the Hundred Years' War finally ended in 1453.

Doing History

BIAS IN PLACE NAMES

Not only do historic place names change, but places often simultaneously have two or more names and pronunciations. For example *Biscay Bay*, referred to in the text, is the English form for *Viscaya*, its Spanish name; *Napoli* is the Italian form for *Naples*. Were this book written in a language other than English these other forms would be used. One is not more "correct" than the other. The choice simply reflects the bias of language.

Behind this bias may lie serious distortions of history, however, for the use of one term, spelling, or pronunciation for a place or person tends to reflect how "the victor writes the history." The pronunciation of *Agincourt* is an example, for the English call it *ag'-in-kort;* properly, in French, the pronunciation is *ä-zhan-kor.* By the choice of pronunciation one may implicitly take sides in a dispute.

Through the use in text or on a map, of a name in the national language, one may make a political point concerning national identity. Thus Ireland's capital city, Dublin, often appears as Baile Atha Calaith and Ireland as Eire. An area called Upper or Higher or even Superior usually simply means father up an important river from other peoples, but the words may easily be mistaken to imply quality.

Finally, local pride and custom may lead to pronunciations that differ markedly from those of the places after which they were named; this is especially true in North America, where the English river Thames (timms) has become the American river Thames (pronounced as spelled), the Egyptian city of Cairo (ky-ro) has become *kay-ro,* and the Greek city of Athens (*ä-thens*) has become *á-thens.*

Meantime, Charles had acted against another institution that might have weakened the Crown. In 1438 the Pragmatic Sanction of Bourges (a solemn royal pronouncement) laid down the policy known as *Gallicanism,* claiming for the Gallican (French) Church a virtually autonomous position within the Roman Catholic Church. It greatly limited papal control over church appointments and revenues in France and asserted the superiority of church councils over popes.

The Burgundian Threat and King Louis XI, 1419–1483

Against one set of enemies, however, Charles VII was not successful—his rebellious vassals, many of them beneficiaries of the new bastard feudalism, who still controlled nearly half of the kingdom. The most powerful of these vassals was the duke of Burgundy, Philip the Good (r. 1419–1467), whose authority extended to Flanders and other major portions of the Low Countries. This sprawling Burgundian realm was almost an emerging national state. It was also a personal state, for Duke Philip had assembled it as much by good fortune as by good management, inheriting some lands and acquiring others by conquest or negotiation. Yet it was also a menacing state that might have interposed itself between France and Germany. Philip behaved as though he were a monarch of the first magnitude. The wealth of the Flemish and Dutch towns enabled him to maintain the most lavish court in Europe, and his resources at least equaled those of the king of France and the Holy Roman emperor.

The decisive trial of strength between France and Burgundy took place under the successors of Charles VII and Philip the Good—King Louis XI, (r. 1461–1483), the Spider, and Duke Charles the Bold (r. 1467–1477). Although the new French king had repeatedly intrigued against his father while he was dauphin, he now energetically pursued the policies that Charles VII had initiated. At his accession Louis was already a crafty and practiced politician who preferred secret diplomacy to open war. He forced his protesting subjects to pay higher taxes but gave men of the middle class responsible posts in his administration. He appeased the pope by withdrawing the Pragmatic Sanction of 1438, but in practice continued most of its restrictions on papal control over the Gallican church. He enlarged the army bequeathed him by his father but conserved its use for the direst emergencies.

Where Louis XI was cautious, Charles the Bold was audacious to the point of folly. He was determined to bridge the gap between Burgundy and the Low Countries and seize Lorraine and Alsace. Since Alsace was a confused patchwork of feudal jurisdictions overlapping northern Switzerland, his designs threatened the largely independent Swiss Confederation. Subsidized by Louis XI, the Swiss defeated Charles three times in 1476 and 1477; in the last battle, at Nancy, Charles was slain.

Since Charles left no son, his lands were partitioned. The duchy of Burgundy passed permanently to France. The Low Countries went to Mary, the daughter of Charles, who married Maximilian of Habsburg, later Holy Roman emperor.

Although Louis XI did not keep all the Burgundian inheritance out of the hands of potential enemies, he shattered the prospect of a middle kingdom. He broke the strength of the Armagnac faction as well, recovered most of the territory held as apanages, and doubled the size of the royal domain. At his death, French bastard feudalism was virtually eliminated. The only major region still largely independent of the Crown was the duchy of Brittany, and this passed to royal control during the reign of Charles VIII (r. 1483–1498), Louis's son and successor. The France of Louis XI was not yet a full-fledged national monarchy, but by his consolidation of territory and by his competent central administration, Louis laid the foundations for a proud, cohesive, confident nation in subsequent centuries.

England: Edward II and Edward III, 1307–1377

England was also emerging as a national monarchy. Bastard feudalism flourished until Edward IV and Henry VII reasserted royal power in the later fif-

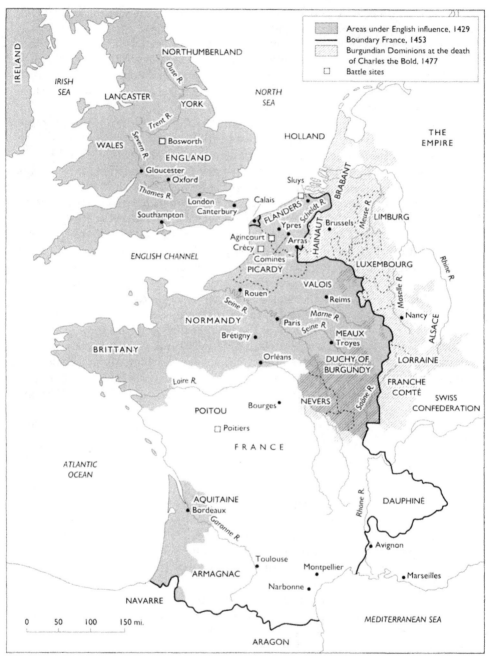

England and France during the Hundred Years' War

teenth century, much as Louis XI did in France. But however close the parallels between the two countries, there was also an all-important difference. Whereas the French Estates General was becoming the servant of the monarchy, the English Parliament was slowly acquiring powers that would one day make it the master of the Crown.

After the death of Edward I in 1307, the political tide turned abruptly against the monarchy. His son, Edward II (r. 1307–1327) was a bored, weak, and inept ruler, dominated by his favorites and by his French queen, Isabella. In 1314 he lost the battle of Bannockburn to the Scots. He also faced baronial opposition. In the Ordinances of 1311 the barons set up as the real rulers of England twenty-one *lords ordainers,* who had to consent to royal appointments, to declarations of war, and to the king's leaving the realm. Parliament repealed the Ordinances in 1322, and noble malcontents gathered around Queen Isabella, who led a revolt against her husband. Imprisoned, then murdered, Edward II was succeeded on the throne by his fifteen-year-old son, Edward III.

The reign of Edward III (r. 1327–1377) was marked by stunning English victories in the early campaigns of the Hundred Years' War and by the great economic crisis following the Black Death. English agricultural laborers demanded better working conditions or left home for the towns. In 1351 Parliament passed the Statute of Laborers, forbidding workers to give up their jobs and attempting to fix wages and prices as they had been before the plague. The law was not a success, and the labor shortage hastened the end of serfdom and paved the way for the disorders that took place under Edward's successor. The cause of the peasants was defended effectively in a vernacular verse satire of Edward's reign, *The Vision Concerning Piers Plowman,* which denounced the corruption of officials and of the clergy.

Attempts to enforce the Statute of Laborers were made by the justices of the peace. The justices were all royal appointees, selected in each shire from the landed gentry. Since they received no pay, they accepted office from a sense of duty or for prestige. As the old shire and hundred courts disappeared, the justices of the peace became the chief local magistrates and the virtual rulers of rural England.

The reign of Edward III also witnessed the growth of English national feeling, fostered by the long war with France. The papacy was a particular target of nationalist suspicion because the popes now resided at Avignon and were thought to be under the thumb of the French. In 1351 Parliament passed the Statute of Provisors restricting the provision (that is, the appointment) of aliens to church offices in England. Two years later Parliament checked the appeal of legal cases to the papal curia by the Statute of Praemunire (a Latin term that refers to the prosecution of a legal case). In 1362 Parliament declared English the official language of the courts, although the Norman French of the old ruling classes persisted in some legal documents.

Nationalism, dislike of the papacy, and widespread social and economic discontent were all involved in England's first real heresy, preached during

Edward's reign by the Oxford scholar John Wycliffe (c. 1320–1384). Advocating a church without property in the spirit of the early Christians, Wycliffe called for direct access by the individual to God without priest as intermediary. He and his followers were also responsible for the first English translation of the Bible, despite the church's insistence that the Latin Vulgate was the sole authoritative version of the Bible. Although his views, called Lollardy, were condemned as heretical, Wycliffe was not sentenced until well after his death, when his body was dug up and burned by order of the Council of Constance in 1478.

The most significant constitutional development of Edward III's long reign was the evolution of Parliament. Division of Parliament into two houses was beginning to appear in the fourteenth century. Edward I's Model Parliament of 1295 had included representatives of the lower and higher clergy, barons, knights of the shire, and burgesses. While the lower clergy had dropped out, the other groups continued to attend. The higher clergy—the lords spiritual—came to Parliament as vassals of the king. In time, the lords spiritual joined with the lords temporal—the earls and barons—to form the House of Lords; the knights of the shire and the burgesses merged to form the House of Commons.

This gradual merger of knights and burgesses was an event of major significance that laid the social foundation for the future greatness of the House of Commons. It brought together two elements, the one representing the gentry, the lower level of the second estate, and the other representing the third estate, which had always remained separate in the assemblies of the Continental states. In the fourteenth century the knights of the shire had little sense of social unity with the burgesses. But some of the smaller boroughs were represented by knights from the countryside nearby. By the end of the fourteenth century the Commons began to choose one of their members to report to the king on their deliberations, and this position developed into the important office of Speaker of the House.

In the meantime, the political foundations of the future greatness of the House of Commons were also being laid. In the fourteenth century the chief business of Parliament was judicial. From time to time the knights and burgesses employed the judicial device of presenting petitions to the king; whatever was approved in the petitions was then embodied in statutes. The growth of parliamentary power was further stimulated by Edward III's frequent requests to Parliament for new grants of money to cover the heavy expenses of the Hundred Years' War. Slowly Parliament took control of the purse strings, while Edward let the royal powers be whittled away imperceptibly.

Richard II and Bastard Feudalism, 1377–1399

When Edward III died, his ten-year-old grandson succeeded as Richard II (r. 1377–1399). Richard's reign was marked by mounting factionalism and peasant discontent. Both conflicts strongly resembled those of their French coun-terparts—the strife between Burgundy and Armagnac, and the Jacquerie of 1358. Just as the Jacquerie opposed attempts to regulate life in ways ulti-mately bound to benefit the nobility and the entrepreneur, so did the Peas-ants' Revolt of 1381.

The social disorders arose out of protests against the imposition of poll (head) taxes, which fell equally upon all subjects; the poorer classes bitterly resented paying their shilling a head for each person over fifteen. Riots pro-voked by attempts to collect the tax led to the Peasants' Revolt. Under the leadership of John Ball, a priest, and Wat Tyler, a day laborer, the peasants burned manor records to destroy evidence of their obligations, murdered the archbishop of Canterbury, and demanded the end of serfdom and the seizure of clerical wealth. When they marched on London, the fifteen-year-old king promised to settle their grievances. But Richard failed to keep his promises and permitted severe reprisals against the rebels.

The most longstanding popular statement of the grievances of the rural population is the legend of Robin Hood, who seems to have been a thir-teenth-century Yorkshire criminal. The first written reference appears in *Piers Plowman*. The legend became firmly entrenched in the fifteenth century, and Robin Hood's adventures became part of the *gest,* some thirty ballads accom-panied by lute and harp. These ballads spoke of economic and social griev-ances, of the constant savaging of open lot and woodland by the followers of noblemen and gentry, of fears of both tyrants and towns.

Under Richard II and his successors, factional strife assumed critical dimensions. During the fourteenth century the baronage had become a smaller and richer class of great magnates, whose relationship to their vassals grew to be based more on cash and less on military service and protection. These great lords recruited the armed following they still owed to the king by hiring small private armies to go to war for them. Soldiers in these armies were bound by written indenture and a retaining fee. This was known as liv-ery and maintenance, since the lord provided uniforms for his retainers, who, in turn, maintained others. Although forbidden by statute in 1390, this prac-tice continued to flourish. The danger from private armies became greater during each interlude of peace in the war with France, when mercenaries accustomed to plundering in a foreign country returned to England.

Strife had begun during the last years of Edward III, when effective control of the government passed from the aging king to one of his younger sons, John of Gaunt, duke of Lancaster. John of Gaunt could mobilize a private army of fifteen hundred men, and his faction persisted under Richard II. New factions also appeared, centered on two of the king's uncles, the dukes of York and Gloucester. After defeating Richard II's supporters in battle, Gloucester had royal ministers condemned for treason in a packed Parlia-ment (1388). Richard II waited a few years and then in 1397 arrested Glouces-ter and moved against his confederates. The king packed Parliament in his own favor and had it pass retroactive treason laws. Richard's confiscation of the estates of his exiled first cousin, Henry of Bolingbroke, son of John of Gaunt, set off a revolution. After Bolingbroke's landing in England, Richard was forced to abdicate in 1399 and was murdered. Bolingbroke became Henry IV (r. 1399–1413), first monarch of the house of Lancaster.

Lancaster and York, 1399–1485

Henry IV owed his position in part to confirmation by Parliament, which was sensitive about allowing any assertion of royal authority. Moreover, Henry faced a series of revolts. The last years of his reign were troubled by poor health and by the hostility of his son, Henry V (r. 1413–1422). Henry V renewed the Hundred Years' War with spectacular victories and reasserted royal power at home, tempered by his need to secure parliamentary support to finance his French campaigns. He also vigorously persecuted the Lollards.

The untimely death of Henry V in 1422 ended the brief period of Lancastrian success, for it brought to the throne Henry VI (r. 1422–1461), a nine-month-old infant who proved mentally unstable as he grew up. As English forces were defeated in the last campaigns of the Hundred Years' War, the feebleness of Henry VI strengthened both the hand of Parliament and the growth of private armed retainers. While corrupt noble factions competed for control of government, a quarrel broke out between Henry VI's queen, Margaret of Anjou, and her English allies on the one side, and on the other, Richard, duke of York, once regent of France and now heir to the English throne. The quarrel led directly to the Wars of the Roses (1455–1485), so named for the red rose, badge of the House of Lancaster, and the white rose, badge of the House of York.

In thirty years of dreary, sporadic fighting, Parliament became the tool of rival factions, and the kingdom changed hands repeatedly. In 1460 Richard of York was killed, and the ambitious earl of Warwick took over the leadership of the Yorkist cause. Warwick forced the abdication of Henry VI and placed on the throne the son of Richard of York, Edward IV (r. 1461–1483). King and kingmaker soon fell out, and Warwick briefly restored the house of Lancaster to the throne (1470–1471). Edward IV quickly regained control, however, and Henry VI and Warwick were killed. With Edward securely established, firm royal government returned to England.

Again, however, the prospect of stability faded, for Edward IV died in 1483. His twelve-year-old son, Edward V, was soon pushed aside by his guardian and uncle, Richard III (r. 1483–1485), last of the Yorkist kings. Able, courageous, and ruthless, Richard III continues to be the focus of much controversy. There is still debate over whether Richard was responsible for the death of Edward V and his younger brother. In any case, factional strife flared up again as Richard's opponents found a champion in the Lancastrian leader Henry Tudor. In 1485, on Bosworth Field, Richard III was slain, and the Wars of the Roses came to an end. The battle gave England a new monarch, Henry VII, and a new dynasty, the Tudors.

Henry VII, 1485–1509

Henry VII (r. 1485–1509) was descended from a bastard branch of the Lancastrian family. His right to be king, however, derived not from this tenuous hereditary claim but from his victory at Bosworth and a subsequent act of Parliament. The new monarch had excellent qualifications for the job of tidying up after the divisiveness of civil war. Shrewd, able, working very closely with his councilors, waging foreign policy by diplomacy and not by arms, Henry VII had much in common with Louis XI of France. Unlike Louis, however, Henry was devout and generous. He formally healed the breach between the rival houses of the roses by marrying the Yorkist heiress Elizabeth, daughter of Edward IV, and deprived the nobles of their private armies by forbidding livery and maintenance.

Henry rewarded many of his advisers with lands confiscated from his opponents at the end of the Wars of the Roses. The king and his councilors more than doubled the revenues of the central government, at times by high-handed methods. When prelates were summoned to make special payments to the king, those who dressed magnificently to plead exemption on the grounds of the cost of high church office were told that their rich apparel proved their ability to make a large payment. Those who dressed shabbily in order to claim poverty were told that their frugality argued that they, too, could afford a large contribution. Such practices enabled Henry to avoid a clash with Parliament because he seldom needed its sanction for taxes.

Henry VII reestablished prosperity as well as law and order in an England weary of rebellion, civil war, and insecurity. He restored the prestige of the monarchy, making it the rallying point of English nationalism. He fixed the pattern for Tudor policy toward the English Parliament. Henry asked Parliament for money as seldom as possible; during the last dozen years of his reign he had to summon only one Parliament, which met for a few weeks in 1504. Even so, when it refused to give him all the monies he wanted, he yielded gracefully and avoided a confrontation.

Spain, to 1492

The decisive event in the early medieval history of the Iberian peninsula was the conquest by the Muslims, who brought almost the whole of the peninsula under their control. In the eighth and ninth centuries, Christian communities free of Muslim domination survived only in the extreme north. Starting in the ninth century, these Christian states had pressed southward until the last Muslim stronghold at Granada fell in 1492. The reconquest of Spain, like the great Crusades to the Holy Land, was a disjointed movement, undertaken in fits and starts by rival states that sometimes put more energy into combating each other than into fighting the Muslims.

Three Christian kingdoms dominated the Iberian peninsula in the middle of the fifteenth century. Castile, the largest and most populous, had assumed the leadership of the reconquest. But the power of the Castilian kings did not

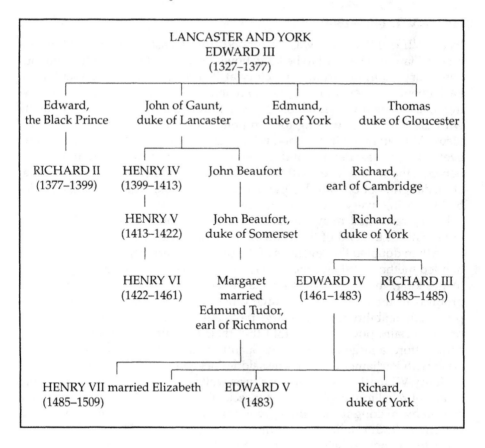

grow in proportion to their territory. The powerful organization of sheep-ranchers, the *Mesta*, controlled vast stretches of Castilian territory. Both the nobility and the towns maintained many rights against royal authority. Both were represented, together with the clergy, in the *Cortes*, the Castilian counterpart of the English Parliament and the French Estates General. The Cortes was, however, largely powerless by the fifteenth century.

To the west of Castile, along the Atlantic coast, lay the second Christian kingdom, Portugal, a former Castilian province that had won independence in the twelfth century. Although still retaining close links with Castile, the Portuguese had developed their own distinctive language and pursued their own national interests, especially in exploration and overseas commerce.

The third kingdom, located in northeastern Spain, was Aragon, which was as much a Mediterranean power as an Iberian one. Its kings controlled the Balearic Islands, ruled lands along the Mediterranean on the French side of the Pyrenees, and had an important stake in southern Italy. In the breakup of the Hohenstaufen Empire, Aragon took the island of Sicily (1282) and King

Alfonso V, the Magnanimous (r. 1416–1458), added Naples in 1435. In Aragon, as in Castile, the oldest established political institutions were those limiting the Crown—the nobility, the towns, and the Cortes, which was much more powerful than in Castile. Moreover, two territories of the Crown of Aragon on the Spanish mainland, Valencia and Catalonia, the latter centered on the prosperous port of Barcelona, had Cortes of their own and were, in effect, separate states.

In 1469 Ferdinand, later king of Aragon (1479–1516), married Isabella, later queen of Castile (1474–1504), and thus made the dynastic alliance that eventually unified Spain. The obstacles confronting them were enormous. Not only was the royal power weak in both states, the inhabitants of Castile and Aragon did not speak the same language. Aragon looked toward the Mediterranean, Castile toward the Atlantic, so that a union of Castile with Portugal might have been more natural.

Ferdinand and Isabella made a good political partnership. He was a cautious realist and skeptical and tolerant in religion. Isabella, on the other hand, was devout to the point of intolerance and enjoyed the pomp and circumstance of the throne. She vested much authority in a new body staffed by royal appointees, the Council of Castile. She allied herself with the middle class of the towns against the nobles and drew military support from town militias rather than from feudal levies. Finding her sovereignty weakened by three large military brotherhoods founded in the twelfth century to advance the reconquest (and controlled by the Castilian nobility), she insisted that Ferdinand become head of each brotherhood.

Although pious, the queen was determined to bring the church under royal discipline, and she prescribed a much-needed purge of ecclesiastical corruption. The Spanish monarchs also obtained from the papacy the right to appoint Spanish bishops. Like the Gallican Church of France, the Spanish Church was half-independent of Rome. The ranking Spanish prelate, Cardinal Jiménez de Cisneros (1436–1517), became Isabella's chief minister and executed her policies of purifying the church, curbing the aristocracy, and courting the towns.

The Inquisition was introduced into Spain in 1478; it was from the first a royal rather than a papal instrument. The Spanish Inquisition sought to promote Spanish nationalism by enforcing universal Catholicism and to create loyal subjects of the Crown by obliging all people to be obedient children of the Church. Its chief targets were New Christians, or *conversos*—those who had been forcibly converted from Judaism to Christianity. The fear it pursued through intense investigation was that Jews were continuing to practice their former religion, but clandestinely. The persecution of conversos drove more than 100,000 to flee to the Low Countries, where they were known as *Marranos*, suggesting their exotic appearance in the eyes of the Dutch and Flemish. In 1492 unconverted Jews were confronted with the alternatives of baptism or exile with the loss of their property; about 150,000 chose exile. Ten years later, it was the turn of the Muslims, who received no choice except baptism. Catholicism thereby won many nominal new adherents who conformed only because they dreaded what the Inquisition had in store for those who wavered in their new faith.

The year 1492, accordingly, may be viewed as the most crucial date in Spanish history. It began, on January 2, with the triumphal entry of Ferdinand and Isabella into Granada, marking the conquest of the last fragment of independent Muslim Spain. Later in the year, the way was opened for immense new conquests when Christopher Columbus sailed from a Castilian port on the first of his voyages to the New World.

Particularism in Germany and Italy

Power in Germany shifted steadily from the emperor to the princes of the particular states. For almost two decades, there was no emperor at all. This was the Great Interregnum (1254–1273), following the death of the last Hohenstaufen king, Conrad IV. During this time the princes grew even stronger at the expense of the monarchy, and the old links between Germany and Italy were cut.

The Princes and the Empire, 1254–1493

The imperial title survived. It went to Rudolf of Habsburg (r. 1273–1291), whose estates lay mostly in modern-day Austria, parts of southern Germany, and parts of Switzerland. Rudolf wanted to establish a hereditary monarchy for his family and make this monarchy as rich and as powerful as possible. He added Austria to the family holdings, and his descendants ruled at Vienna until 1918. Rudolf made concessions to the French in the west to get their support for the new Habsburg monarchy.

After 1270, consequently, the French moved into imperial territories that had once belonged to the old Carolingian middle kingdom. The German princes, however, opposed the Habsburg policy of appeasing the French. Thus, during the century following the Interregnum two parties developed in Germany. The Habsburg party, eastern-based and pro-French, favored a strong hereditary monarchy. The opposition party, western-based and anti-French, was against a strong hereditary monarchy.

Toward the middle of the fourteenth century, the princes as a class secured a great victory, which was embodied in the Golden Bull of 1356, issued by the emperor Charles IV. It affirmed that imperial majesty derived from God, that the German electoral princes chose the emperor, and that the choice of the majority of the electors needed no confirmation by the pope. The electors were to number seven: three ecclesiastical princes—the archbishops of Mainz, Trier, and Cologne—and four secular princes—the count palatine of the Rhine, the duke of Saxony, the margrave of Brandenburg, and the king of Bohemia. The rights of the four secular electors were to pass to their eldest sons, and their territories could never be divided. Each of the seven electors was to be all but sovereign in his own territory.

Throughout the fourteenth century, the German princes faced the threat of new political fragmentation, especially from their administrative officials, the *ministeriales.* To levy taxes, the princes had to obtain the consent of the nobles and knights, along with that of the other two estates—the clergy and the towns. The estates regularly won privileges from the princes in exchange for money. This period also saw the rise of the *Hansa* (league of merchants) of North German commercial towns and the increasing prominence of sovereign "free cities," such as Hamburg and Frankfurt, all over Germany.

After about 1400 the princes who were not electors gradually adopted for their own principalities the rules of primogeniture (inheritance by the first-born) and indivisibility that the Golden Bull had prescribed for the electoral principalities. The princes were assisted in their assertion of authority by the spread of Roman law, which helped them make good their claims to absolute control of public rights and offices. Gradually, in dozens of petty states, orderly finance, indivisible princely domains, and taxation granted by the estates became typical.

With numerous sovereign princes firmly established and free cities enjoying virtual independence, the empire had become almost meaningless. It had lost control not only over the western lands taken by France but also over other frontier areas, notably Switzerland. By the early sixteenth century the Swiss, backed by France, had checked both Burgundian and German attempts to subjugate them. The Swiss Confederation, although nominally still subject to the Empire, was in fact an independent entity. Thus, another national state was emerging, although one without a strong central authority.

In 1438 the Holy Roman emperorship, although still elective, passed permanently to the house of Habsburg. Fifty-five years later Maximilian I (r. 1493–1519) became emperor without being crowned by the pope. He had acquired great riches by marrying Mary of Burgundy. Maximilian reestablished firm Habsburg power in Austria and its dependencies. He also arranged marriages for his children and grandchildren that promised to add vast new territories to the family possessions and that would make his grandson, Charles V, ruler of half of Europe.

Despots and Condottieri in Italy, 1268–1513

In Italy the medieval struggle between popes and emperors had promoted the growth of independent communes or city-states, particularly in northern Italy. In the twelfth and thirteenth centuries the communes were oligarchic republics. The ruling oligarchies, however, were torn by the strife between the pro-papal Guelfs and the pro-imperial Ghibellines. Meantime, something close to class warfare arose between the wealthy, on the one hand, and the small shopkeepers and wage earners, on the other. Dissension grew so bitter that arbitrary one-man government seemed the only remedy. Sometimes a despot seized power; sometimes he was invited in from outside by the contending factions; often he was a *condottiere,* a mercenary commander the states had hired under contract to fight their wars. One of the first great condottieri was an Englishman, Sir John Hawkwood, who as a soldier of fortune sold himself to various communes. In the fifteenth century the most celebrated

Germany and the Baltic in the Fifteenth Century

condottieri were drawn from noble dynasties such as the Gonzaga of Mantua, or were ambitious commoners such as Francesco Sforza, who became duke of Milan (r. 1450–1466).

By the fifteenth century the fortunes of war and politics had worked significant changes in the map of Italy. Many city-states that had been important a century or two earlier were sinking into political obscurity. Several small states now dominated Italian politics—Naples in the south, the States of the Church in the center, and the duchy of Milan and the republics of Florence and Venice in the north.

The kingdom of Naples, which included Sicily, had long been subject to foreign domination. In 1266 Charles of Anjou conquered the territory. The kingdom of Sicily revolted (1282) and passed to the control of Aragon, and eventually to the Spain of Ferdinand and Isabella. Naples remained under Angevin rule until 1435, when it was taken by Alfonso the Magnanimous of Aragon. On his death it became independent once more under his illegitimate son Ferrante (Ferdinand I, r. 1458–1494). Under Angevin and Aragonese rule the area never fully recovered the prosperity and cultural leadership it had earlier enjoyed.

The States of the Church also experienced a material decline in the fourteenth and early fifteenth centuries. While the papacy was at Avignon, Rome passed to the control of rival princely families; outlying papal territories fell to local lords or despots. The angry Romans, determined to bring the papacy back to their city permanently, intimidated the French-dominated College of Cardinals into electing an Italian as Urban VI. The new pope alarmed the cardinals by plans for drastic reform, and thirteen of them proceeded to declare his election invalid and chose a rival to rule the Church from Avignon, "Clement VII" (r. 1378–1394). (The quotation marks indicate that he does not rank as a legitimate pope and distinguish him from the sixteenth-century Pope Clement VII.) These events inaugurated the Great Schism (1378–1417), when there were two popes, each with his own College of Cardinals—one at Rome, the other at Avignon.

Against the scandal of the Great Schism, the body of the Church rallied in the Conciliar movement, which began when both Colleges of Cardinals agreed to summon a general council of five hundred prelates and representatives from European states. The Council of Pisa (1409–1410) deposed both papal claimants and elected an Italian, "John XXIII" (r. 1410–1414). Since neither of the rival popes accepted the council's actions, there were now three popes. A second general council, meeting at Constance (1414–1417), finally ended the Great Schism and elected Martin V (r. 1417–1431), a Roman aristocrat, thus restoring the formal unity of Western Christendom.

On other issues, however, the Conciliar movement was less successful. The Council of Constance tried the Bohemian reformer Jan Hus (c. 1369–1415) for doctrinal heresy and had him burned at the stake in violation of a guarantee of his safety. The movement Hus had started continued until the Hussites were again granted communion at the Council of Basel in 1436. Neither this council nor its successors, which met sporadically until 1449, managed to

The Florentine Andrea del Verrocchio's dramatic monument (1488) of the condottiere Bartolomeo Colleoni, who became generalissimo of Venice in 1454.   (Alinari/Art Resource. NY)

purge the church of corruption and worldliness. And their efforts to transform the papacy from an absolute monarchy into a constitutional one by making general councils a permanent feature of ecclesiastical government were thwarted. Nevertheless, important limitations were placed on the pope's authority. A notable example was the Pragmatic Sanction of Bourges, which in 1438 gave the Gallican Church a large measure of autonomy.

With the Conciliar movement defeated, the popes concentrated once more on central Italy. Beginning with Sixtus IV (r. 1471–1484), the office of Pope was held by a series of ambitious men. They were often highly cultivated and very secular as well. They restored Rome as a center of art and learning and began the reconquest of the papal dominions outside Rome. A Spanish pope from the Borgia family, Alexander VI (r. 1492–1503), made notable progress in subjugating the lords of central Italy and breaking the power of the Roman princely families. Alexander was greatly aided by his son, who employed violence, treachery, and poison to gain his ends. The most redoubtable of these militant popes was Julius II (r. 1503–1513). The pontificate of Julius II marked the summit of papal temporal power, which receded thereafter because of the wounds inflicted on the Church by the Reformation and the damage sustained by Italy as the battleground in wars between the Habsburgs and Valois.

Milan, 1277–1535

Milan lay in the midst of the fertile plain of Lombardy. It was the terminus of trade routes from northern Europe and was also a textile and metalworking center. It had played a major political role since the twelfth century, when it headed the Lombard League. Milan was then a republic, run by the nobility in conjunction with a *parlamento,* or great council, in which all citizens of modest means could participate. This precarious balance between aristocracy and democracy was upset by outbreaks of Guelf and Ghibelline factionalism. In 1277 authority was seized by the noble Visconti family, who in 1395 finally secured recognition from the emperor as dukes of Milan.

When the direct Visconti line died out in 1447, Francesco Sforza usurped the ducal office in 1450. The most famous of the Sforza dukes was a younger son of Francesco, Ludovico Il Moro (1451–1508). Ludovico made the court of Milan one of the most brilliant in Europe by assembling a retinue of outstanding artists and intellectuals, most famously Leonardo da Vinci (1452–1519). His craftiness could not protect him against the armies of France and Spain, which invaded Italy in the 1490s. Driven from his throne in 1500, Il Moro died in French imprisonment eight years later. The duchy of Milan came under Spanish control in 1535 and remained there for almost two hundred years.

Florence, to 1569

The Republic of Florence, like that of Milan, was a fragile combination of aristocratic and democratic elements. It was badly shaken by Guelf-Ghibelline rivalries and by the emergence of an ambitious wealthy class of bankers and merchants. In the twelfth century the commune had acquired a dominant position.

Florence exemplified the growth of social mobility, new wealth, extensive trade, and complex credit operations. Increasingly society was based on the need to work cooperatively, as best shown by the widespread use of credit in both public and private finance. There grew a productive tension between the cult of poverty (and insecurity) that was deeply rooted in monastic and philosophical Christian thought and the desire for wealth (and security) that lay at the base of the growth of the Italian cities. The factionalism, therefore, expressed very major concerns in a changing society.

In the late 1200s Guelf capitalists prevailed over the Ghibelline aristocrats and revised the constitution of the republic so that a virtual monopoly of key government offices rested with the seven major guilds, which were controlled by the great woolen masters, bankers, and exporters. They denied any

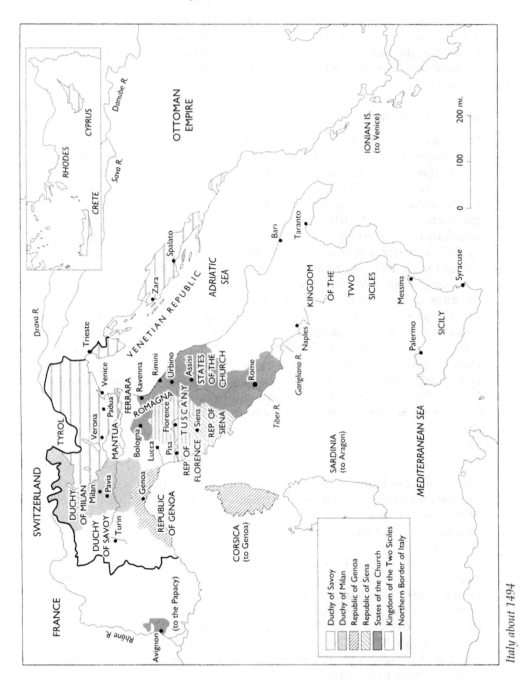

Italy about 1494

effective political voice to the artisans and shopkeepers of the fourteen lesser guilds, as well as to Ghibellines, many nobles, and common laborers. But feuds within Guelf ranks soon caused a new exodus of political exiles, including the poet Dante.

Throughout the fourteenth century and into the fifteenth, political factionalism and social and economic tensions tormented Florence, although they did not prevent a remarkable cultural growth. The politically unprivileged sought to make the republic more democratic; they failed in the long run because of the oligarchy's resilience and also because the reformers themselves were torn by the hostility between the lesser guilds and the *ciompi*, or poor day laborers. The English king Edward III's repudiation of his debts to the Florentine bankers, followed in the 1340s by disastrous bank failures, weakened the major guilds enough to permit the fourteen lesser guilds to gain supremacy.

Unrest persisted, however, reaching a climax with the revolution of the ciompi in 1378. Wool carders, weavers, and dyers gained the right to form their own guilds and to have a minor voice in politics. Continued turbulence permitted the wealthy to gain the upper hand over both the ciompi and the lesser guilds. The prestige of the reestablished oligarchy rose when it defended the city against the threat of annexation by the aggressive Visconti of Milan. Finally, in the early 1400s, a new rash of bankruptcies and a series of military reverses weakened the hold of the oligarchy. In 1434 some of its leaders were forced into exile, and power passed to a political champion of the poor, Cosimo de' Medici.

For the next sixty years (1434–1494) Florence was ruled informally by the Medici, who were perhaps the wealthiest family in all Italy. Their application of the graduated income tax bore heavily on the rich, particularly on their political enemies, while the resources of the Medici bank were employed to weaken their opponents and assist their friends. They operated quietly behind the facade of republican institutions. Cosimo, for example, seldom held any public office and kept himself in the background.

The grandson of Cosimo was Lorenzo, ruler of Florence from 1469 to 1492 and known as the Magnificent. Although possessing the wide-ranging interests admired by his contemporaries, Lorenzo was not without flaws. His neglect of military matters and his financial carelessness, which contributed to the failure of the Medici bank, left Florence poorly prepared for the wars that were to engulf Italy in the late 1400s.

Venice in the Fifteenth Century

The third great north Italian state, Venice, enjoyed a political stability that contrasted with the turbulence of Milan and Florence. By the fifteenth century the Republic of Saint Mark, as it was called, was in fact an empire that controlled the lower Po valley on the Italian mainland, the Dalmatian coast of the Adriatic, the Ionian islands, and part of mainland Greece. The Po territories had been annexed to secure the defenses and food supply of the island capital, and the others were the legacy of its aggressive role in the Crusades.

A map of Florence in 1490. *(Scala/Art Resource, NY)*

The Venetian constitution assumed its definitive form in the early fourteenth century. Earlier, the chief executive had been the *doge,* or "duke," first appointed by the Byzantine emperor, then elected; the legislature had been a general assembly of all the citizens. However, the Venetian merchants feared that a powerful doge might establish a hereditary monarchy, and they found the assembly unwieldly and unbusinesslike. Accordingly, they relegated the doge to a ceremonial role and transformed the old assembly into the Great Council, whose membership of 240 men was limited to the families listed in a special Golden Book. The Great Council, in turn, elected the doge and the members of the smaller councils, which really ran the government. Foremost among these was the Council of Ten, charged with maintaining the security of the republic.

The Venetian system gave a permanent monopoly of political power to the old merchant families listed in the Golden Book. Yet the oligarchs of Venice, while denying the majority a voice in politics and sternly repressing all opposition, instituted many projects that served the general welfare, from neighborhood fountains to a great naval arsenal. They treated the subject cities of the empire with fairness and generosity, and developed a corps of diplomats to serve the far-reaching concerns of a great commercial power. Venice was unique among Italian states for its political calm and order.

"The School of Europe"

The Italian states of the fifteenth century have been called "the school of Europe," instructing the rest of the Continent in the new realistic ways of power politics. Despots such as Il Moro or Cesare Borgia, or Lorenzo the Magnificent, or the oligarchs of Venice might well have given lessons in statecraft to Henry VII of England or Louis XI of France. In international affairs, the experiments with diplomatic missions made by Venice, by the Visconti of Milan, and by the Gonzaga family in Mantua marked an early stage in the development of permanent diplomatic embassies. Italian reliance on condot-tieri in warfare foreshadowed the increased use of mercenaries and the aban-donment of the old feudal levies.

However, Italy also furnished an object lesson in how not to behave polit-ically. By the close of the fifteenth century it was evident that the balance established among the Italian states was too precarious to preserve their independence. Beginning with the French invasion of 1494, Italy became a prize for the new national dynastic imperialists of France, Spain, and the Habsburg realm. The Italians of the Renaissance, like the Greeks of antiquity whom they resembled, were victimized by stronger neighbors and penalized for their failure to form a united Italy.

These lessons from "the school of Europe" were first drawn by Niccolò Machiavelli (1469–1527), a diplomat who served the restored Florentine republic from 1494 to 1512 and was exiled when the Medici returned in 1512. Soon after, he wrote *The Prince* and dedicated it to the Medici ruler in the vain hope of regaining political favor. *The Prince* presented low opinion of human beings in general:

> They are ungrateful, changeable, simulators and dissimulators, runaways in danger, eager for gain; while you do well by them they are all yours; they offer you their blood, their property, their lives, their children . . . when need is far off; but when it comes near you, they turn about.*

The politics of *The Prince* follow directly from its estimate of human nature:

> Since . . . a prince is necessitated to play the animal well, he chooses among the beasts the fox and the lion, because the lion does not protect himself from traps; the fox does not protect himself from wolves. The prince must be a fox, there-fore, to recognize the traps and a lion to frighten the wolves. . . . By no means can a prudent ruler keep his word—and he does not—when to keep it works against himself and when the reasons that made him promise are annulled. If all men were good, this maxim would not be good, but because they are bad and do not keep their promises to you, you likewise do not have to keep yours to them.†

The Prince was a prescription against the severe political maladies afflicting Italy in the early 1500s. But what precisely was Machiavelli's diagnosis of Italy's ills, and what precisely was his recommended prescription? Scholars do not entirely agree. Some believe that *The Prince* is to be taken literally and that Italy's desperate plight in the face of foreign invasion required a desper-ate remedy. Others argue that Machiavelli's intention was satirical and that he was warning Italians against relying on excessive despotism, even during a national emergency.

When *The Prince* is set next to Machiavelli's twenty-fold longer work, *The Discourses on the First Ten Books of Livy* (the Roman historian), it is far more dif-

---

*Niccolò Machiavelli, *The Prince*, in *The Chief Works and Others*, trans. Allen Gilbert (Durham, N.C.: Duke University Press, 1965). l. 62, © 1965 Duke University Press.
†Ibid., l, 65.

ficult to argue that the representation of human nature in *The Prince* is Machiavelli's own belief. In *The Discourses,* Machiavelli addressed the problem of building a stable and lasting government, not within the peculiarly volatile context of early sixteenth-century Italy, but as an abstract question. There he presents a very different argument, closer in spirit to the man who served in Florence's short-lived republican experiment.

The Prince may well have been a bitter satire on the excesses of despotic princes, so many of whom in Renaissance Italy were former mercenaries, and the deformations of civic virtue that courts and courtier culture engendered. It was taken, however, by such powerful rulers as the Holy Roman Emperor Charles V as a handbook for princes, the most rational in a long line of such handbooks. Whether the expression of satire or detached reason, *The Prince* presented a vision of politics that has proven more influential than any other single text in the formation of the modern state. In it, Machiavelli separated religious ethics from the conduct of government, the ruler from his representation to his subjects, and "Realpolitik" from appearances and, perhaps most importantly, argued for conscious and rational instrumentalism in pursuit of a stable state. The work was the first of its kind, even as the practices it supported were already to be found in the rules of the Tudor Henry VII, the Valois, Louis XI, Ferdinand of Aragon, the Sforza, the Medici, and the Borgia dynasties in Italy.

These were very different rulers from their predecessors. None would be canonized for saintly behavior. Henry VII, Louis XI, and Ferdinand all laid foundations for the new states of the early modern period through calculation, a "ruthlessness" that contemporaries marked, and an instrumentalism in the pursuit of stability. The attention to self-representation, the calculated use of diplomacy and bureaucracy, the clear understanding of the extent and limits of their authority, and their efforts to increase their "power" all make manifest how life had changed during the later Middle Ages.

SUMMARY

The transition from medieval to modern times was marked by the consolidation of royal power, the decline of serfdom, the revolt against the medieval church, and the increasing importance of a money economy. These changes were hastened by the calamity and hardships of the late Middle Ages, including the Hundred Years' War, the Black Death, the Great Schism in the church, and the threat of Turkish invasion.

In France, the consolidation of royal power was interrupted by the Hundred Years' War (1337–1453). The war broke out after Edward III of England laid claim to the French throne. England gained early victories at Crécy (1346) and Poitiers (1356) and captured the French king.

A peasant revolt, the Jacquerie, and factional strife between Armagnacs and Burgundians contributed to French inability to unify against the English. After the battle of Agincourt (1415), the French king, Charles VI, adopted Henry V of England as heir to the throne. Rallying behind Joan of Arc, whose mystical faith inspired French patriotism, French armies began to drive the English back. Although Joan was burned at the stake for witchcraft, the new French king Charles VII regained control of his lands.

By the end of the Hundred Years' War, the French monarch had gained important powers from the Estates General: the right to keep a standing army and the right to collect the taille. Louis XI (1461–1483), a crafty politician, centralized royal administration, eliminated bastard feudalism, and laid the foundations for absolutism in France.

In England, a strong national monarchy also had emerged by the late 1400s. However, unlike France, where the Estates General was subservient to the Crown, the English Parliament had power to grant money and thereby exert control over the monarch.

During the fourteenth and fifteenth centuries, England was affected by social and economic dislocations as a result of the Black Death. The emergence of English nationalism was reflected in the official use of English in place of Norman French. In Parliament, two houses began to emerge, and a significant alliance evolved between knights and burgesses in the House of Commons.

Henry VII (r. 1485–1509), a shrewd ruler who established the Tudor dynasty, restored property, law, and order after the factional strife of the Wars of the Roses (1455–1485). He also centralized royal authority and inaugurated new fiscal policies.

In Spain, three Christian kingdoms had emerged by the fifteenth century: Castile, Portugal, and Aragon. A dynastic marriage between Ferdinand of Aragon and Isabella of Castile led to the consolidation of royal power in Spain. With the support of the Church, Spain imposed religious uniformity, forcing tens of thousands of Spanish Jews and Muslims to convert. By 1492, Ferdinand and Isabella had ousted the Muslims from their last stronghold in Granada and embarked on a policy of religious and national intolerance that would mark the Spanish monarchy for centuries to come.

In Germany, the principle of an elective monarchy triumphed in the fourteenth century and was confirmed in the Golden Bull of 1356. Sovereign princes and free cities ruled their own territories. In the west, the Swiss Confederation became virtually independent of the Holy Roman Empire. After 1483, Holy Roman emperors, although elected, were always members of the house of Habsburg.

In Italy, individual city-states rather than any central authority prevented the development of national awareness. Of the three most powerful states of northern Italy—Milan, Florence, and Venice—only Venice enjoyed political stability under merchant oligarchs. Venice introduced the idea of establishing diplomatic embassies throughout Europe.

The Florentine diplomat Niccolò Machiavelli (1469–1527) wrote two books, *The Prince* and *The Discourses*, which embodied ideas that would shape the modern world: the primacy of secular over religious interests, the realities of power politics, and the importance of national identity.

THREE

The Renaissance

∞

Renaissance—rebirth—is the name traditionally bestowed upon the remarkable outpouring of intellectual and artistic energy and talent that accompanied the passage of Europe from the Middle Ages to the modern epoch. Yet "Renaissance" to a large extent was the creation of nineteenth-century scholars who, looking back on the intense flowering of culture, sought a name by which to designate it. The term is also often extended to politics and economics.

Most scholars accept that the Renaissance started in Italy around 1300 and continued for three centuries, during which the economic, intellectual, and cultural currents flowing from its homeland eventually reached France, the Low Countries, Germany, England, and also, although with diminished force, Spain and Portugal. By 1600, it had virtually ended, giving way to a culture called *baroque* and a new approach to classical art.

Few scholars would date the start of the Renaissance later than 1350. Many argue for two "Renaissances": one a period of revival based on the old learning and spread through traditional methods; the other a period of innovation in which much new knowledge was generated and spread by a new medium, print—which meant that a far wider community could share in and debate the changes. Still other scholars find three distinct periods to the Renaissance, coinciding roughly with the "three ages of mankind": youth, maturity, and decline. There was a Renaissance of the twelfth century as well as the greater flowering of the fifteenth century, however the term might be used.

It is extremely difficult to establish the degree to which the term *Renaissance* should be interpreted literally. Were the classical values of ancient Greece and Rome in fact reborn at the close of the Middle Ages? If so, for whom? Only for an elite group with the money and time to explore the meanings of the classics? Or for a far broader part of the population, although in ruder and less evident ways? Could such a rebirth alone account for the extraordinarily productive careers of Renaissance writers, sculptors, painters, architects, musicians, and scientists? Until the middle of the nineteenth century most educated people would have answered yes to all these questions.

Today this simple answer no longer suffices. Today it is almost universally agreed that a great Christian civilization had, in fact, matured during the

Middle Ages and that the cultural heritage from classical antiquity had never disappeared from the West. During this time European society had gradually shifted from an oral to a print culture, from Gothic to Italic ways of writing, and from the preservation of knowledge to the expansion of information through the power of printing. Some historians contend that the cultural rebirth had begun in the "Carolingian Renaissance," or the "Renaissance of the twelfth century" centered at the court of Eleanor of Aquitaine. But to claim that the germ of the Renaissance had sprouted long before 1300 is to go too far.

The thinkers and artists of the Renaissance owed much to their medieval predecessors, and they were often as religious and as "feudal" as their forebears. Yet they were also materialistic, skeptical, and individualistic. Human beings were attempting to create things, to do things, to study things as ends in themselves because they enjoyed them, derived a sense of accomplishment from them, and felt they were contributing to their own security and well-being, rather than doing things as a means to the glorification of God and to salvation.

A Money Economy

Trade

The areas of Europe to the west of the Adriatic Sea and the Elbe River were changing from the more subsistence-oriented economy of the early Middle Ages to a money economy, from an economy based in good measure on home-grown produce paid for in kind to one relying heavily on imports paid for in money or letters of credit. By the fifteenth century the West had long been importing the spices of the East; salt from the mines of Germany or the sea-salt pans of the Atlantic coast; and the wines of the Rhine, Burgundy, and Bordeaux. The furs of eastern Europe, the wool of England and Spain, and the woolen cloth of Flanders and Italy commanded good markets. At the close of the Middle Ages supplies of palatable food and warm clothing were steadily increasing.

Trade slumped during the serious economic depression of the early 1300s and in the prolonged aftermath of many wet summers, the Black Death, and the Hundred Years' War. Recovery came in the fifteenth century, and by the late 1400s the trade of the West could, for the first time, be compared in relative volume and variety with that of the Roman Empire, of Byzantium at its peak, and of Norman and Hohenstaufen Sicily. Meantime, Western merchants developed more elaborate commercial procedures and organizations.

In the fourteenth and fifteenth centuries the membership of the *Hansa* (the German word means "league") included almost a hundred towns, among which Lübeck, Hamburg, Bremen, and Danzig were the leaders. Its policies were determined by meetings of representatives from the member towns, usually held at Lübeck. The weakness of the Holy Roman Empire and the fact that many of the Hanseatic towns began as autonomous frontier outposts enabled the Hansa to play a virtually independent political and military role, besides exercising great economic power.

The Hansa was not the first important confederation of commercial towns in Europe; alliances of communes in Lombardy and in Flanders had blocked the ambitions of Hohenstaufen emperors and French kings, respectively. The Hansa, however, operated on a grander scale; its ships carried Baltic fish, timber, grain, furs, metals, and amber to western European markets and brought back cloth, wine, and spices. Hanseatic merchants, traveling overland with carts and pack trains, took their Baltic wares to Italy. The Hansa maintained large depots at Bruges, London, Venice, Novgorod, and Bergen on the Norwegian coast. These establishments resembled colonial outposts of a Hanseatic empire. The Hansa itself had its own legal code (the Law of Lübeck), its own diplomats, and its own flag.

After 1500, however, the fortunes of the Hansa declined rapidly. The shift of trade routes from the Baltic to the Atlantic ended the prosperity of many Hanseatic towns. The loosely organized Hansa was no match for the stronger monarchical governments growing up along the rim of its Baltic preserve. Internally, the Hansa was weakened by the mounting conservatism of its merchants and by rivalries among member towns and competing merchant families. Only a minority of the member towns usually sent representatives to the deliberations in Lübeck, and very few of them could be counted on for men and arms in an emergency. Moreover, Hanseatic trading activities were carried on in a relatively primitive fashion by a multitude of individual merchants who entered temporary partnerships for a single venture rather than establishing permanent firms.

The truly big business of the last medieval centuries was to be found in Augsburg, Nuremberg, and the cities of the Mediterranean: Venice, Genoa, Pisa, Lucca, Florence, Milan, and a dozen others in Italy; Marseilles, Montpellier, and Narbonne in France; and Barcelona in Spain. Venice furnishes an excellent case study. The East-West trade brought wealth to Venetian merchants: from the East, spices, silk, cotton, sugar, dyestuffs, and the alum needed to set colors; from West, wool and cloth. The area of Venetian business was enormous, from England and Flanders to the heart of Asia, which the thirteenth-century Venetian Marco Polo (1254–1324) crossed to reach China.

The main carrier of Venetian trade was the galley. By 1300 the designers of the Venetian arsenal (originally a government-operated shipyard) had transformed the traditional long, narrow, oar-propelled galley of the Mediterranean into a swifter and roomier merchant vessel, relying mainly on sails and employing oarsmen chiefly to get in and out of port. In the fifteenth century these merchant galleys had space for 250 tons of cargo. Records from the early fifteenth century show about forty-five galleys sailing from Venice annually to Flanders, southern France, the Black Sea, Alexandria, Beirut, and Jaffa in the Holy Land. The Flanders fleet, which touched also at London and Southampton, provided a service between Italy and northwestern Europe that was cheaper and more secure than the overland route.

The state supervised the activities of these galleys. Since the average life of galleys was ten years, government experts periodically tested their seaworthiness, and the arsenal made needed replacements. The government provided for the defense of the galleys and their cargoes by requiring that at least twenty of the crew be bowmen. The captains of the Flanders galleys were directed to protect the health of the crew by enlisting a physician and a surgeon. The Venetian Republic also maintained an ambassador in England to smooth the way for its merchants.

Ship design changed slowly, but as more and more galleys ventured out into the Atlantic, the differences between northern European and Mediterranean designs began to disappear. The great medieval ship was the full-rigged three-master that could be adapted to carracks (ships that carried bulk cargoes), to caravels (ships that crossed the Atlantic), to galleons (ships that brought treasure back from the Americas to Spain), to merchantmen for the Baltic trade, and finally to the *fluyt*, a Dutch ship best used for grain, wine, and alum, which became the model for Europe's commercial fleets.

With these changes went better instruments, improved charts, and clearer lines of authority for ships' captains. Improved navigation tied the world of commerce closer together, sped cargoes that otherwise might spoil, created a community of instrument makers, and made possible the pursuit of cargoes around Africa. Sailing in tropical waters brought changes in ship design, new cargoes, knowledge of disease, and new forms of finance. For example, shipworm, which rotted the bottoms of wooden ships, was far more active in the tropics; ships sailing in those waters therefore had to be replaced far more often. This, together with the increase in sailing distances and the need to carry cargoes further and to sail at greater speeds, led to ever more complex commercial arrangements. Europeans hoisted sail before they saddled horse, and watercraft became the first tools in the European conquest of the world.

Industry

The expansion of trade stimulated industry. The towns of Flanders had developed the weaving of woolen cloth in the thirteenth century, with many workers and high profits. In the early fourteenth century perhaps two hundred masters controlled the wool guild of Florence, which produced nearly 100,000 pieces of cloth annually and employed thirty thousand men.

The earlier practice of grouping in a single guild all artisans engaged in making a single product was giving way to the modern division (and tension) between capital and labor, and, within the ranks of labor, between the highly and the less skilled. In late fourteenth-century Florence, strife was intense among the seven great guilds, the fourteen lesser guilds, and the *ciompi* (workers excluded from the guild membership).

Despite the growth of capitalism, Europe had not yet experienced a full industrial revolution, and most "manufacturing" continued to be what the Latin roots of the word suggest—a "making by hand." But a few advanced crafts showed modern trends: increase in output, mass production of standardized articles, and specialization of the labor force. In Lübeck, Hanseatic capitalists promoted the mass output of rosaries by hiring beadmakers and supplying them with materials; in the Habsburg lands of central Europe the silver mines inaugurated round-the-clock operations by dividing their workers among three eight-hour shifts; in Florence twenty or more different specialized crafts participated in woolen production—washing, combing, carding, spinning, weaving, dyeing, and so forth. But the actual work was subcontracted to small domestic shops according to the putting out system; instead of the worker's going to a mill or a factory, the piece work went to the worker's home.

The largest industrial establishment in Europe was probably the Venetian arsenal (shipyard), which normally employed a thousand men. These *arsenalotti* formed a pyramid of skills, with unskilled laborers at the bottom; at the next level, sawyers, who cut the timbers for the galleys, and caulkers, who made the wooden hulls seaworthy; then pulley makers and mast makers; and at the top, highly skilled carpenters, who shaped the lines of the hull. By the sixteenth century, the process of adding a superstructure to the hull and outfitting the vessel was so efficient that it took the arsenalotti only two months to complete and equip a hundred galleys for a campaign against the Turks.

Banking

The expansion of trade and industry promoted the rise of banking. The risks of lending were great, but so, too, were the potential profits. In 1420 the Florentine government vainly tried to put a ceiling of 20 percent on interest rates. Bankers were money changers, for only experts could establish the relative value of the hundreds of coins in circulation. Bankers also facilitated the transfer of money over long distances by bills of exchange, which bankers bought and sold and on which they took a commission. Letters of credit, which represented sums of money not physically transferred, were also safer than coins, since they could easily be hidden and carried by a cleric or other unsuspected person.

The great European bankers were Italians. By the late 1200s Italian bankers had become the fiscal agents of the pope. In the thirteenth century the Florentine banking families of the Bardi and the Peruzzi financed imports of English wool and the export of finished cloth; both firms advanced large sums to the kings of England and France at the outbreak of the Hundred Years' War, and both failed in the 1340s when Edward III defaulted on his debts. The repercussions of this banking failure included new attempts to democratize the Florentine government and the revolt of the ciompi against the tyranny of the wool guild. Florentine banking rallied in the fifteenth century under the dynamic Cosimo de' Medici, whose activities involved companies for woolen and silk manufacture, as well as Medici bank and branch firms in Venice, Rome, Milan, Avignon, Geneva, Bruges, and London. However, the inefficiency of branch managers together with the extravagance of

Lorenzo the Magnificent caused the failure of the Medici bank before the end of the century.

Meanwhile, money and banking were thriving elsewhere. The golden ducats of Venice joined the florins of Florence in international popularity, and the Bank of St. George, founded at Genoa in 1407, eventually took over much of the Mediterranean business done by Spanish Jews before their persecution in the late 1400s. In France, Jacques Coeur of Bourges (1395–1456) used private wealth to secure public office and was master of the mint and superintendent of royal expenditure for Charles VII. In Germany powerful banking families flourished in the cities of Augsburg and Nuremberg. The most famous was the Fugger family of Augsburg, whose founder was a linen weaver and trader in the late fourteenth century; his sons and grandsons imported textiles and luxuries from Venice and began buying silver and lead mines. In the late 1400s the Fuggers became bankers to the Habsburgs and, after the failure of the Medici bank, to the papacy as well. In the 1540s the family fortune may have exceeded half a billion present-day dollars. Thereafter it dwindled, as the flood of gold and silver from America ended the central European mining boom and as the Fuggers themselves made extensive loans to the Habsburg Philip II of Spain, who suffered repeated bankruptcies. In 1562, 1563, and in the seventeenth century the family firm went bankrupt each time the Spanish monarch suspended payments.

Town and Countryside

Augsburg's total population at the height of Jacob Fugger the Rich's power probably never exceeded 40,000. One set of estimates for the fourteenth century puts the population of Venice, Florence, and Paris in the vicinity of 100,000 each; that of Genoa, Milan, Barcelona, and London at about 50,000; and that of the biggest Hanseatic and Flemish towns between 20,000 and 40,000. Most Europeans still lived in the countryside.

The urban minority, however, was beginning to bring important changes to the life of the rural majority. Merchants often invested their wealth in agricultural properties; nobles who acquired interests in towns usually retained their country estates; and peasants often moved to town as workmen or became artisans on the land. Town governments sometimes improved adjacent farmland on the pattern established by the medieval communes of Milan and Siena, which had drained nearby marshes to increase the amount of cultivable land in order to assure a more dependable food supply. But individuals, whether of town or country, were being drawn together into wider communities by the changes in economic, social, and political organization.

The development of a money economy greatly altered the agrarian institutions of the West. Money became important for the exchange of surpluses. Many manors could specialize in a single crop, like grain or wool, olives or grapes, and therefore could purchase items they no longer produced. The lords of these one-crop manors became capitalists on a modest scale. The more enterprising demanded that their peasants pay rent in money rather than in commodities or work. The sheep-raising capitalists of sixteenth-century England won the right of *enclosure*—fencing off for their flocks common lands where peasants had traditionally pastured their own livestock. In Spain the *Mesta* secured rights to vast tracts of pasture. Urban businessmen wanted property in a form that they could readily buy and sell, free from the restrictions of feudal tenure; they wanted laborers they could hire and fire, free from the restrictions of serfdom. All these desires, together with the labor shortage and peasant unrest created by the Black Death, spelled the end of serfdom.

Thus, at the heart of economic and social relationships, the cash network of the capitalist was beginning to replace the medieval complex of caste and service. The ordinary person probably earned more by becoming a wage-earning worker or rent-paying tenant farmer instead of a serf. Yet something was also lost—the tenuous security, inherited job, the right to certain lands. In towns and cities pressures also mounted, as the guilds became more exclusive and the separation between wealthy master and ordinary worker widened.

So, too, merchants and urban artisans moved in the fourteenth and fifteenth centuries to control the government of the towns in which they lived. Towns throughout Europe witnessed a "revolution," in which an alliance of guildmasters and wealthy merchants curtailed the authority and the jurisdiction of local nobility and articulated organs of government. The Medici, originally rural weavers, epitomize something of the transformation of cities: In three generations, they rose from wage laborers to bankers to monarchs, from the unenfranchised to the virtual rulers of Florence. This alliance of merchants and artisans, made possible within the context of cities, came to be called "the bourgeoisie." The term "bourgeois" refers strictly to those who live in cities; our modern usage reflects its transformation from defining a place of dwelling to describing an economic stratum with its own values. Merchants and wealthy masters encroached upon the political power of nobles and the economic preeminence of lords. They also changed both the market in art and the subject matter of art. The "Renaissance" was also a time of unprecedented portraiture, the great majority of which were of the bourgeois, commissioned by the prosperous citizens of cities. New sorts of secular themes emerged, as did a sense of the artist as "genius," a perception made possible by a competitive market for artistic talent.

Finally, urban elites also began to transform both the location of learning and its character. Private libraries, not only of monarchs but also of wealthy merchant and banking families, challenged monastic libraries, often offering collections monastic libraries could not match. The Medici were famous collectors of classical texts. Lorenzo de' Medici brought Greek scholars from Byzantium to Florence, with them founding the Platonic Academy, where Europeans and Byzantines studied the corpus of Platonic writings and translated much of it into Latin. This was a learning based not upon rote memorization and repetition but upon the purchase and collection of rare classical texts, which emphasized linguistic knowledge over the mastery of abstruse points of doctrine, and promulgated a new handwriting, that of the notary and public secretary, over monastic hands.

Although a time of profound economic transformation, the Renaissance was not a period of economic boom. A variety of factors induced periodic depressions. Commercialization was diffused unevenly, while agriculture went through phases of dynamism and of inertia. International trade patterns disrupted traditional economies, plunging some societies into debt while others prospered. Overall prosperity increased but by no means uniformly or consistently.

Printing, Thought, and Literature

The communications transformation brought on by the printing press, the enormous significance of the book as a force for change, and the simple fact that printing preceded the Protestant revolt on which the Reformation fed are all aspects of a profound shift in perspective that, perhaps more than any other change, defines the transition from medieval to modern. Humanity began to secularize, to particularize, to conceive of knowledge as growth rather than as discovery. Scientific inquiries were made widely known and were thus liberated from the scribes of the monasteries and the libraries of the very rich, by the dramatic shift from script to print.

Those historians who most emphasize the significance of technology in promoting human change, and who see the development of print as perhaps the most sweeping technological revolution between the wheel and the steam engine, also argue that there was essentially two stages to the Renaissance: the earlier, which preceded the printing press, and the later, which accompanied the spread of print. The Renaissance clearly did have two phases, the difference between the two being a matter of degree. Printing was the revolutionary event that made possible the diffusion of scientific knowledge, turned science into a revolutionary force, and closed the gap between the practice of artisans and the theories of scholars.

The introduction of print penetrated rural society more slowly than urban society. Perhaps as many as 10 percent could sign their names, but some learned their letters and how to keep accounts from printed materials, and a few sons of laborers found their way to a university. More important was the change brought about by print in the custom of the *veillée*—the gathering of villagers together two or three nights each week, or farm families telling each other stories about ghosts or werewolves, such gatherings eventually turning into dances or an interchange of gossip, that is, of news. To the evening gathering was added, in the sixteenth century, the practice of listening to traditional storytellers who enriched their repertoire by referring to a few books. In time someone—often the rural schoolteacher—would use the veillée for reading aloud to the village. *Aesop's Fables*, the *Romance of the Rose*, or the vernacular Bible were thus read. The *Shepherds' Calendar*, full of practical agricultural advice illustrated by woodcuts, was also read aloud.

The Vernaculars and Latin

The vernaculars of the western European countries emerged gradually, first as the spoken languages of the people, then as vehicles for popular writing, finally achieving official recognition. Many vernaculars—Spanish, Portuguese, Italian, and French—developed from Latin; these were the Romance (Roman) languages. Castilian, the core of modern literary Spanish, attained official status in the thirteenth century when the king of Castile ordered that it be used for government records. In Italy the vernacular scarcely existed as a literary language until the eve of the Renaissance, when Dante employed the dialect of his native Tuscany in the *Divine Comedy*, and it was not until the early sixteenth century that Tuscan Italian emerged over the rival dialect of Rome as the medium for vernacular expression.

In medieval France two families of vernaculars appeared: Southern Frenchmen spoke the *langue d'oc*, so called from their use of oc (the Latin *hoc*) for "yes"; their northern cousins spoke the *langue d'oïl*, in which "yes" was *oï* (the modern *oui*). The epic verses of *The Song of Roland* were composed in the *langue d'oïl*, while the troubadours at the court of Eleanor of Aquitaine sang in Provençal, a form of the *langue d'oc*. By 1400 the *langue d'oïl* of the Paris region was well on its way to replacing Latin as the official language of the whole kingdom; Provençal eventually died out. Another offshoot of the *Langue d'oc* survives in Catalan, used in both Spain and France at the Mediterranean end of the Pyrenees.

In Germany and in England the vernaculars were derived from an ancient Germanic language. The *minnesingers* of thirteenth-century Germany composed their poetry in Middle High German, predecessor of modern literary German. The Anglo-Saxons of England had spoken a dialect of Low German. English achieved official recognition in the fourteenth century; meantime, it was coming into its own as a literary language with such popular works as *Piers Plowman* (see Chapter 2) and Chaucer's *Canterbury Tales*.

Some of the vernaculars became international languages. In the Near East the Italian that had been introduced by the crusaders was the *lingua franca*, the Western tongue most widely understood; by the seventeenth century it would be replaced by French and in the twentieth by English. Meantime, Latin remained the international language of the church and of the academic world. Scholars worked diligently to perfect their Latin and, in the later Renaissance, to learn Greek and sometimes Hebrew. They have been called *humanists* because they were devotees of what Cicero had termed *studias humanitatis*, or humane studies, which still included rhetoric, grammar, history, poetry, and ethics.

Humanism drastically changed attitudes toward the classical heritage. The medieval schoolmen had not disdained this heritage; they admired and copied its forms but transformed or adapted its ideas to fortify their own Christian views. The humanists of the Renaissance transformed their medieval heritage in the more secular spirit of their own age and in the light of their own more extensive knowledge of the classics. Reverence for the classics did not prevent some humanists from becoming enthusiastic advocates of the vernacular; the reverse was also true, as vernacular writers studied Cicero to improve their own style.

Writers of the Early Italian Renaissance

In the work of Dante Alighieri (1265–1321) we find the first expression of characteristics that would define Renaissance literature. While his magnificent poem the *Divine Comedy* has structural affinities with Gothic cathedrals—the Christian mystical numbers one and three dominate the organization of the whole, of each book, and of each canto—he wrote it in vernacular Italian. The poem, moreover, is peopled with hundreds of individuals, each person distinguishable not only by vice or virtue, but by voice and personality. Virgil, Plato, Socrates, and Caesar dwell in Limbo, at once recognized for their classical virtue and differentiated from all the Christians by their designation as virtuous pagans. And the poem is an exploration of love: love perverted, love inadequate, and love divine. It draws upon the tropes of troubadour poetry, but ultimately represents one of the most complex conceptualizations of a central human emotion in the Western tradition. In each of his works, moreover, Dante's voice is self-consciously distinctive, seeking not to blend himself within the authority of tradition, but to speak as a unique human being of singular gifts and singular spirit.

The pursuit of fame and an unabashed enthusiasm for things classical marked the next major Italian literary figure, Petrarch (Francesco Petrarca, 1304–1374). Since his father was a political exile from Florence, the young Petrarch lived for a time at the worldly papal court in Avignon and studied law at the University of Bologna. As a professional man of letters he collected and copied the manuscripts of ancient authors, produced the first accurate edition of the Roman historian Livy, and found in an Italian cathedral forgotten letters by Cicero that threw new light on Cicero's political activities.

Ironically, the writings of Petrarch most admired in modern times are not those in his cherished Latin but those he esteemed the least—vernacular love poems he addressed to his adored Laura, who died during the Black Death. In these lyrics Petrarch perfected the verse form known as the Italian sonnet—fourteen lines long, divided into one set of eight lines and another of six, each with its own rhyme scheme. Almost despite himself, therefore, he proved to be one of the founders of modern vernacular literature.

Petrarch exemplified emerging humanism by his devotion to the classics and his deep feeling for the beauties of this world. He criticized medieval schoolmen for their emphasis on dialectical logic, their dependence on Aristotle as an infallible authority, and their preoccupation with detail. But he admired Augustine almost as much as he admired Cicero, believing that the religious teachings of the one and the Stoic morality of the other could counter the materialism he observed around him.

Petrarch's friend and pupil, Giovanni Boccaccio (1313–1375), shared his master's estimate of humanity, but not his confidence in the possibility of human improvement. Boccaccio, son of a Florentine merchant, spent part of his youth at the frivolous court of Naples and turned to letters after his apprenticeship in banking left him disillusioned. He learned Greek and aided his master in tracking down old manuscripts, finding a copy of Tacitus in the Benedictine abbey on Monte Cassino. His *Decameron* recounts stories told by a group of young Florentines who have moved to a country villa during the Black Death. Most of the plots in the *Decameron* were not original with Boccacio, who retold these earthy tales in a graceful and entertaining way and with a lighthearted disenchantment based on his own worldly experience.

Classical Scholarship

The men of letters of this period may be divided into three groups: First were the conservers of classical culture, heirs of Petrarch's humanistic enthusiasm for the classical past; second were the vernacular writers who took the path marked out by the *Decameron*, from Chaucer at the close of the fourteenth century down to Rabelais and Cervantes in the sixteenth; and third were the synthesizers—philosophical humanists who tried to fuse Christianity, classicism, and other elements into a universal human philosophy.

The devoted antiquarians of the fifteenth century uncovered a remarkable number of ancient manuscripts. They ransacked monasteries; they pieced together the works of Cicero, Tacitus, Lucretius, and other Latin authors; they collected Greek manuscripts through agents in Constantinople. To preserve, catalog, and study these literary treasures, the first modern libraries were created. Cosimo de' Medici supported three separate libraries in and near Florence and employed forty-five copyists. Humanist popes founded the library of the Vatican, and even the minor duchy of Urbino in northern Italy had a humanist court and a major library.

Greek scholars made the journey from Byzantium to Italy. One of the earliest of them, Manuel Chrysoloras (1368–1415), came to Italy to seek help for the beleaguered Byzantines against the Turks and remained to teach at Florence and Milan. He did literature a great service by insisting that translations into Latin from the Greek should not be literal, as they had been in the past, but should convey the message and spirit of the original. The revival of Greek studies reached maturity in the 1460s with the emergence of the informal circle of Florentine humanists known as the Platonic Academy. The Greek language, however, never equaled Latin in popularity because of its difficulty, a fact that discouraged interest in the Greek drama and led most humanists to study Plato in Latin translation.

Lorenzo Valla (c. 1407–1457) represented classical scholarship at its best. Valla passed much of his adult life in Rome and Naples. Volatile and quarrelsome, he also commanded both immense learning and the courage to use it against the most sacred targets. He even criticized the supposedly flawless prose of Cicero and took Thomas Aquinas to task for his failure to know Greek. His own expert knowledge of the language led him to point out errors and misinterpretations in the Vulgate (St. Jerome's Latin translation of the Bible), and thereby to lay the foundation for humanist biblical scholarship.

Valla's fame rests above all on his demonstration that the Donation of Constantine, one basis for justifying papal claims to temporal domination, was a forgery. He proved his case by showing that both the Latin in which the Donation was written and the events to which it referred dated from an era several centuries after Constantine. When Valla published this exposé in 1440, he was secretary to Alfonso the Magnanimous, king of Aragon, whose claim to Naples was being challenged by the papacy on the basis of the Donation itself.

The philosophical humanists aspired not only to universal knowledge but also to a universal truth and faith. They were centered at Florence, attracted by the Platonic Academy founded in 1462 by Cosimo de' Medici, who entrusted the commission of translating Plato to Marsilio Ficino (1433–1499), a medical student turned classicist who also translated some of the Neoplatonists' works from Greek into Latin. The opportunity for stressing the compatibility of Neoplatonism with Christianity exerted a strong attraction on Ficino and his circle.

Ficino argued that religious feeling and expression were as natural to humanity as barking was to dogs. Humanity, he wrote, has the unique faculty called intellect. He coined the term *Platonic love* to describe the love that transcends the senses and may lead to mystical communion with God. Ficino seemed to be attempting a synthesis of all philosophy and religion.

The attempt was pressed further by Ficino's pupil, Giovanni Pico della Mirandola (1463–1494). Pico crowded much into his thirty-one years: He knew Arabic, Hebrew, Greek, and Latin; he studied Jewish allegory, Arab philosophy, and medieval Scholasticism. Pico's tolerance was as broad as his learning. In his short *Oration on the Dignity of Man,* he cited approvingly Chaldean and Persian theologians, the priests of Apollo, Socrates, Pythagoras, Cicero, Moses, Paul, Augustine, Muhammad, Francis of Assisi, Thomas Aquinas, and many others.

Together with Ficino, Pico helped to found the humane studies of comparative religion and comparative philosophy. He strengthened Ficino's idea that humanity was unique—the link between the mortal physical world and the immortal spiritual one. This concept lay at the core of Renaissance style.

However, the person who epitomized the most mature expression of the impulse to draw on all wisdom was Desiderius Erasmus (1466–1536). Trained first by the Modern Devotion, then at Louvain and Paris, he continued his studies throughout his life in London, Oxford, Basel, and Italy. He particularly relished the free atmosphere of small cities like Louvain in the Low Countries, Basel in Switzerland, and Freiburg in the Rhineland. Building on Valla's scholarship, Erasmus published a scholarly edition of the Greek New Testament. He compiled a series of *Adages* and *Colloquies* to give students examples of good Latin composition. Most influential was his satirical *The Praise of Folly,* in which he contrasted the spontaneous natural reactions of the supposedly foolish with the studied and self-serving artificiality

Erasmus, as painted by Hans Holbein in 1523.   *(Erich Lessing/Art Resource, NY)*

of those who claimed to be wise. Erasmus mocked any group inflated by a sense of its own importance—merchants, philosophers, scientists, courtiers, clerics, and kings.

Erasmus coupled a wry view of human nature with faith in the dignity of humanity. He joined a love of the classics with respect for Christian values. He had little use for the fine-spun arguments of Scholasticism and was a tireless advocate of what he called "the philosophy of Christ"—the application of the doctrines of charity and love Jesus taught. Yet his edition of the Greek New Testament raised disquieting doubts about the accuracy of the Latin translation in the Vulgate and therefore of Catholic biblical interpretations, and his attacks on clerical laxity implied that the wide gap between the lofty ideals and the corrupt practices of the church could not long endure. Both his fidelity to the Christian tradition and his humanist convictions committed Erasmus to the position that the only worthy weapons were reason and discussion. Perhaps because he sought change without violence, he has also become enormously popular with twentieth-century humanists.

Medieval values were gone in the works of the Frenchman François Rabelais (1490–1553). Rabelais studied the classics, particularly Plato and the ancient physicians, practiced and taught medicine, and created two of the great comic figures of letters—Gargantua and his son Pantagruel. The two are giants, and everything they do is of heroic dimensions. The abbey of Theleme, which Gargantua helps to found, permits its residents a wildly unmonastic experience:

> All their life was spent not in lawes, statutes or rules, but according to their own free will and pleasure. They rose out of their beds, when they thought good; they did eat, drink, Labour, sleep, when they had a mind to it and were disposed for it. . . . In all their rule, and strictest tie of their order there was but this one clause to be observed, DO WHAT THOU WILT.*

To Rabelais free will meant self-improvement on a grand scale. Gargantua exhorts Pantagruel to learn *everything;* he is to master Arabic in addition to Latin, read the New Testament in Greek and the Old in Hebrew, and study history, geometry, architecture, music, and civil law. He must also know "the fishes; all the fowls of the air; all the several kinds of shrubs and trees, . . . all sorts of herbs and flowers that grow upon the ground; all the various metals that are hid within the bowels of the earth." "In brief," Gargantua concludes, "let me see thee an abyss, and bottomless pit of knowledge."†

Rabelais leaned heavily on oral traditions and other forms of popular culture. He discovered the people who spoke and wrote in the vernacular; he enjoyed the carnival atmosphere of ordinary life, and he put popular forms together with his knowledge of the classics, theology, medicine, and law. He drew upon folksongs, ballads, and German and French chapbooks, with less than customary respect for the barriers between types of audiences. He understood that there was an underculture of wanderers, sailors, and women who desired and created their own literary forms. By depicting them in his writings, he was at once a humanist who truly saw the unity among all people, an innovator producing a new genre, and a subversive whose language brought to popular culture academic respectability.

In a sense Rabelais personified the tension between the carnal and the spiritual in Renaissance life, for he drew upon both. He saw himself as an exponent of the "philosophy of Christ," yet the very word *Rabelaisian* came to mean bawdy, vulgar, even obscene. He understood how the peasantry, in particular, ritualized the tension in their lives in both Lent and Carnival. Car-

---

*Rabelais, *Gargantua and Pantagruel,* trans. Sir Thomas Urquhart and Peter Anthony Motteux (London: Gibbings, 1901), I, pp. 165–67.
†Ibid., II, 32–35.

Brueghel's Combat of Carnival and Lent *(1559), the original of which hangs in the* Kunsthistorisches Museum, Vienna. *(Erich Lessing/Art Resource, NY)*

nival was a time of holiday, an end in itself, with emphasis on food, the body, and sex. (*Carne* meant that "meat" could be eaten before the long Lenten fast; *carne* also meant "the flesh," in the sexual sense.) Symbols of lust were openly displayed at Carnival; aggression was expressed toward animals, women, and Jews; and the widespread use of costumes freed men and women to reverse roles, to justify disorder, and to do things for which they would not be blamed, since, even if recognized behind their masks, they were not "themselves."

Against Carnival, traditional popular culture set Lent, as shown in a famous painting by Pieter Brueghel, *Combat of Carnival and Lent* (1559). While Carnival was represented as a fat man eating and drinking licentiously, Lent was depicted as a thin woman, going without food or sex, that is, depriving herself of whatever was most valued for pleasure. Religious reformers increasingly sought to distinguish Lent from Carnival, to use the popular pastimes of the peasantry for didactic purposes. The Catholic reformers sought to modify, the Protestant reformers to eliminate, Carnival. In this tension between the mortification of Lent and the release of Carnival, both so intense in Rabelais, the diversity of Renaissance life is well revealed; in the triumph of Lent in the seventeenth century, the success of the discipline of the Reformation would be demonstrated.

Science and Religion

In 1948, Herbert Butterfield argued in lectures at Cambridge University for a "Scientific Revolution" that took place in the seventeenth century. Since then, a number of scholars have contrasted the benighted Middle Ages with the heroic individuals, such as Galileo Galilei (1564–1642), of the sixteenth and seventeenth centuries, who stood bravely against institutions of superstition and tradition, in particular the Church. The story, we have come to learn, is considerably more complicated. Medieval schoolmen were responsible not only for the preservation of Aristotelian texts, whose categories still inform scientific thought, but also for integrating Arab science and mathematics into the Western curriculum. Our numeric system, an enormous improvement in efficiency over Roman numerals, is Arabic, adopted in the West during the Middle Ages; zero, perhaps the single most important number for its conceptual power, comes to the West through the Arabic number system.

"Science" now connotes a very specific kind of knowledge derived from the consistent application of specific methods. That meaning is very recent. The word itself comes from the Latin word *scientia*, the noun derived from *scio*, a kind of practical knowledge, a skill. For most of its history, "scientia" was distinguished from philosophy and theology, the fields of abstract thought, and, perhaps more importantly, from the activity *cogito*, the active thinking of a philosopher or theologian.

The Renaissance's relation to "science" is paradoxical. Humanists collected all sorts of classical texts, among them treatises by Galen on the human body and by Ptolemy on cartography, as well as, at long last, all of Aristotle's works. But they tended to treat those texts as almost sacred, close to the Bible in their authority and their veracity. Their critical skills were turned not to testing the truthfulness of this or that classical author, but to establishing the authoritative edition of his work.

It would not be until the "New World" overwhelmingly demonstrated the flaws in that classical tradition that the majority of European scholars would turn to question that classical heritage, its premises, and its conclusions. Ptolemy, for example, had assumed the known world covered 180° longitude, underestimating the earth's circumference by roughly one quarter—particularly significant if one is sailing across the Atlantic with limited supplies of food and fresh water.

Galen, as another example, had taught that the blood moved from one side of the heart to the other by passing through invisible pores in the thick wall of tissue separating the two sides of the organ; actually, as William Harvey (1578–1657) was to show in 1616, the blood gets from the one side to the other by circulating through the body and lungs. Galen's theory of invisible pores kept Leonardo da Vinci from anticipating Harvey; when his anatomical investigations led him to the brink of discovery, he backed away because he could not believe that Galen might have erred.

Da Vinci (1452–1519) exemplifies both the shortcomings and the achievements of Renaissance science. He had little concern for systematic cataloging of observations and the publication of his findings and speculations. Yet Leonardo also showed remarkable inventiveness, drawing plans for lathes, pumps, war machines, flying machines, and many other contraptions, not all of them workable but all highly imaginative. He had a passionate curiosity about almost everything concerning human beings and nature. His accurate drawings of human embryos differed radically from the older notion of the fetus as perfectly formed miniature human being. His geological studies convinced him that the earth was far older than the scholars of his time thought it to be. The Po River, he estimated, must have been flowing for 200,000 years to wash down the sediments forming its alluvial plain in northern Italy.

With the "discovery" of the "New World"—the very formulation captures how profoundly Europeans had accepted the veracity of classical descriptions—observation acquired a kind of authority it had had only unevenly in the Middle Ages. Leonardo's experiments in optics—both how the eye works and with telescopes and microscopes—was but the beginning of an explosion in interest in optic theory in the sixteenth and seventeen centuries. Perspective, the new "realism" of Renaissance painting, and the extraordinary detail of Dutch still life painting all have as their point of departure a new sensitivity to the human eye and its power of observation. Following upon Leonardo's drawings and notebooks, optic theorists of the sixteenth and seventeenth centuries would formulate new conceptualizations of the functioning of the human eye and the functioning of light, and sixteenth-century northern humanists, such as Montaigne and Rabelais, would put at the center of their work the question of perception. Indeed, Montaigne would formulate an utterly new form of writing, the *essai*, an inconclusive attempt, to reflect rhetorically his own insight that perception and knowledge are inseparable for each and every human being. Or, as he would argue some eighty years after the first encounters, no human knowledge is absolute, perfectly abstracted from human experience and all its differentiations.

"Science" was not a unified field before the Enlightenment, but small, often discrete steps taken by men, some of whom were in correspondence with one another, others of whom worked in isolation, unaware of the work of others. Many, but not all, had in common a classical education, a familiarity with the works of Aristotle on categories and on the natural world, the natural history of Pliny, as well as Greek mathematics. That education was made possible by humanists' philological skills, their dedication to the collection of texts, and their absolute commitment to the most accurate version of each classical text. Many of those who would "discover" a piece of what only in hindsight can be seen in its fullness as the puzzle of scientific knowledge, many of those who worked out this or that small piece of the puzzle were tinkerers or, like Copernicus, clergy. Their pursuit of a single question—Why do the planets move as they do?—over years led to new ways of conceiving larger problems, such as How is the (solar) system organized? But it is important to see the discreteness of the individual's pursuit of questions and the idiosyncrasies of "method"— the absence of a clearly defined body of knowledge called "science."

Invention, Technology, Medicine

The most important invention of the Renaissance—the technology for printing books—furnishes a case history of how many individual advances contribute to an end result. The revolution in book production began in the twelfth century, when Muslims in Spain introduced a technique first developed by the Chinese in the second century and began to make paper by shredding old rags, processing them with water, and then pressing the liquid out of the finished sheets. The cost of the new product was only a fraction of that of the sheepskin parchment or calfskin vellum employed for manuscripts. The sheepskin required splitting to make parchment, and thus was expensive and labor-intensive, while the new process could be done far more quickly and cheaply.

The next step came when engravers, adapting another Chinese technique, made a mirror image of a drawing on a wood block or copper plate that could make many identical woodcuts or engravings. Sentences were then added to the plates or blocks to explain the drawings. Finally, movable type was devised, each minute engraved piece of type representing a single letter that could be combined with other pieces to form words, sentences, a whole page, and then salvaged to be used again. This crucial invention was perfected during the 1440s. Johann Gutenberg (c. 1397–1468), who used to receive the credit for its invention, has been the focus of a scholarly controversy. Although the first printed Bibles are still referred to by his name, others may have done the printing.

The new invention gained wide popularity because printed books were not only much cheaper than manuscripts but also less prone to copyists' errors. By 1500 the total number of volumes in print had reached the millions, and Italy alone had some seventy-three presses employing movable type. The most famous of them, the Aldine Press in Venice (named for its founder, Aldus Manutius, 1450–1515), sold inexpensive editions of the classics.

Once books were available, the world was transformed. As with most technologies, the long evolution of printing would turn upon the steady improvement in a basic component, in this case paper. It would not be until the eighteenth century that relatively inexpensive paper would be developed, when methods were found to produce paper from plant fibers. While rag-content paper (the paper made from linen and cotton rags) continued to be manufactured, the rush to the new paper began with the production in the West of the first such book, in France in 1784. Even so, it would not be until 1870 that a technique would be perfected, in Sweden, for the use of wood pulp for papermaking.

Although no other single invention can be compared with printing for quick and decisive effects, many innovations ultimately had comparable influence. Gunpowder, for example, also brought from China to medieval Europe, was used in the later campaigns of the Hundred Years' War. In navigation important marine aids came into general use, particularly the magnetic compass and sailing charts. Engineers solved some of the problems of extracting and smelting silver, iron, and other ores.

The wide publication of printed books with clear anatomical illustrations also advanced medical skills, which were further improved by the partial lifting of a thirteenth-century ban against dissection of human cadavers. Pharmacology also progressed, thanks to experiments with the chemistry of drugs made by an eccentric Swiss physician, Paracelsus (Theophrastus Bombastus von Hohenheim, c. 1493–1541). He rejected Galen's theory of disease and proposed that chemical remedies be applied to specific diseases. The French surgeon Ambroise Paré (c. 1510–1590) laid the foundations for modern surgery by developing new techniques, notably that of sewing up blood vessels with stitches rather than cauterizing them with a hot iron. Yet many so-called physicians were quacks, and many teachers of medicine merely repeated the demonstrations that Galen had made more than a thousand years earlier.

A striking exception was furnished by the physicians and scholars of the University of Padua. They maintained a tradition of scientific inquiry that presaged the seventeenth-century triumphs of the experimental method. In 1537 a young Belgian named Andreas Vesalius (1514–1564) rejected Galen's notion of invisible pores in the wall of tissue within the heart because he simply could not find such pores. In 1543 Vesalius published *De humanis corporis fabrica* (Concerning the Structure of the Human Body), prepared with concern for anatomical accuracy and detail, and illustrated with elaborate woodcuts.

Growth in medical knowledge probably had little direct impact on life span, however. Until the early eighteenth century, the typical operating theater in a hospital—if there was one—was much like a butcher shop. Indeed, patients were often led to an operation blindfolded so that they would not be frightened by seeing the operating instruments, which were only modified butcher's tools. As in a butcher shop, the floor was covered with sawdust to soak up the flow of blood, and most operations involved amputations by sawing. The patient was drugged with opium or alcohol. The operation was performed quickly to forestall surgical shock, and perhaps half of the patients died—either from the operation itself or from infection afterward.

As we have seen, the Black Death coincides with the customary dates for the beginning of the Renaissance. The idea of quarantine was introduced in 1346, and regulations concerning the quarantine of suspected carriers of disease were fully in place in Venice by 1485. Nonetheless, plagues continued until the last major outbreak in Marseilles in 1720. The prevalence of thatched roofs from which rats or fleas might fall assured a high level of infection. Leprosy, commonplace in Europe from the sixth century, declined in part from change in climate and in part because of changing patterns of disease competition. As tuberculosis became more common in the Renaissance, the infectious chain of Hansen's disease (the proper name for leprosy) may have been interrupted, as the one called forth antibodies that forestalled the slower-moving bacillus associated with the other. Yaws declined dramatically, while syphilis broke out equally dramatically in the fifteenth century.

Disease patterns were influenced more by social and economic conditions than by medical knowledge. The growing use of woolens, changes in household sanitation, and the virtually free interchange of infections between the Old and the New Worlds after the discovery of America altered the balance of disease and immunities. The Old World introduced measles, for example, to the New, while taking from it exotic foods—including corn, the tomato, and the potato—and, ultimately, the plant louse (*phylloxera*), that virtually destroyed European vineyards in the 1880s. At the same time, the rise of the city, the growth of closer communities, and easier communication throughout Europe between 1500 and 1700 lessened the probability of devastating epidemics, as the frequent circulation of disease also quickened the adaptability of the human species. Despite the growth of scientific knowledge about disease, however, the general public continued to rely on magic, witchcraft, alchemy, and astrology for protection against the unpredictable.

Astronomy

The year 1543 marked the publication of Copernicus's *De revolutionibus orbium coelestium* (Concerning the Revolutions of Heavenly Bodies). Born in Poland of German extraction, Nicolaus Copernicus (1473–1543) studied law and medicine at Padua and other Italian universities and spent thirty years as canon of a cathedral near Danzig. His work in mathematics and astronomy led him to attack the hypothesis of the geocentric (earth-centered) universe. In its place he advanced the revolutionary new hypothesis of the heliocentric (sun-centered) universe.

The concept of the geocentric universe included an elaborate system of spheres. Around the stationary earth there revolved some eighty spheres, each, as it were, a separate sky containing some of the heavenly bodies, each moving on an invisible circular path, each transparent so that mortals could see the spheres beyond it. This picture of the universe had already come under attack before Copernicus, for observers could not make it tally with the actual behavior of heavenly bodies. Copernicus used these earlier criticisms and his own computations to arrive at the heliocentric concept.

The Copernican hypothesis had radical implications. It destroyed the idea of the earth's uniqueness by suggesting that it acted like other heavenly bodies. Nevertheless, once Copernicus had reversed the roles of the sun and the earth, the heavens were still filled with spheres revolving along invisible orbits, only now they moved about a stationary sun.

Music

In the medieval curriculum music was grouped with the sciences because mathematics underlies musical theory and notation. The mainstay of medieval sacred music was the Gregorian chant, or *plainsong*, which relied on a single melodic line. At the close of the Middle Ages musicians in the Low Countries and northern France developed the technique of *polyphony*, which combined several voices in complicated harmony. When French and Flemish musicians journeyed to Italy in the fifteenth century, they introduced polyphonic music and borrowed in return the popular tunes of the dances and

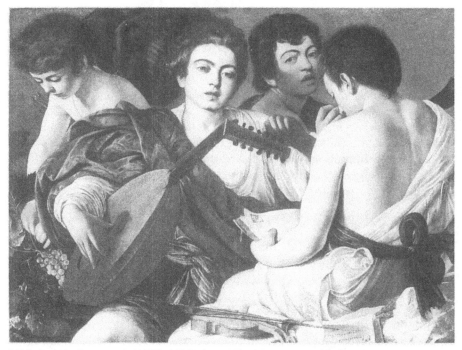

Michelangelo Caravaggio (1565–1609) shows The Musicians *with their instruments: a lute, a fiddle, and a cornet.* *(The Metropolitan Museum of Art, Rogers Fund, 1952)*

folk songs they encountered in southern Europe. The end products of the interaction were the sacred and secular polyphonic compositions of Josquin des Pres (c. 1450–1521) at the court of Louis XII and the masses of Giovanni Palestrina (c. 1526–1594), choirmaster in the Vatican.

The secularism and individualism of the Renaissance and its taste for experimentation also affected music. New instruments were developed or imported: the violin, double bass, and harpsichord; the organ, the kettle-drum, and the lute. Paid professional singers staffed the choirs of Antwerp cathedral and of the Vatican; a retinue of musicians became a fixture of court life. German artisans, calling themselves mastersingers, organized choral groups. Music had also become part of popular culture; the French *cabaret*, the Spanish *venta*, the German *Wirtshaus*, the Polish *gospoda*, the English pub—all rang to popular folk songs.

The Renaissance and the Church

In the nineteenth century, the Swiss historian Jacob Burckhardt characterized the Renaissance as a "secular age." Since World War II, scholars have distin-guished among Renaissance humanists: While Marsilio Ficino and Pico della Mirandola were deeply fascinated with ancient hermeticism, Lorenzo Valla and Desiderius Erasmus were using their philological skills to illumine the deeper meaning of Scripture. All, moreover, were Christian: None repudiated Christianity or refused to participate in its central rituals.

We have seen something of the relationship of the Renaissance to science. The conflict between Galileo, whose Jesuit training introduced him to Aristotle, and the Church was the conflict between a written text, Scripture, and what Galileo called the book of nature: what he observed with his human eyes. Scripture depicted an earth-centered universe, but the available data from observation supported a different theory, a sun-centered universe. Galileo's theories about the universe, however, were not what got him in trouble, but his argument, a purely theoretical argument, for something analogous to atoms. That argument, which was founded not in observation but in speculation, put at risk the central Catholic doctrine of transubstantiation. It was heresy because embracing it would bring tumbling down the entire edifice of the Eucharist as Catholics understood it. Much was at stake in the debate between speculation and biblicism.

The relationship of the Renaissance to the Reformation is much contested. For more than a century, Burckhardt's characterization shaped the perception of the Renaissance, his argument for the Renaissance as the age of the "individual" shaping both the understanding of the Renaissance and the ways in which Martin Luther's words and deeds in the sixteenth century were construed.

Scholars all agree on one explicit and important relation between the Renaissance and the Reformation: Erasmus's work—collecting, collating, and then publishing a scholarly edition of the Greek New Testament—itself one manifestation of the humanists' philological and textual commitments made possible the biblicism not only of Luther, but of hundreds who would call for the Reformation of the Church. Erasmus understood himself to be performing an act of great piety in providing Christianity with its most authentic and therefore authoritative text of the Holy Scriptures. But he himself also recognized the singular power of "the Word," as Scripture came to be called, to call into question all sorts of contemporary practices of the church. Erasmus and Valla moreover shared with Luther an "anticlericalism," that is, an explicit and public criticism of the current practices and life of the clergy: their arrogance, their lethargy, their excesses of food and drink, their ignorance—the plethora of ways in which they deviated from the model of piety Christ had embodied in his own life.

Where Renaissance humanists, Erasmus in particular, differed from Luther was in their respect for the textual tradition. Luther privileged Scripture alone (*sola scriptura*) as the authority by which to judge contemporary practices, beliefs, and doctrine. Erasmus, in keeping with humanism's respect for ancient texts, set Scripture within a context of human commentary and discussion, arguing directly against Luther for the necessity that any one reading of scripture be tempered with the knowledge of other, and manifestly diverse, but also finally human readings. Luther and Erasmus broke not on the authority of Scripture—both shared the humanist's respect for the veracity of the text—but on how it was to be interpreted. As we shall see in the next chapter, Luther was as much and as little an "individual" as anyone else in that age, but he held human interpretation to be far less trustworthy than his humanist predecessors had.

Perhaps the worst shortcomings existed at the top, in the papacy itself. In the fourteenth and early fifteenth centuries the papacy had abandoned Rome for Avignon and gone through the crisis of the Great Schism and the Conciliar movement. It emerged from these ordeals with its power reinvigorated, but its spiritual prestige was gravely damaged. For three quarters of a century after 1450 the papacy was occupied by men who scored political and military successes and lavished money on learning and the arts. While they bequeathed to posterity the Vatican Library, the Sistine Chapel, and the early parts of the Basilica of St. Peter, they also increased the burden of ecclesiastical taxation. Papal indifference to spiritual functions enfeebled the church at a time when it needed firm control and reform.

The papacy had entered into its long period of being influenced by affairs of state, at first German, then French, then Spanish in the Counter-Reformation, followed by another period of French dominance again, then again Spain. The popes themselves remained learned, but they were less pious and more diverse and politically wise. The first popes were Greek-speaking, then Latin. The first German was elected in 996, the first Frenchman in 999, the only Englishman in 1154, the first Spaniard in 1455. Diversity would not be matched, however, by popes drawn from the outer regions of a Church that would shortly experience vast overseas expansion.

The Fine Arts

Even more than the writers and preachers of the Renaissance, its artists displayed an extraordinary range of originality in their interests and talents. They found patrons both among the princes of the church and among merchant princes, condottieri, and secular rulers. They took as subjects their own patrons and the pagan gods and heroes of antiquity, as well as Christ, the Virgin, and the saints. Although their income was often meager, they enjoyed increasing status both as technicians and as creative personalities.

The artists liberated painting and sculpture from subordination to architecture. The statues, carvings, altarpieces, and stained glass contributing so much to Romanesque and Gothic churches had usually been only parts of a larger whole. In the Renaissance the number of freestanding pictures and sculptures steadily increased.

Important advances in painting came with the further development of chiaroscuro, stressing contrasts of light and shade, and with the growing use of perspective. In the early Renaissance painters worked in fresco or tempera; in fresco they applied pigments to the wet plaster of a wall, and the painters had to work swiftly before the plaster dried; in tempera they mixed pigments with a sizing, often of eggs, which allowed them to work after the plaster had dried but gave the end product a muddy look. Oil paints overcame the deficiencies of fresco and tempera by permitting leisurely, delicate work and ensuring clearer and more permanent colors.

Without Leonardo, Michelangelo, and other Italian artists of genius, the Renaissance could never have become one of the great ages in the history of art. In sculpture it rivaled the golden centuries of Greece; in painting it transformed a rather limited medium into a dazzling new instrument. It is no wonder that historians often use Italian designations for these centuries; *trecento, quattrocento,* and *cinquecento* (literally, "300s," "400s," and "500s," abbreviated references to the 1300s, 1400s and 1500s).

Florence was the artistic capital of the Renaissance in Italy. Lorenzo the Magnificent subsidized the painter Sandro Botticelli (c. 1444–1510) as well as the humanists of the Platonic Academy. Court painters were commonplace in other states, both in Italy and elsewhere. In Milan, Il Moro made Leonardo da Vinci in effect his minister of fine arts and director of public works; after Sforza's fortunes collapsed, Leonardo found new patrons in Cesare Borgia, the pope, and the French kings Louis XII and Francis I.

The mixture of worldly and religious motives among patrons also characterized the works they commissioned. Artists applied equal skill to scenes from classical mythology, to portraits of their secular contemporaries, and to such religious subjects as the Madonna, the Nativity, and the Crucifixion. Often the sacred and the secular could be found in the same picture; for example, in the *Last Judgment,* in the Arena Chapel, Giotto portrayed Scrovegni, who had commissioned the work, on the same scale as the saints.

Patronage, like art, was a complex matter. Many patrons were lay men and women who wanted a religious painting for their houses; many were corporate and ecclesiastical, such as religious brotherhoods who wished a painting on the theme of the saint after whom their church was named; many were corporate and secular, such as the wool guild, who might wish to illustrate a specific theme; many were individual and ecclesiastical, such as the popes, archbishops, and bishops of the church; and there was always the state, as when the Florentine government commissioned Michelangelo to make a bronze David (as opposed to his marble David). Patrons could and did dictate the trends in themes, the use of materials, the placement of finished objects. Thus commerce, prestige, a sense of place, the desire to honor an occasion, and social customs all shaped art and were in turn shaped by the artists' responses to their commissions.

Renaissance artists at first painted classical and pagan subjects like Jupiter or Venus as just another lord and lady of the chivalric class. Later they restored the sense of historical appropriateness by using classical settings and painting the figures in the nude; at the same time, however, they also created an otherworldly quality. When Botticelli was commissioned by the Medici to do *The Birth of Venus* (1485), he made the goddess, emerging full grown from a seashell, more ethereal than sensual, and he placed the figures in the arrangement usual for the baptism of Christ. In *Primavera* (c. 1478), Botticelli's allegory of spring, the chief figures—Mercury, Venus, the Three Graces, Flora (bedecked with blossoms), and Spring herself (wafted in by the West Wind)—are all youthful, delicate, and serene.

Leonardo da Vinci completed relatively few pictures, since his scientific activities consumed much of his energy. Moreover, his celebrated mural, *The*

Last Supper (1495–1498), began to deteriorate during his own lifetime because the mold on the damp monastery wall in Milan destroyed the clarity of the pigments he used. Luckily, Leonardo's talent and his extraordinary range of interests can also be studied in his drawings and notebooks. The drawings include preliminary sketches of paintings, fanciful war machines, and doodles, along with realistic portrayals of human embryos and of deformed suffering individuals.

In composing *The Last Supper* Leonardo departed dramatically from previous interpretations. He divided the apostles into four groups of three men around the central figure of Christ. His second departure was to choose the tense moment when Jesus announced the coming betrayal and to place Judas among the apostles, relying on facial expression and bodily posture to convey the guilt of the one and the consternation of the others.

Michelangelo Buonarotti (1475–1564), although best known as a sculptor, ranks among the immortals of painting as a result of the frescoes he executed for the Sistine Chapel in the Vatican. He covered a huge area with 343 separate figures and spent four years working almost alone, assisted only by a plasterer and a color mixer, painting on his back atop a scaffold, sometimes not even descending for his night's rest. He began over the chapel entrance with *The Drunkenness of Noah* and ended above the altar with *The Creation*. God appears repeatedly. Hovering over the waters, he is benign; giving life to the motionless Adam or directing Eve to arise, he is gently commanding; creating the sun and the moon, he is the formidable, all-powerful deity.

Both Michelangelo and Leonardo had received their artistic training in Florence. Titian (1477–1576) was identified with Venice, and the rich reds and purples that are his hallmark exemplify the flamboyance and pageantry of that city. At the start he was engaged to do frescoes for the Venetian headquarters of German merchants, and he went on to portraits of rich merchants, Madonnas, altarpieces for churches and monasteries, and a great battle scene for the palace of the doge. He was offered commissions by half the despots of Italy and crowned heads of Europe.

Painting in Northern Europe

In northern Europe the masters of the fifteenth century were influenced by their Gothic traditions as well as by Titian and other Italians. The ranking northern painters included two Germans, Albrecht Dürer (1471–1528) and Hans Holbein (c. 1496–1543), and two from the Low Countries, Hieronymus Bosch (c. 1450–1516) and Pieter Brueghel (c. 1525–1569). Dürer received commissions from the emperor Maximilian and Brueghel from wealthy businessmen of Antwerp and Brussels. Holbein executed portraits of Henry VIII and his courtiers as well as a likeness of Erasmus that catches the humanist's wit and intelligence.

Dürer created what has been termed the first great Protestant art, in which he simplified traditional Christian themes by pruning them of what Lutherans regarded as Catholic trimmings. But this was only one facet of Dürer's many-sided talent; his fascination with nature led him to include wild crea-

Although religious themes continued to be popular during this period, figures became more fleshy and lifelike. Here the Florentine Masaccio (1401–1428), who revolutionized art during his short lifetime, provides his version of The Expulsion of Adam and Eve *from the Garden of Eden. Light slants in sharply from an outside source to create a sense of distance; the figures are caught in motion and despair. Deprived of God, Eve cries out, and both Adam and Eve hide their nakedness, having learned of evil. Neither figure attempts to resist the angel who expels them.   (Erich Lessing, Art Resource, NY)*

tures in many pictures; his realistic and compassionate portrait of his aged mother might almost have been taken from Leonardo's notebooks; and his improvements in the techniques of woodcuts and engravings enabled him to mass-produce his own drawings as illustrations for printed books.

Northern art was fascinated with the monstrous and supernatural. Dürer depicted this Gothic strain in a series of woodcuts of the Four Horsemen and other grim figures of the Apocalypse. Bosch made his paintings graphic sermons filled with nightmarish apparitions illustrating the omnipresence of sin and evil and foreshadowing the techniques and effects of the surrealists of the twentieth century. Brueghel's works contained coats-of-arms that fight, shellfish that fly, and monstrous hybrids that have insect wings, artichoke bodies, and flower heads. Other paintings of Brueghel's were realistic and sensitive comments on human misery in a time long before social services, such as *The Blind Leading the Blind*. Brueghel also favored two types of painting otherwise neglected in the period. One was the landscape; his series illustrating farming activities through the year was in the tradition of late medieval books of hours, but with new attention to the changing light and atmosphere of the seasons. The other was the densely populated scene of everyday life and popular culture—children's games and peasant weddings, dances, and festivals.

Sculpture

Renaissance sculpture and painting were closely related, and Italian pictures owed some of their three-dimensional quality to the artists' study of sculpture. The first Renaissance sculptor was Donatello (1386–1466), whose statue of the condottiere Gattamelata in Padua was even then a landmark in the history of art. The subject is secular, the treatment classical. Donatello created the first statue of a nude male since antiquity, a bronze David who, however, looked more like a handsome youth than the inspired slayer of Goliath. Yet Donatello's wooden statue of Mary Magdalene, all lank hair and skin and bones, was a saint who looked the part.

Still another gifted Florentine, Andrea del Verrocchio (1435–1488), extended the concern for social and political realism. His statue of the condottiere Colleoni in Venice, mounted on a muscular horse, is more dynamic than Donatello's Gattamelata. Painter, goldsmith, teacher of Leonardo, and student of architecture, geometry, music, and philosophy, Verrocchio ranked among the universal men of the Renaissance. So did Benvenuto Cellini (1500–1571), goldsmith, engraver, devotee of high living, and author of a noted autobiography. Cellini boasted as patrons two popes as well as King Francis I of France and the Medici duke of Tuscany, who commissioned an elegant statue of Perseus (1553) holding aloft the head of Medusa.

Florence commissioned Michelangelo's colossal statue of David, a muscular nude more than sixteen feet high, fashioned from an enormous block of marble abandoned by another sculptor. Michelangelo went on to carry sculpture to a summit it had not attained since the age of Pericles. He showed his ingenuity in solving technical problems with his *Pietà* (c. 1499), in St. Peter's, which shows the Virgin mourning the dead Christ. It was exceedingly difficult to pose a seated woman with a limp adult body across her lap, yet Michelangelo succeeded triumphantly.

Architecture

In 1546, at the age of seventy, Michelangelo agreed to become the chief architect of St. Peter's in Rome. St. Peter's exemplifies many of the features that

Botticelli's Primavera, *also called* Allegory of Spring. *(Scala/Art Resource, NY)*

distinguish Renaissance architecture from Gothic. Gothic cathedrals were topped by great spires and towers; St. Peter's was crowned by Michelangelo's massive dome, which rises 435 feet above the floor. Gothic buildings, with their great windows, pointed arches, and high-flung vaults, create an impression of aspiration and grace, of scarcely being earthbound; St. Peter's appears indestructible and utterly stable because of its heavier walls, stout columns, and round arches.

Renaissance architects shared the humanists' enthusiasm for Platonic concepts of perfect ideas and perfect geometrical forms. Andrea Palladio (1508–1580), the leading architectural theorist of the cinquecento, stressed the symbolic value of designing churches on the plan of the Greek cross, which had four arms of equal length, in contrast to the Latin cross used in Gothic churches, which had one long arm forming the nave. If the ends of the arms of the Greek cross were rounded and the spaces between the arms filled with rounded chapels, then the structure became a circle. Palladio himself designed many elegant structures: the Church of San Giorgio Maggiore on an island at the mouth of the Grand Canal in Venice, palaces, public buildings, villas, and a Greek theater in the area of Vicenza, his home town. He also wrote a four-volume study on architecture that spread the influence of the Palladian style.

In Renaissance Europe private individuals could afford lavish residences, and the increasing prevalence of law and order meant that a home no longer needed to be a fortress. Elaborate villas dotted the Italian countryside; in the cities the characteristic structure was the *palazzo,* an imposing townhouse combining business and residential apartments; many examples survive throughout Italy.

The Art of Daily Living

Indoors, Renaissance buildings reflected the improving standard of life among the affluent. Smaller rooms were easier to heat than the vast drafty halls of the Middle Ages, and items of furniture began to multiply beyond the medieval complement of built-in beds, benches, cupboards, and tables. Although chairs were still largely reserved for the master of the house and important guests, benches or stools were becoming more common. Chests were often elaborately painted or carved. New articles of furniture served more specialized purposes: the bookcase to house the new printed books (medieval manuscripts had been kept in chests), the writing desk, and the jewel cabinet, a miniature chest on high legs often encrusted with ivory or inlaid work.

The popularity of brooches, pendants, and other forms of jewelry with intricate gold settings attested both to the wealth and to the taste of upper-class Renaissance men and women. Silversmiths made elaborately etched helmets, shields, and suits of armor better suited for show than for military use. Fine glass was highly esteemed, particularly the elaborate and delicate work that was made in Venice. Both the less affluent and the rich had embroidered household linens and brass and pewter utensils.

When Italians of the Renaissance looked into the mirror, they saw a gown or tunic surmounted by a cape or cloak, the whole made of increasingly colorful and elegant material. Personal cleanliness advanced with the custom of the weekly bath and change of body linen; bodily wastes were disposed of in an outside privy or in a "close-stool" (commode) indoors. In Italy table manners became more complex, with the substitution of the fork for the fingers, the fading out of the custom of tossing bones and other debris from a meal onto the floor beneath the table, and the use of easily cleaned tiles or mosaics for flooring. Elsewhere changes came more slowly. In England the fork was not in common use until the seventeenth century, and the floor of the great hall in many houses was still covered with rushes; a fresh layer of rushes and fragrant herbs was added from time to time to counter the stench and insects from the lower layers.

The peasantry probably lived better after the Black Death than before, for those who survived could demand higher wages and use those wages to buy better food, including meat for special occasions. By the mid-fifteenth century, however, white bread and meat were again exclusively for the rich, and the peasant was once again reduced to hard bread and gruel as population increased and the bargaining power of labor declined. The worker in the field expected to wear dirt as though it were clothing. Privacy did not exist for any purpose, and even the rich used corridors and decorative bushes to urinate

The Written Record

THE ARTIST'S LIFE

Benvenuto Cellini's fame rests as much on his *Autobiography* as on his art. Begun in Florence in 1558, it is filled with court gossip, attacks on fellow artists, and accounts of Cellini's often riotous life. It could take him months, even years, to complete a single commissioned work of art, for he faced many distractions. One of his most famous works, a great figure of Perseus (son of Zeus in Greek myth), took an especially long time, interrupted as it was by other commissions, difficult working conditions, poor workmanship by some assistants, and the death of his brother-in-law.

While the workshop for executing my Perseus was in building, I used to work in a ground-floor room. Here I modelled the statue in plaster, giving it the same dimensions as the bronze was meant to have, and intending to cast it from this mould. But finding that it would take rather long to carry it out in this way, I resolved upon another expedient, especially as now a wretched little studio had been erected, brick on brick, so miserably built that the mere recollection of it gives me pain. So then I began the figure of Medusa, and constructed the skeleton in iron. Afterwards I put on the clay, and when that was modelled, baked it.

I had no assistants except some little shopboys, among whom was one of great beauty; he was the son of a prostitute called La Gambetta. I made use of the lad as a model, for the only books which teach this art are the natural human body. Meanwhile, as I could not do everything alone, I looked about for workmen in order to put the business quickly through; but I was unable to find any. . . . I set about to do my utmost by myself alone. The labour was enormous: I had to strain every muscle night and day; and just then the husband of my sister sickened, and died after a few days' illness. He left my sister, still young, with six girls of all ages, on my hands. . . . So I went home with despair at heart to my unlucky Perseus, not without weeping. . . . At the end of three days news was brought to me that my only son had been smothered by his nurse, which gave me greater grief than I have ever had in my whole life. However, I knelt upon the ground, and, not without tears, returned thanks to God, as I was wont, exclaiming, "Lord, Thou gavest me the child, and Thou has taken him; for all Thy dealings I thank Thee with my whole heart." This great sorrow went nigh to depriving me of reason; yet, according to my habit, I made a virtue of necessity, and adapted myself to circumstances as well as I was able. . . . Nevertheless, I felt convinced that when my Perseus was accomplished, all these trials would be turned to high felicity and glorious well-being.

Benvenuto Cellini, *The Autobiography of Benvenuto Cellini*, trans. John Addington Symonds (New York: Modern Library Edition, 1942), pp. 382–83, 399–401, 412.

or defecate. The world stank. At nightfall people were deprived of their sense of sight, for candles were very expensive.

For the rich, luxury did not mean comfort. Travel was difficult, for roads were bad and highway robbers common. There was neither underwear nor soap in any quantity. The perfumes of the East were used to cover the body odors of the West. There was much concern for fashion among men as well as women; the size of a bow, the length of a sleeve, the nature of a ruffle were important matters.

In Renaissance Italy and Spain, blacks were present in significant numbers and had important roles, since the wealthy found it fashionable to have as many black servants as possible. Thousands of slaves were sold in Genoa, Venice, Barcelona, Seville, and Marseilles. From the twelfth century on, the cult of St. Maurice, a black man who had been martyred in the fourth century, grew. Because St. Maurice was depicted as a knight, the nobility gave him special attention. Black Madonnas were venerated in churches in Poland and Spain. Free blacks were employed in Venice as gondoliers and dock workers, and throughout the western Mediterranean were entertainers and professional fools, or individuals kept for family amusement and as exotic representatives of "the other," the cultures that stood outside the courts and upper middle class. Attitudes toward blacks were ambiguous: Medieval and early Renaissance art often portrayed the devil as black, but black was also the color of humility and grief. In the sixteenth century, as European vessels began to explore the coasts of Africa, more and more blacks began to appear in port cities.

Galenic medicine also shaped at least the formal medieval and early modern representations of women. The theory of humors posited specifically that the female body was composed of cold and wet humors, the physiological basis for what was held to be unpredictable behavior. A number of medical theorists viewed the womb as definitive of female nature: Its presence largely determined women's speech and senses. In the prescriptive literature, women were often represented as overly sensual, or volatile, a force for disorder. Some of that sense of women permeates accusations of women, some 80 percent of all accusations, for witchcraft. Although women such as Hildegard of Bingen and Heloise demonstrated two centuries earlier an unquestionable ability to read Latin and to enter into the subtleties of scholarship, universities remained the prerogative of men, as did many different sorts of learning, from theology to medicine. As one learned woman writer, Christine de Pisan (c. 1363–1431), wrote in 1405, "Alas, God, why was I not born into this world as a member of the masculine sex?"

Perhaps nowhere is the fissure between the veneer of the Renaissance and its lived reality as wide as in the difference between various scholars' representations of "woman" and the lived realities of individual women. As early as the thirteenth century, women were investing in business. As we have already seen, women were often trusted advisors and partners to their husbands in trade and craft. Noblewomen exercised greater or lesser authority over their domains, according to a wide and differing range of factors. In the sixteenth century, one of the great Renaissance monarchs, Elizabeth I of Eng-

---

| A Closer Look |

THE COURTIER

The Italian Baldassare Castiglione (1478–1529) was said to be "one of the finest gentlemen in the world." Over many years he wrote out the code of the Renaissance patrician. The ideal courtier should know Greek and Latin, the Italian poets, horsemanship and military skills, music and painting. He should excel in sport, like the knight of old, should hunt, wrestle, swim, "play at tennis." He should also receive a good education in "orators and historiographers, and also in writing both rhyme and prose, and especially in this our vulgar tongue." The following is from Castiglione's work, *The Courtier.*

It is not unreasonable to say also that the old can love without blame, and more happily than the young; taking this word old, however, not in the sense of decrepit or as meaning that the organs of the body have already become so weak that the soul cannot perform its operations through them, but as meaning when knowledge in us in its true prime. I will not refrain from saying this also: I think that, although sensual love is bad at every age, yet in the young it deserves to be excused, and in some sense is perhaps permitted. For although it brings them afflictions, dangers, toils, and the woes we have said, still there are many, who, to win the good graces of the ladies they love, do worthy acts, which (although not directed to a good end) are in themselves good; and thus from that great bitterness they extract a little sweetness, and through the adversities which they endure they finally recognize their error. Hence, even as I consider those youths divine who master their appetites and love according to reason, I likewise excuse those who allow themselves to be overcome by sensual love, to which they are so much inclined by human weakness: provided that in such love they show gentleness, courtesy, and worth, and the other noble qualities which these gentlemen have mentioned; and provided that when they are no longer youthful, they abandon it altogether, leaving this sensual desire behind as the lowest rung of that ladder by which we ascend to true love. But if, even when they are old, they keep the fire of the appetites in their cold hearts, and subject strong reason to weak sense, it is not possible to say how much they should be blamed. For like senseless fools they deserve with perpetual infamy to be numbered among the unreasoning animals, because the thoughts and ways of sensual love are most unbecoming to a mature age.

---

land, would patronize such luminaries of Renaissance arts as William Shakespeare. The Renaissance was a time of new kinds of wealth, as well as new ways of displaying that wealth. The wives of prosperous merchants and masters, duchesses, princesses, the queens—all shaped letters and the arts through patronage. Female artisans, such as Artemisia Gentileschi, and women of letters, such as Marguerite de Navarre, participated in the creation of Renaissance culture through their own works of painting, poetry, sculpture, and literature. We have only begun to understand the extent and the nature of women's agency in the Renaissance.

Typologies of gender in the Renaissance may have been less important for the daily lives of individual women than they were in the discourse of politics. The ideal relation of wife to husband was one model for articulating the hoped-for relation of subject to ruler. An "orderly" marriage was a trope for an orderly state, the relations articulated not in terms of dominance, but of natural order, the sovereignty of the husband not the product of force or artifice, but of his natural superiority of reason and, in Machiavelli's term, of *virtú*. The Renaissance, like the Middle Ages, remained very much a hierarchical society, in which "nature" and God determined the proper ordering of the world: within each marriage, each family, each household, each town, and the state.

SUMMARY

Scholars have debated what the Renaissance was and when it began. However, most accept that it began in Italy about 1300 and lasted for about three centuries. The outpouring of intellectual and artistic energy was not only marked by a revival of interest in classical Greek and Roman values but also owed a debt to medieval Christian civilization.

During the Renaissance, the economy of western Europe changed from one based on barter to one based on money. Improvements in ship design and better navigational instruments resulted in the expansion of seaborne trade. Industry, especially textiles, metals, and shipbuilding, also grew.

Early forms of capitalism such as mass production and specialization emerged. To finance growing trade and industry, banking expanded. Kings, popes, and merchants borrowed large sums from Italian bankers. Banking families, such as the Fuggers in Germany, gained power and wealth.

Towns expanded, bringing change to people in surrounding areas. The money economy led to the raising of cash crops on the manor and the payment of rent in money. Lines were blurred between classes as money replaced the medieval social system based on caste and service. Moreover, the bourgeoisie arose as a new business class and generously supported Renaissance learning and art.

During the Renaissance, vernacular, or popular, literature emerged, although Latin remained the language of scholarship. The development of printing brought on a communications revolution in which the printed book became a profound force for change.

Petrarch exemplifies the mixture of the old and the new in the Renaissance. In France, the language of the Paris region replaced Latin as the official language.

Renaissance scholars such as Lorenzo Valla, who revealed the forgery of the Donation of Constantine, uncovered, preserved, and studied ancient manuscripts. A number of humanists sought to blend Christian and classical traditions, helping to found the studies of comparative religion and comparative philosophy. One, Erasmus, brought all the humanistic, linguistic, and philological expertise to bear on the text of Scripture, producing an edition of the Greek New Testament that would prove the foundation of Reformation within his own lifetime.

The influx of classical works after the Fall of Constantinople in 1453 had consequences for the study of classical science and mathematics, as well as classical philosophy, history, and poetry. In 1492, the authority of Ptolemy, as well as of Greek and Roman natural history, would be irreparably weakened, as Europeans confronted fully the contradiction between what they saw and what that classical tradition had taught them to expect. Leonardo da Vinci in many ways epitomizes the Renaissance scholar: He explored questions we now consider the domain of science, but his observations never led him to reject the classical tradition.

With the perfecting of movable type in the 1440s and the development of the printing press, books became cheaper and had fewer errors. Printed handbooks became available on many specific subjects.

Copernicus launched a revolution in astronomy in 1543 by putting forth the heliocentric theory of the universe. Within 150 years the Copernican revolution was confirmed by the work of Galileo and Newton.

Music reflected the Renaissance emphasis on secular and individual concerns. New instruments were developed, and music became part of popular culture.

The Great Schism had damaged the prestige of the Church. In addition, the burden of church taxation to support the lavish Renaissance papacy and indifference to the need for reform left the Church open to attack.

In the fine arts, an extraordinary outpouring of creativity occurred in painting and sculpture. Botticelli, Michelangelo, Leonardo, and Raphael found patrons among Renaissance popes and rulers and produced works reflecting a mixture of worldly and religious themes.

In the fifteenth century, northern European painters such as Dürer, Holbein, Bosch, and Brueghel were influenced by Gothic as well as Italian Renaissance styles. Notable in some of their works were elements of the monstrous and supernatural.

Many leading painters such as Michelangelo and Cellini were also sculptors and masters of other arts. The great work of Renaissance architecture was St. Peter's in Rome, crowned by Michelangelo's massive dome.

The wealthy enjoyed great luxury, although not comfort, while daily life for peasants remained pretty much unchanged, and would do so until the nineteenth century. That luxury encompassed unprecedented lay patronage of arts and music, in which women had an increasingly influential role. In an age of female regents, such as Catherine de' Medici, and female monarchs, such as Mary Tudor and Elizabeth I, a number of treatises depicted "woman" as by nature disorderly, unpredictable, and unstable. The paradox of the Renaissance is perhaps best captured in this: Even as the most learned of men depicted "woman" as inferior in mind, discipline, and moral character to "man," we can hear more individual women's voices and see more individual women acting in the Renaissance than at any time previously.

FOUR

Exploration and Expansion

∞

In the fifteenth century, Portugal initiated an unprecedented expansion that carried first Portuguese, then Spanish and Italian, then Dutch, and finally English and French merchants, missionaries, adventurers, and settlers as well as sailors ultimately to every quarter of the globe. What Europeans called "the known world"—meaning the world known to them—spread outward at a breathtaking pace. In the age of Homer, that "known world" had encompassed little more than the eastern Mediterranean. While the Romans expanded that world to Britain and the eastern reaches of modern-day Germany, as well as southward into Egypt and Ethiopia, their world remained centered on the Mediterranean: It was the defining body of water. Explorations in the Middle Ages did not transform Europe's sense of itself in the world, but the changes in technology and in cartography introduced in the late Middle Ages made possible the long sea voyages of the late fifteenth century, and with them the "discovery" both that the Atlantic was larger than any "known" body of water and, more stunningly, that it was also bounded by another continent.

The Expansion of the West

Westerners were not the first people to migrate over vast reaches of water. Even before the Viking voyages in the Atlantic, the Polynesians had settled remote Pacific islands. But the Polynesians and other early migrants were not societies in expansion; they were groups of individuals on the move. The expansion of the West was different. From its beginning in ancient Greece and Rome, records were kept, maps were made, and the nucleus always remained in touch with its offshoots.

Modern Western expansion, which began in the mid-fifteenth century, differed in four important ways from the expansions that had carried the cultures of the ancient Near East as far as western and northern Europe. First, this modern expansion was much faster and covered more ground. Most of the whole world was revealed to Europeans within the three centuries after 1450. Second, this modern expansion was the first time Western society crossed great oceans. Ancient and medieval Western navigation had clung to the narrow seas and the shorelines; now Westerners crossed the Atlantic and the Pacific, far from the protecting land for weeks at a time. Third, this expansion carried Westerners well beyond the familiar orbit of relations with Byzantines and Muslims into relations with a bewildering variety of races, creeds, and cultures. Fourth, Europe possessed a margin of superior material and technological strength that enabled Western society to extend its influence around the world. An important element of that margin was the possession of firearms.

The strength by which Europeans overcame the world was a compound of technological and economic power plus political and social organization, which permitted superior military enterprise. This material advantage was applied by a half dozen competing Western states, each quite willing to arm and organize the local population against its Western competitors. The French in North America armed the indigenous peoples against the British, and the British armed them against the French. In the Far East, the French, British, Portuguese, Dutch, Spanish, and later the Germans and Americans intrigued against one another. So great was the Western advantage that the rivalries of competing powers did not delay the process of expansion as much as stimulate and hasten it.

The motives for expansion were, of course, mixed. Although often moved by greed, by sheer despair over their lot at home, or by enthusiasm for new things, those who carried out the expansion were also convinced that they were doing God's work and that they were carrying with them a better way of life. The acquisition of empire is usually laid to four primary motivations: the human desire for glory, the desire to serve God, the hunger for gold in all its forms, and the strategic need to seize certain areas or resources to achieve the other three ends. While specific empire builders may have held one of these motives uppermost, all were compatible.

The magnetic compass helped make ocean voyages possible. Without the compass, earlier mariners had been helpless, except when clear weather gave them sun or stars as guides. Not only were better instruments and better methods of determining a ship's position at sea available by the fifteenth century, but shipbuilders were constructing vessels that were longer and narrower than the traditional Mediterranean ships and better able to withstand the long swells of the ocean.

Moreover, the rising political and economic power of the Atlantic states led their merchants to search for new routes to India, since the old Near Eastern route was controlled by the Ottoman Turks and by the Italians. Historians who interpret developments first in terms of economics also suggest that Europeans discovered new worlds because the aggressive drives inherent in rising capitalism sent them on their way. Yet the explorations of the Europeans were also guided by the new spirit of empirical science.

Nothing makes clearer the consecutive, planned, deliberately scientific nature of these early modern explorations and settlements than the contrast with the sporadic, unplanned, and often mythical nature of earlier oceanic

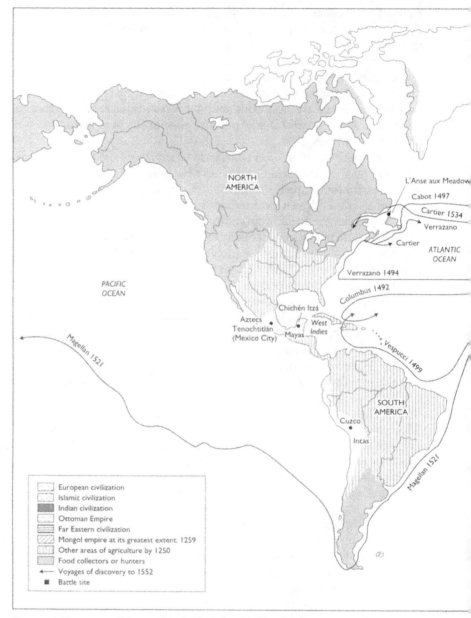

European Voyages and Encounters with Other Civilizations

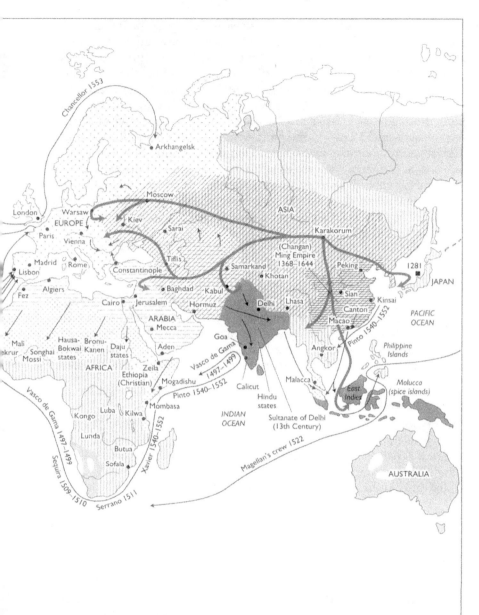

navigations. Tradition is full of tales of these early voyages. The Phoenicians, the Irish, the Norse, the Welsh, and Breton fishermen have all been credited with the "discovery" of America. Of all these tales of pre-Columbian discovery, that of the Vikings reaching the North American continent in 986 is supported by the firmest evidence. There is no doubt that the Norse settled Iceland, that they had outposts in Greenland, and that they founded a small settlement about 1000 at L'Anse aux Meadows in northern Newfoundland. Their heroic sagas credit Leif Ericson with reaching a Wineland (or Vinland), which almost certainly was somewhere along the present New England or Canadian coasts. Yet even if hundreds of Europeans reached the New World before Columbus, they did not establish a permanent link between the two worlds; they were not explorers supported by a state or a group of merchants expecting a full report, and they were, above all, not urged on by purposes either social or scientific.

East by Sea to the Indies

Over the broad sweep of the growth of European empires, there was a strong tendency for one nation to dominate for a century or so and then decline. The fifteenth and sixteenth centuries tended to be dominated by the Iberian states, the seventeenth century by the Dutch, the eighteenth by the French, and the nineteenth by the British. The first on the scene were the Portuguese.

Prince Henry and the Portuguese

Prince Henry of Portugal (1394–1460), known as "the Navigator," was a deeply religious man who may well have been moved by a desire to convert the populations of India and the Far East. Indeed, many in the West were convinced that these distant peoples were already Christian, and for true salvation needed only to be brought in direct contact with the Roman Catholic church.

Prince Henry and his associates wanted to promote Portuguese commerce and national power as well as the Christian faith. They went about their work carefully, sending out frequent, well-equipped expeditions. Their vessels discovered Madeira and the Azores, uninhabited islands in the Atlantic where the Portuguese and other Europeans then began to settle first about 1420.

The main thrust southward gradually crept along the harsh desert coast of Africa where the Sahara meets the Atlantic, until in 1445 the Portuguese moved eastward past Cape Verde. Whether Henry himself believed that Africa could be circumnavigated with the right technology is not certain, but according to legend the Phoenicians had done it, and Greco-Roman geographers had argued that Africa was surrounded by ocean. The problem was that a return voyage was almost impossible against the winds and currents unless a huge arc could be plotted out into the Atlantic, and vessels—adapted from Arab and Mediterranean craft—could be developed to withstand such waters.

By 1472, after Prince Henry's death, the Portuguese reached the end of the bulge of West Africa at the Cameroons and were disheartened to see that the coast was once more trending southward. But they kept on, stimulated by royal patronage, and in the next generation two great explorers finished the task. In 1488 Bartholomeu Dias (1450–1500), blown far south by a great storm, turned northeast and found that he had rounded the great cape later called Good Hope. He was followed by Vasco da Gama (c. 1460–1524), who set out in 1497 with four ships to reach India and worked northward along the east coast of Africa, coming soon to an area of Arab trading where the route to India was well known. Da Gama secured a pilot and reached the Malabar coast of India at Calicut ten months and fourteen days out from Lisbon. The Portuguese now had an ocean route to the East.

In 1500 Pedro Cabral (c. 1464–c. 1520) started out to repeat da Gama's voyage to India. But by now the Portuguese were used to long voyages on the open ocean. Cabral kept boldly southward from the bulge of Africa and then bore westward to make a landfall on the bulge of the South American continent in what is now Brazil. He at once sent a ship to Portugal to announce his discovery. Six years previously, by the Treaty of Tordesillas (1494), Spain and Portugal had agreed to partition their newly discovered lands along a north-south line about a thousand miles west of the Azores, so eastern Brazil fell within the Portuguese sphere.

The main Portuguese push, however, continued toward India and the Far East. Explorers were followed by traders aided and protected by the state, which aimed to set up a monopoly of commerce with the newly found lands. The great figure of early Portuguese imperialism was Afonso de Albuquerque (1453–1515), governor of the Indies from 1509 to 1515, under whom the Portuguese founded their trading center at Goa in India. From Goa they organized regular trade routes toward southeast Asia and China. By 1557 they had established a base at Macao on the Chinese coast near Canton and had begun to trade with the Japanese.

New Encounters: Africa

The two new worlds thus opened to Europeans were very different both from Europe and from each other. Africa was humid, relatively thinly populated, and thought to be poor by European standards. India, China, and much of southeast Asia were thickly populated, with great wealth accumulated in a few hands and with much that Europeans wanted in the way of spices, silks, and other luxuries. Africa was temporarily bypassed, although the many coastal stations that the Europeans founded in West Africa soon carried on a flourishing trade in slaves.

The African tribes on the great westward bulge of the continent had already left their mark on history. Medieval Ghana controlled a much larger area than its modern namesake until it was overthrown by Muslim invaders from North Africa in the eleventh century. When the Portuguese reached West Africa, parts of the interior were controlled by the empire of Mali, centered at Timbuktu, on the upper Niger River. Caravans organized by North African traders came to Timbuktu to buy gold and slaves and to sell wares from the Mediterranean.

In the interior of central and southern Africa there were politically complex tribal states, especially at Zimbabwe and among the kingdoms of the Kongo, Luba, Lunda, and Kuba. But these cultures were little known to the Europeans, who judged Africa by what they encountered near the coasts, where the societies were much less complex. These cultures were so different from those of Europe that few Europeans made any effort to understand them. Nor did the Europeans do much to undermine these indigenous cultures. Except for the southern tip of Africa, where the Dutch began settlement in the seventeenth century, Africa south of the Sahara was not directly subject to colonialism until the annexations and partitions of the nineteenth century.

India

India had been marginally in touch with Europe for several thousand years. Throughout the Middle Ages the Arabs had served as a link in trade, and in the sixteenth century a direct link was forged between the West and India, never to be loosened.

When the Portuguese reached India, Muslim invaders were consolidating their rule. The Muslim empire was misleadingly called Mogul (Mughal or Mongol), for its rulers were Turks from central Asia. It had little hold over the regions of southern India where Europeans first established their footholds. Local Indian rulers, whether Muslim or Hindu, were ready prey to European promises of aid against the other. All the European powers found it easy not merely to win Indian princes to their side but to raise and train native armies to fight under Portuguese, French, Dutch, or British flags.

Some of the more isolated parts of India in the Deccan, or southern peninsula, were inhabited by tribes that seemed to Europeans to have stepped out of the Stone Age. Some on the northern edges were warrior tribes, much like those who had invaded Europe from the highlands of Central Asia. In the great valleys of the Indus and the Ganges and in the richer parts of the Deccan, there was a wealthy, populous society basically Hindu in culture— although when the Europeans arrived it was dominated in many areas by Muslim invaders.

Hindu society was the result of a mix between earlier native groups and invaders from the north. The early history of India, however, is still controversial, and there is no full agreement on how numerous these invaders were or just where they came from, although the invasion apparently took place between 2000 and 1200 B.C.

According to the Hindu laws of caste, men and women were by the fact of birth settled for life in a closed group that pursued a given occupation and occupied a fixed social position. There were over a thousand castes, plus a group at the bottom without caste, the "untouchables." The ruling groups were of two main castes, the *Brahmins*, or priests, and the *Kshatriya*, or warriors. The third main caste, the *Vaisya*, was based largely on vocation or trade. In theory, marriage between members of different castes was forbidden, as was change of caste through social mobility.

The priestly caste, the Brahmins, enjoyed exceptional prestige and authority. The Brahmin faith had strains of an otherworldly belief, shunning the evils of the life of the flesh and seeking salvation through mystic and ascetic denial. With this went a doctrine of the transmigration of souls, in which a sinful life led to reincarnation as lower animal life, and a virtuous life led, at least in some forms of Hindu belief, to ultimate freedom from flesh of any sort and reunion with the All-perfect. Official Brahminism acquired a series of rigid and complicated rituals, but the religion of the common people carried over from earlier times an elaborate polytheism—gods and goddesses who were fleshly indeed by post-Greek European standards. Against all this worldliness there had arisen in the sixth century B.C. a great religious leader, Gautama Buddha. Buddhism accepts the basic Brahmin concept of the evil of this world of the flesh, but it finds salvation—the *nirvana* of peaceful release from the chain of earthly birth and rebirth—in a life that is ascetic but not withdrawn, a life of charity and good works.

Although Buddhism died out in India, it spread with great power to China, Japan, and southeastern Asia. In these lands it took two forms that still exist. In Tibet, China, and Japan, the *Mahayana* (Great Vehicle) continued to emphasize Buddha's strong ethical desire to make nirvana available to all. In southeastern Asia and Ceylon (present-day Sri Lanka), the *Hinayana* (Lesser Vehicle) prevailed; in theory, the Hinayana relies more on ritual, and its monks are wholly detached from the world.

China

China, too, resisted the West. China also saw its armed forces beaten whenever they came into formal military conflict with European or European-trained armies or fleets. It, too, was forced to make many concessions to Europeans—to grant treaty ports, and above all, *extraterritoriality*, that is, the right of Europeans to be tried in their own national courts for offenses committed on Chinese soil. Yet China, unlike India, was never annexed by a European power and never lost its sovereignty.

Like the other civilizations bordering the great nomadic Eurasian heartland, this ancient civilization was subject to periodic incursions by nomadic tribes; it was against such incursions that the Great Wall was built in the third century B.C. On the whole, the Chinese protected their institutions against the victorious nomads, whom they absorbed after a few generations. Early in the seventeenth century Mongolian tribes established a state of their own in eastern Manchuria, to the north of China proper. In 1644 they seized the Chinese capital of Peking and established a dynasty that lasted until 1911. But the Manchus, like other outsiders before them, left Chinese institutions almost untouched.

Chinese history is filled with the dynamic rise and fall of dynasties; with periods of effective governmental centralization and periods of "feudal" dis-

This Mogul painting from late sixteenth-century India shows Portuguese naval mercenaries attacking a local population. One man wears armor in the hot climate. One vessel carries a horse for the commander to use after landing. As this picture is a non-Western rendition, it provides a clear sense of how Westerners were viewed through Eastern eyes.   (The British Library/The Heritage Image Collection)

integration; with wars, plagues, and famines; and with the gradual spread of Chinese culture to Canton, Vietnam, Korea, and Japan. Within this flux were many elements of continuity. At the base of Chinese social life was a communal village organization held together by very strong family ties, a cult of ancestor worship, and a tradition of hard work on farms. At the top of this society was an emperor, the Son of Heaven.

The business of running this vast empire was entrusted to the *mandarins*, a bureaucracy of intellectuals, or at least of those who could pass examinations in literary and philosophical classics. The mandarin class had served the state for thousands of years, and its existence was one of the reasons for the extraordinary stability of Chinese society. Although in theory this class was open to talent, the necessary education was too expensive and too difficult for any but a few gifted, lucky, and persistent poor boys.

In China the upper class took little interest in mysticism and otherworldliness. They accepted the world and were concerned with human relations, with politeness and decorum; their conventional Confucianism was a code of manners and morals, not a sacramental religion. Confucius (551–479 B.C.), a sage who flourished in the fifth century B.C., was a moralist who taught an ethical system of temperance, courtesy, and obedience to those who were wise and good. Most frustrating for Europeans such as the Jesuit Matteo Ricci, the Chinese, perhaps reflecting the influence of Confucius, remained indifferent to Western ideas and institutions.

The Growth and Decline of the Portuguese Empire

Along the coasts of Africa, India, and China, the Portuguese established a series of trading posts over which they hoisted their flag as a sign that these bits of territory had been annexed to the Portuguese Crown. Such posts were often called factories after the *factors,* or commercial agents, who were stationed there to trade with the local population. The Portuguese offered guns, knives, cheap cloth, and fascinating items of all sorts that provided access to a new technology. In return they got gold and silver, pepper and other spices, silks and other luxuries, and, finally, raw materials such as cotton and, in Brazil, tobacco and sugar.

Two guiding principles of this trade were accepted by almost all European contemporaries. First, in this trade the mother country was the dominant partner and would provide manufactured goods and services, while the colony produced raw materials. Second, nationals of other European lands were excluded from this trade; they could not deal directly with the colony or share in the commerce between mother country and colony. The Portuguese, in sum, followed a policy of *mercantilism,* referring not to individual merchants but to a mercantile, or commercial, system based on central control for the benefit of the imperial state through authority over shipping, trade, and production.

Armed forces were essential to this colonial system. Relatively small land forces proved sufficient both to keep "the natives" under control and to ward off rival Europeans from the trading posts. A large and efficient navy was also necessary to protect the sea routes of a colonial power. Pirates were often an unofficial adjunct of a navy, called privateers and operating only against enemies or neutrals.

Few Portuguese settled either in the hot coastlands of Africa or in the already heavily populated lands of India and the Far East; nor did they attempt to transform these populations into pseudo-Portuguese. Many local residents were enlisted in the armed forces or used as domestic help or in subordinate posts such as clerks, and they inevitably learned something of the language and culture of the colonial power without abandoning their own. But neither among the tribes of Africa nor among the Indian and Chinese people did the process of Europeanization go very deep. The Portuguese left the old ruling chiefs and classes in local authority much as they had found them. The local upper classes monopolized most of the limited European wares; very little that was Western touched the people or tempted them away from their traditional ways.

There was one exception. The Portuguese did attempt to Christianize the indigenous groups they encountered. Some of these attempts involved force, as at Goa, where the Portuguese pulled down all the temples and made it impossible to practice the traditional religion. From the first, the earliest missionaries underestimated the obstacles they were to encounter. Many missionaries were in a sense partly converted themselves; that is, they came to be attached to their charges and were convinced that they were almost Christians already.

From the start, difficulties arose between the missionaries, anxious to protect those they regarded as their charges, and the traders and colonial officials, driven by material incentives to exploit the local population. To local chiefs and monarchs, converts were potential traitors, likely to be more loyal to their Western faith than to their own rulers. Money and manpower were always serious problems for the missionaries, with so many to convert and tend, and with so few people and so little money to do the work. Measured in statistical terms, the effort to convert India and the Far East to Christianity did not make a serious impression on the people; there were fewer than a million converts by 1600. The greatest missionary successes tended to occur in areas of Buddhism, then in a state of decay, and the greatest failures in areas of Islam, for Muslims seldom abandoned their faith for any other.

The Portuguese soon had to yield to newer rivals. Their banking, their business methods, their initiative were not equal to competition with the aggressive, expanding powers of northwest Europe. Although monopolizing the import of pepper from the East, they sought the assistance of the more knowledgeable merchant community of Antwerp in distributing the pepper to European markets. The cloth and other wares that they traded in the East were often imported from competing European countries with more developed industries. After the sixteenth century the Portuguese ceased to add to their empire and to their wealth, and they sank back to a secondary place in international politics. A great epic poem, the *Lusiads* (1572) of Liuz de Camöes (c. 1524–1580), was their monument, written at the height of their empire.

The sixty years of union between the Spanish and Portuguese monarchies, 1580–1640, accelerated the decline of Portugal's imperial fortunes by involving it in prolonged worldwide warfare with Spain's great adversary, the Dutch republic. Better-equipped and better-disciplined Dutch forces drove the Portuguese from most of their posts in present-day Indonesia and from Ceylon and parts of the Indian coast. Yet a Portuguese empire did survive along the old route around Africa to Goa, on the island of Timor off southeast Asia, at Macao, and in Brazil.

West by Sea to the Indies

In the earliest days of concerted effort to explore the oceans, the rulers of Spain had been too busy disposing of Muslim Granada and uniting the separate parts of Spain to patronize scientific exploration as the Portuguese had done. But Spanish traders were active, and Spain was growing in prosperity. When Portuguese mariners found the three groups of Atlantic islands—Azores, Madeira, and Canaries—a papal decree assigned the Canaries to the Crown of Castile and the others to Portugal. Once the marriage of Ferdinand and Isabella had united Aragon and Castile, Queen Isabella wanted to catch up with the Portuguese. So in 1491, when the fall of Granada seemed imminent, she commissioned Christopher Columbus to try to reach India by sailing west.

Columbus and Later Explorers

Columbus (1451–1506), born in Genoa, was an experienced sailor and had gone at least once to the Gold Coast of Africa; he may also have sailed to Iceland. His central obsession, that the Far East ("the Indies") could be reached by sailing westward from Spain, was not unique. No educated person in 1492 seriously doubted that the earth was round, but as it turned out most scholars had underestimated its size by 25 to 30 percent. The major problem was a practical one; if one accepted Ptolemy's ancient estimate of the circumference of the earth, no ship of the time could complete so great a voyage. But Columbus insisted that the wealthy island of Cipangu (Japan) was only twenty-four hundred miles due west, a distance easily within the range of ships and crews.

Columbus might not have been able to set out had his sole aim been that of reaching the Indies. But he was also charged to discover and secure for the Spanish Crown new islands and territories. Therefore, even if he did not reach the Indies, there seemed a chance that he would reach something new.

Setting out from Palos near Cadiz on August 3, 1492, in three very small ships, he made a landfall on an island in the Bahamas on October 12, and eventually discovered the large islands we know as Cuba and Santo Domingo (modern-day Haiti and the Dominican Republic). Since he assumed that he had reached the Indies, he called the people he encountered there "Indians." On a second voyage in 1493, Columbus went out with seventeen ships and some fifteen hundred colonists, explored further in the Caribbean, and laid the foundations of the Spanish empire in America. On his third voyage, in 1498–1500, he reached the mouth of the Orinoco River in South America, but he encountered difficulties among his colonists and was sent home by the royal governor, who took over the administration of the Indies for the Crown. Columbus was released on his return to Spain, and in 1502–1504 he made a fourth and final voyage, in which he finally reached the mainland at Honduras in August 1502. He died in comparative obscurity in Spain.

News of Columbus's voyage soon spread by word of mouth in Europe, for printing was still in its infancy. The most effective spreading of the word about the New World in print was done by another Italian navigator in the Spanish service, Amerigo Vespucci (c. 1454–1512), who wrote copiously about his explorations in the immediate wake of Columbus. Vespucci's letters came to the attention of a German theoretical geographer, Martin Waldseemüller (c. 1470–c. 1522), who in 1507 published a map blocking out a landmass in the southern part of the New World that he labeled, from the Latinized form of Vespucci's first name, America.

After Columbus, discoveries multiplied. Juan Ponce de León (c. 1474–1521) reached Florida in 1513, and Vasco Nuñez de Balboa (1475–1519) in 1513 crossed the Isthmus of Panama and saw the the wide Pacific. Many other Spaniards and Portuguese in the first two decades of the sixteenth century explored in detail the coasts of what was to be Latin America.

Maritime exploration then turned to the problem of getting around the Americas and into the Pacific by sea. North America proved an obstacle indeed, for the great rivers barely penetrated the great continent, the breadth of which was totally unknown. The St. Lawrence River looked more promising, and to its first French explorers it seemed like the sought-for strait; but it too gave out, and the rapids near Montreal that showed it was only another river received the ironic name of Lachine (China). Not until 1903–1906 was the ice-choked "Northwest Passage" in the Arctic finally traversed by an English expedition.

However, the "Southwest Passage" was found only a generation after Columbus. Ferdinand Magellan (c. 1480–1521), a Portuguese in the Spanish service, set out in 1519 with a royal commission to find a way westward to the Spice Islands of Asia. Skirting the coast of South America, he found the difficult, fog-bound passage that bears his name, the Straits of Magellan, reached the Pacific, and crossed it by a route not precisely known. After they reached the islands now known as the Philippines, Magellan was killed in a skirmish with a hostile chief. One of his captains, however, kept going along the known route by the Indian Ocean and the coast of Africa. On September 8, 1522, the *Victoria* and a crew of eighteen men—out of five ships and 243 men that had sailed in 1519—reached Cadiz. For the first time, circumnavigation of the earth had proved empirically that the world was round.

The Growth of the Spanish Empire

By the Treaty of Tordesillas Spain and Portugal had divided the world open to trade and empire along a line cut through the Atlantic, so that Brazil became Portuguese. This same line extended across the poles and cut the Pacific, so that some of the islands Magellan discovered came into the Spanish half. Spain conveniently treated the Philippines as if they, too, were in the Spanish half of the globe, although they were actually just outside it.

The Spaniards in the New World soon explored and acquired thousands of square miles of territory. The original explorers by sea were followed by the *conquistadores*, often of the now-impoverished lesser nobility the *hidalgos*— half explorer, half soldier-administrator, and all adventurer. Of the conquistadores, two in particular—Hernando Cortés (1485–1547) and Francisco Pizarro (c. 1478–1541)—conquered vast territories. With a handful of men they seized the two most civilized regions of the New World: the Aztec empire of Mexico, taken by Cortés with 600 men in 1519–1521, and the Inca empire of Peru, taken by Pizarro with 180 soldiers in 1531–1533.

Other Spaniards in search of gold, salvation, glory, and excitement toiled up and down these strange new lands: Francisco Vasquez de Coronado (c. 1510–1554), Hernando de Soto (c. 1500–1542), and Alvar Cabeza de Vaca (c. 1490–c. 1556) in the southwest of what became the United States; Sebastian Cabot (c. 1484–1557) on the great Paraguay and Parana river systems; Pedro de Valdivia (c. 1502–1553) in Chile; Pedro de Alvarado (1485–1541) in Guatemala; and Pedro de Mendoza (c. 1487–1537), a Basque who with many Austrians, Flemings, and Saxons reached La Plata (the area around the River Plate in present-day Argentina and Uruguay) in 1536 and founded Buenos Aires.

The toll in lives of Spanish exploration was staggering, especially in South America. A single expedition to Peru in 1535 lost 150 Spaniards, 150 slaves, and 11,000 Indians. The sea passages were often horrendous; by 1540 more than 2,000 men and twelve ships had been lost trying to find the route ultimately mapped out by Magellan. As late as 1925 an entire expedition disappeared in the interior of Brazil.

The indigenous cultures of the Americas crumbled under the impact of the Europeans. From Mexico to Bolivia, Paraguay, and Patagonia (in southern Argentina), millions of people survive today who are descendants of those peoples. Any understanding of Latin America requires some knowledge of their cultural and social traditions. But the structure of the Aztec and the Inca empires has totally disappeared.

Well before the end of the sixteenth century, the work of the conquistadores was over, and the first of the true European colonial empires had been established in Latin America. Only in northern Argentina and in central Chile was the native population eliminated and replaced by a population almost entirely from the Old World. Over vast reaches of Mexico and Central and South America, a thin layer of Spanish or Portuguese formed the top of society and made Spanish or Portuguese the language of culture. Beneath them a class of "mixed blood," the *mestizos*, was gradually formed from the intermingling of Europeans and indigenous peoples, and in many regions the Indians continued to maintain their old ways of life almost untouched. Where the Indians were exterminated, as in the Caribbean, or where they proved insufficient as a labor force, as in Brazil, African slaves were imported in the millions.

Geography and the circumstances of settlement by groups of adventurers in each region created several separate units tied together only by their

dependence on the Crown. Geography alone was a fatal obstacle to any subsequent union of the colonies. Between such apparently close neighbors as
present-day Argentina and Chile, for instance, lay the Andes, crossed only
with great difficulty through high mountain passes; between the colonies of
La Plata and those of Peru and New Granada lay the Andes and the vast tropical rainforests of the Amazon basin, still almost unoccupied in the twentieth
century.

Nonetheless, the Spaniards transported to the New World the centralized
administration of Castile. At the top of the hierarchy were two viceroys: From
Lima, Peru, the viceroy ruled for the Crown over the Spanish part of South
America, except Venezuela; from Mexico City the viceroy ruled over the
mainland north of Panama, the West Indies, Venezuela, and the faraway
Philippines. Each capital had an *audiencia,* a powerful body staffed by professional lawyers and operating both as a court of law and as an advisory
council. During the sixteenth century audiencias were also established in
Santo Domingo, Guatemala, Panama, New Granada, Quito, Manila, and
other major centers. A special Council of the Indies in Madrid formulated
colonial policy and supervised its execution.

This centralized, paternalistic government was less rigid in practice than in
theory; given the vast areas and the varied peoples under its control, it had to
be. In time the bureaucracy came to be filled largely with colonials who had
never been in the home country, and who developed a sense of local patriotism and independence. Madrid and Seville were simply too far away to
enforce all their decisions. It proved especially impossible to maintain the
rigid monopolies, which sought to confine trade wholly to the mother country, and to prohibit or severely limit domestic industry in the colonies.

The hand of Spain was heaviest in the initial period of exploitation, when
the rich and easily mined deposits of the precious metals in Mexico and Peru
were skimmed off for the benefit both of the Spanish Crown, which always
got its *quinto,* or fifth, and of the conquistadores and their successors. By the
early seventeenth century, when the output of precious metals began a long
decline, the economy and society of Spanish America had stabilized. Colonial
products—sugar, tobacco, chocolate, cotton, hides, and much else—flowed
out of Latin America in exchange for manufactured goods and for services.
Creoles (American-born subjects of European descent) and *mestizos* (persons
of mixed European and Amerindian descent) were the chief beneficiaries of
this trade. Above the African slaves in the social pyramid, but well below the
mestizos, was the native population. This was a system of social caste based
on blood and culture rather than on the nineteenth-century concept of "race,"
one that never became as rigid as that in North America.

Everywhere, but especially in the Caribbean, the Europeans tried to use
native labor on farms, in the mines, and in transport. The results were disastrous, for epidemics of smallpox and other diseases that had been introduced
by the Europeans took a terrible toll of the native population. In the West
Indies the Carib Indians were utterly wiped out. In central Mexico the total
population fell from about 25 million when Cortés arrived to only some 2.5

The Written Record

THE HAZARDS OF EXPLORATION

A routine entry from the journal of Antonio Pigafetta (c. 1491–c. 1536), who completed the circumnavigation of the globe begun by Magellan, tells of daily pain and deprivation.

On Wednesday the twenty-eighth of November, one thousand five hundred and twenty, we issued forth from the said strait [of Magellan] and entered the Pacific Sea, where we remained three months and twenty days without taking on board provisions or any other refreshments, and we ate only old biscuit turned to powder, all full of worms and stinking of the urine which the rats had made on it, having eaten the good. And we drank water impure and yellow. We ate also ox hides which were very hard because of the sun, rain, and wind. And we left them four or five days in the sea, then laid them for a short time on embers, and so we ate them. And of the rats, which were sold for half an écu [French silver coin] apiece, some of us could not get enough. Besides the aforesaid troubles, this malady was the worst, namely that the gums of most part of our men swelled above and below so that they could not eat. And in this way they died, inasmuch as twenty-nine of us died. . . . For during this time we had no storm, and we saw no land except two small uninhabited islands, where we found only birds and trees. Wherefore we called them the Isles of Misfortune. . . . And I believe that nevermore will any man undertake to make such a voyage.

Antonio Pigafetta, *Magellan's Voyage: A Narrative Account of the First Circumnavigation,* trans. and ed. R. A. Skelton (New Haven, Conn.: Yale University Press, 1969), I, p. 57. Another version of this manuscript adds that the men ate sawdust from planks; the disease referred to was scurvy.

---

million eighty years later. Conquest may have been preceded by a "disease frontier" in which smallpox and influenza had so weakened the Indian groups that they could not resist the major European military attacks. However, a biological exchange also took place; although the origin of syphilis is still disputed, many historians of medicine believe that it was brought from the West Indies, where it was mild, to western Europe, where it became virulent.

Attempts to regiment native labor in a plantation system or to put it on a semimanorial system of forced labor, known as the *encomienda*, proved almost as disastrous. The encomiendas grouped farming villages whose inhabitants were "commended" to the protection of a conquistador or colonist. The "protector" thereby acquired both a source of income and an economic base for potential defiance of central authority.

Against these forces there were counteracting forces. The New Laws of 1542 forbade the transmission of encomiendas by inheritance, thereby inhibiting feudal decentralization. These laws also forbade the enslavement of Indians, who were regarded as wards of the Crown. The cause of the indigenous people was championed by men of great distinction, notably by Bartolomé de las Casas (1474–1566), "Father of the Indians" and bishop of Chiapas in Mexico, who fought vigorously to limit slavery.

Unlike their counterparts in Africa and Asia, the Indian peoples in the New World were converted to Christianity. More than Spanish pride was involved in the grandiose religious edifices constructed by the colonists and in their elaborate services; many priests wished to fill the void left by the destruction of the Indians' temples and the suppression of the complex pagan rituals. Church and state in the Spanish and Portuguese colonies in the New World worked closely together. The Jesuits in Paraguay tried to set up a benevolent despotism and paternalistic utopia for the Guarani Indians. On the northern fringes of the Spanish world, a long line of missions in California and the Southwest held the frontier.

In their close union of church and state, in their very close ties with the home country, in their mercantilist economics, and in other respects, the Portuguese settlements in Brazil resembled those of the Spaniards elsewhere in Latin America. Yet there were significant differences. The Portuguese settlements were almost entirely rural; many black slaves were imported into tropical Brazil, and both because there were more slaves and because the white males often drew no sexual color line, the races became more thoroughly mixed than they did in most Spanish colonies except Cuba. Finally, perhaps because of the relative proximity of Brazil to Europe, the Portuguese had more troubles with rival nations than the Spaniards did.

The North Atlantic Powers

Spain and Portugal enjoyed a head start of nearly a century in founding empires of settlement. The northern Atlantic states soon made up for their late start, however. As early as 1497 John Cabot (d. c. 1498) and his son Sebastian, Italians in English service, saw something of the North American coast and gave the English territorial claims based on their explorations. In the first half of the sixteenth century the explorations of another Italian, Giovanni da Verrazano (c. 1485–1528), and a Frenchman, Jacques Cartier (1491–1554), gave France competing claims, which were reinforced in the early seventeenth century by the detailed exploration of Samuel de Champlain (c. 1570–1635). Dutch claims began with the voyages of Henry Hudson (d. 1611), an Englishman who entered Dutch service in 1609.

English, Dutch, and Swedes in North America

The English did not immediately follow up the work of the Cabots. Instead, they put their energies into breaking into the Spanish trading monopoly. In 1562 John Hawkins started the English slave trade; his nephew, Francis Drake, reached the Pacific and claimed California for England under the name of New Albion. Drake returned to London by the Pacific and Indian oceans, completing the first English circumnavigation of the globe (1577–1580). Under Sir Humphrey Gilbert (c. 1539–1583) in 1583 the English staked out a claim to Newfoundland, which gave them a share in the great fishing grounds off northeastern North America.

In 1584 Sir Walter Raleigh (c. 1552–1618) unsuccessfully attempted to found a settlement on Roanoke Island (in present-day North Carolina) in an area the English named Virginia, after their Virgin Queen, Elizabeth. Early in the next century the English established two permanent footholds at Jamestown in Virginia (1607) and at Plymouth on Massachusetts Bay (1620). Both were established by chartered trading companies with headquarters in England; both cherished high hopes that they would find great stores of precious metals. Both were disappointed in these hopes and only just managed to survive the years of initial hardship. Tobacco, first cultivated in 1612, and John Smith (1580–1631), explorer and propagandist for colonization, saved the Virginia colony; furs (notably beaver), salted cod, and Calvinist determination saved Plymouth. Both colonies gradually built up an agricultural economy supplemented by trade with England and the West Indies. Neither received more than a few tens of thousands of immigrants from abroad. Yet both these and the later colonies expanded by natural increase in a country of abundant and productive land. By 1763 there were fourteen mainland British colonies with nearly 3 million inhabitants.

Before these English mainland colonies could be secure, two foreign groups had to be pushed out. The Dutch had founded New Amsterdam (1626) at the mouth of the Hudson and had begun to push into the fur trade. This made them rivals of the English and of the French, farther north in Canada. In their wars with England in the 1660s, however, the Dutch lost New Amsterdam, which was annexed by the English in 1664 and renamed New York.

The Swedes founded Fort Christiana (1638) on the Delaware near present-day Wilmington. But New Sweden was never a great enterprise and in 1655 was absorbed by the Dutch. Pennsylvania, chartered to the wealthy English Quaker William Penn (1644–1718) in 1681, replaced the Swedes and Dutch on the Delaware.

The arch of colonies, in which Pennsylvania formed the keystone, reached from Nova Scotia to Georgia and numbered fourteen, each founded separately and each with its own charter. New England was for the most part settled by Calvinist Independents (Congregationalists), committed to local self-government and distrustful of landowning aristocracy. The southern colonies were settled for the most part by Anglicans used to the existence of social distinctions and to large estates. In Virginia the Church of England became the established church; in Massachusetts the Puritan Congregationalists set up their own state church. Geography, climate, and a complex of social and economic factors drove the South toward plantation monoculture of tobacco, rice, indigo, or cotton and drove New England and the Middle Colonies toward small-scale farming, industry, and commerce by independent farmer-owners and artisans.

*The toovne of Pomeiock and enclosed forme of their houses covered
and enclosed some w matts, and some w borcks of tree. All compassed
abowt w smale poles stock thick together in steed of a wall.*

*Much of our knowledge of life in North America at the time of the arrival of the Europeans
comes from the work of the English artist John White (fl. 1585–1590), who was one of the
first settlers in Virginia. Sixty-three of his watercolors have survived, and they provide much
historical and anthropological detail. This one shows a native village as seen by Sir Walter
Raleigh's expedition in 1585.   (New York Public Library Picture Collection)*

The colonists came from an England in which the concept of freedom of
religion was only beginning to emerge. It was in many ways logical that the
Virginians and the New Englanders set up state churches. Yet these immigrants represented too many conflicting religious groups to enforce anything
like the religious uniformity that prevailed in the Spanish colonies or in
French Canada. Moreover, some of the colonies were founded by groups that
from the first practiced religious freedom and separated church and state. In
Pennsylvania, founded by Quakers who believed firmly in such separation;
in Maryland, founded in part to give refuge to the group most distrusted at
home, the Catholics; in Rhode Island, founded by Roger Williams (c.

1603–1683) and others unwilling to conform to the orthodoxy of Massachusetts Bay—in these colonies there was something like religious freedom.

The seeds of democracy existed, although the early settlers readily accepted class distinctions. No formal colonial nobility ever arose, however, partly because land was relatively cheap; and the early tendency to develop a privileged gentry or squirearchy in the coastal regions was balanced by the freedom of the frontier and by careers open to talent in the towns. Government by discussion was firmly planted in the colonies from the start, and all of them had some kind of legislative body.

This was the critical difference between the English colonies in the New World and the Spanish and French colonies. In Spain and France the home governments were already centralized bureaucratic monarchies; their representative assemblies were no more than consultative bodies with no power over taxation. Royal governors in Spanish America and in New France could truly dominate their provinces. But England was a parliamentary monarchy. Although the Crown was represented in most colonies by a royal governor, the English government had no such extensive bureaucracy as the Spanish and French had. Royal governors in the English colonies had hardly even a clerical staff and encountered great difficulty in raising money from their legislatures. Furthermore, in all the colonies the established landowners, merchants, and professionals participated not only in colonial assemblies but also in local government. Finally, the settlers brought with them the common law of England, with its trial by jury and its absence of a highly bureaucratic administrative code.

The French in North America

To the north and west of the fourteen colonies, in the region of the St. Lawrence basin, the French built upon the work of Cartier and Champlain. The St. Lawrence River and the Great Lakes gave the French easy access to the heart of the continent, in contrast to the Appalachian ranges that stood between the English and the Mississippi River. The French were also impelled westward by their search for furs, which are goods of great value and comparatively small bulk, easily carried in canoes and small boats. Moreover, led by the Jesuits, the Catholic French showed far greater missionary zeal than did the Protestant English. The priest, as well as the *coureur des bois* (literally, "rover of the forest," or fur trapper), led the push westward.

The sieur de La Salle (1643–1687) discovered the mouth of the Mississippi River. In 1682 he took formal possession of a vast region for France. His work was built upon that of a young American-born Frenchman, Louis Joliet (1645–1700), a fur trader, and Father Jacques Marquette (1635–1675), one of six Jesuit missionaries in the vast interior who had passed far enough down the great river before turning back to prove that it flowed into the sea. Able French colonial governors further enhanced French strength, prestige, and authority among the native peoples. By 1712 the French had built up a line of isolated trading posts, with miles of unoccupied land between, thinly populated by

Native Americans who were coerced or persuaded into cooperation, so that the territory of New France and that of Louisiana (named after Louis XIV) were linked.

Impressive though this French imperial thrust looked on the map, it was far too lightly held to be able to push the English into the sea. It was a trading empire with military ambitions, and except in Quebec it never became a true colony of settlement. Enough French settlers simply did not go overseas, and those who did spread themselves out over vast distances as traders and adventurers.

The Two Indies, West and East: Areas of Conquest

The French, Dutch, and English all sought to gain footholds in South America, but had to settle for the unimportant Guianas. They thoroughly broke up the Spanish hold on the Caribbean, however. In early modern times these islands were one of the great prizes of imperialism. Cheap slave labor raised tobacco, fruits, coffee, and, most profitably, cane sugar.

By 1715 the French, Dutch, and English had also laid the bases of trading and colonial empires in Asia and Africa. India proved to be the richest prize and the most ardently fought for. The Mogul Empire could not keep the Europeans out of southern India, but it did confine them mainly to the coastal fringes. Gradually during the seventeenth century both the French and the English established themselves in India. The English defeated a Portuguese fleet in 1612 and immediately got trading rights at Surat on the western coast. Although the Mogul emperor Aurangzeb (r. 1658–1707) tried to revoke their rights in 1685, he soon found their naval and mercantile power too much to withstand. In 1690 the English founded Calcutta. Meanwhile, the French had gotten a foothold near Madras at Pondichéry and soon had established other stations. By the beginning of the eighteenth century the stage was set for a decisive struggle for overseas empire between France and Britain—a struggle now known as the Great War for Empire—which lasted until 1763.

Both countries operated through chartered trading companies: the English East India Company (1600) and the French Compagnie des Indes Orientales (1664). The companies were supported by their governments. Although both countries became involved in Indian politics and warfare to support their trading companies, neither attempted extensive permanent settlement in the East.

The Dutch entered even more vigorously into the competition, founding their own East India (1602) and West India (1621) companies. In sharp contrast to the close government supervision exerted by Spain and Portugal, the Dutch granted these private business ventures full sovereign powers. They had the right to maintain their own fighting fleets and armies, declare war and wage it, negotiate peace, and govern dependent territories. The Netherlands East India Company succeeded in pushing the Portuguese out of Ceylon and then concentrated on southeastern Asia, especially the East Indies. Here again they pushed the Portuguese out and effectively discouraged interlopers. Through it all the company paid its shareholders an annual dividend averaging 18 percent. Despite their rapid decline as a great power in the eighteenth century, the Dutch had so firm a hold in Java and Sumatra that their empire in Indonesia was to last until the mid-twentieth century.

Africa and the Far East: Areas of Influence

To reach the East all three of the northern maritime powers used the ocean route around Africa that the Portuguese had developed in the fifteenth century. All three secured African posts, with the Dutch occupying the strategic Cape of Good Hope at the southern tip of the continent in 1652. While the Cape was at first a repair and replenishing station for Dutch ships on the long voyage to the East, it had a temperate climate, and a small colony of settlement grew up peopled by Dutch and by some French Huguenots. In West Africa the Dutch took the Portuguese posts on the Guinea and Gold Coasts.

The French, too, worked down the Atlantic coast, taking Senegal (1626) at the westernmost point of the African bulge, and later reaching the large island of Madagascar and taking the smaller one of Mauritius in the Indian Ocean, from the Dutch. The British secured a foothold at the mouth of the Gambia River near Senegal (1662) and made further acquisitions at the expense of the French and the Dutch. Thus by the eighteenth century a map of Africa and adjacent waters would have shown a series of coastal stations controlled by various European powers. The interior remained for the most part unexplored, untouched except by slavers and native traders.

The Far East, too, was not truly opened to Western imperialism until the nineteenth century. In China the Portuguese clung to Macao, and the Dutch obtained a station on Taiwan (1624), an island that the Portuguese had named Formosa (meaning "beautiful"). The Jesuits were tolerated by the Chinese, but they made few converts. Generally the Chinese considered most Europeans barbarians who should be paying them tribute.

In Japan the reaction against European penetration was even stronger than in China. The Portuguese had won trading privileges in the sixteenth century, followed by the Dutch in 1609. Meantime, the great Jesuit missionary Francis Xavier (1506–1552) began preaching in 1549. Many Japanese became Christians. The Tokugawa family, the feudal rulers of Japan from 1600 to 1868, feared Christianity. They saw it as a threat both to national traditions and to their own rule because of the opportunities it might give European powers to intervene in Japanese politics and intrigue with their enemies. They therefore decided to close their land entirely to foreign dangers. In the early seventeenth century they suppressed Christianity with brutal force and sealed off Japan. Foreigners were refused entry, and Japanese were refused exit. Even the building of oceangoing ships was forbidden. The Dutch, who had persuaded the Japanese that Protestants were less subversive than Catholics, were allowed under strict supervision to retain an island in Nagasaki harbor.

The Written Record

A Japanese Folk Tale

The age of exploration, discovery, and conquest was a two-way street, for the non-Western culture often reacted quickly and effectively to the arrival of Europeans. The following Japanese tale, a clever variant on the dictim that in the land of the blind the one-eyed man is king, suggests one form of interaction.

Once upon a time there was a man who did nothing all day long—he just waited and hoped that suddenly he would meet with unexpected good fortune and become rich in an instant without any effort.

And thus he lived for many a year, until one day he heard tell that there was a certain island inhabited by people who had only one eye.

"At last! That will be my good fortune," thought the man to himself. "I'll travel to that island, I'll catch one of these one-eyed creatures and bring him back and show him in the marketplace for a penny a look. In a short while I shall be a rich man."

And the more he thought about it, the more he liked the idea.

Finally he made up his mind. He sold the little that he had, bought a boat and set off. After a long journey he reached the island of the one-eyed creatures and, indeed, hardly had he stepped ashore when he saw that the people there really had only one eye each.

But of course the one-eyed people noticed that here was a man with two eyes, and a few of them got together and said:

"At last! So this will be our good fortune! Let's catch him and show him off to the marketplace for a penny a look. We'll soon be rich men!"

No sooner said than done. They seized the two-eyed man and carried him off to the-marketplace, where they showed him for a penny a look.

And that's the sort of thing that happens to people who sit and wait for unexpected good fortune.

From *The Fairy Tale Tree: Stories from All Over the World*, retold by Vladislav Stanovsky and Jan Vladislav, trans. Jean Layton (New York: Putnam's, 1961), p. 242. Copyright © 1961 by Artia. Reprinted by permission of G. P. Putnam's Sons.

Russia

Russian exploration and conquest of Siberia matched European expansion in the New World, both chronologically (the Russians crossed the Urals from Europe into Asia in 1483) and politically, for expanding Muscovite Russia was a "new" monarchy. This Russian movement across the land was remarkably rapid—some five thousand miles in about forty years. Thus the Russian advance left vast unabsorbed areas behind the line of formal settlement. The enormous flatlands of the Siberian river basins made movement relatively easy and the tribal population of Siberia appears on the whole to have cooperated with the Russians.

East by Land to the Pacific

The victories of Ivan the Terrible over the Volga Tatars led to the first major advances, with private enterprise leading the way. By the end of the sixteenth century the Stroganov family had obtained huge concessions in the Ural area, where they made a great fortune in the fur trade and discovered and exploited Russia's first iron mines. The Stroganovs hired bands of Cossack explorers, who led the eastward movement; Timofeyevich Yermak, "Conqueror of Siberia" (d. 1584), whose exploits took on legendary proportions, extended control to the mouth of the Tobol. At a suitable point on a river basin, the spearhead of the advance party would build a wooden palisade and begin to collect furs from the surrounding area. Almost before the defense of each new position had been consolidated, the restless advance guard would have moved hundreds of miles farther eastward to repeat the process, until the Pacific was reached at Okhotsk in the 1640s.

The government followed with administrators and tax collectors, soldiers and priests, as each new district was opened up. A Siberian bureau in Moscow had nominal responsibility for government of the huge area, but decisions had to be made on the spot because of slow communications. Thus the Siberians always tended to have the independence traditionally associated with the wide open spaces. Because Okhotsk and its surrounding area along the Pacific were intensely cold and the ocean frozen for much of the year, the Russians were soon looking enviously southward toward the valley of the Amur River, which flowed into the Pacific at a point where the harbors were open year-round.

Explorations in this area brought the Russians into contact with the Chinese, upon whose outer lands they were now encroaching. But the Chinese government of the period had little interest in these regions. In 1689 the Chinese signed with Moscow the Treaty of Nerchinsk. The treaty stabilized the frontier, demilitarized the Amur valley, and kept the Russians out of Manchuria, though it recognized the Russian advances farther north. It also provided the two powers with a Mongolian buffer zone that acknowledged Chinese overlordship. Thus, with great speed the Russians had acquired an empire with extensive natural resources and had staked out a future as an Asian power with interests in the Pacific.

North by Sea to the Arctic

Henry Hudson had found not only the Hudson River but also Hudson Bay in the far north of Canada. In 1670 English adventurers and investors formed the Hudson's Bay Company, originally set up for fur trading along the great bay to the northwest of French Quebec. In the late sixteenth century the Dutch had penetrated far into the European Arctic, had discovered the island of Spitsbergen to the north of Norway, and had ranged eastward across the sea named after their leader, William Barents (d. 1597). Early in the eighteenth century the Russians also explored most of the long Arctic coasts of Siberia, and a Dane in their service, Vitus Bering (1681–1741), discovered the Aleutian Islands and the sea and strait that now bear his name separating northeastern Siberia from Alaska, proving conclusively that Asia was not connected with North America.

The Impact of Expansion

The record of European expansion contains pages as grim as any in history. The African slave trade—begun by the Africans and the Arabs and turned into a profitable seaborne enterprise by the Portuguese, Dutch, and English—is a series of horrors, from the rounding up of the slaves by local chieftains in Africa, through their transportation across the Atlantic, to their sale in the Indies.

American settlers virtually exterminated the native population east of the Mississippi. There were, of course, exceptions to this bloody rule. In New England missionaries such as John Eliot (1604–1690) did set up little bands of "praying Indians," and in Pennsylvania relations between the Quakers and Native Americans were excellent. Yet the European diseases, which could not be controlled, together with alcohol, did more to exterminate the Native Americans than did fire and sword.

Seen in terms of economics, however, the expansion of Europe in early modern times was more complex than simple "exploitation" and "plundering." There was, in dealing with the native populations, much giving of "gifts" of nominal value in exchange for land and goods of great value. The almost universally applied mercantilist policy kept money and manufacturing in the home country. It relegated the colonies to producing raw materials—a role that tended to keep colonies of settlement relatively primitive and economically dependent.

While Europeans took the lion's share of colonial wealth in the early modern centuries, some of the silver from America financed European imports of spices and luxuries from Asia. Few of the improvements in public health and sanitation that Europeans would bring to the East later on had yet come about, nor had greater public order come to India or Africa, as it eventually would. Most fundamentally, colonialism undermined lifestyles and social arrangements that had survived for centuries without offering equally stabilizing substitutes. As a result most native societies were rendered chronically unstable and insecure.

The West has in its turn been greatly affected by its relations with other peoples. Tobacco, brought into Spain in the midsixteenth century, became essential to the pleasure of many Europeans. Maize, or Indian corn (in Europe *corn* refers to cereal grains in general), was imported from the New World and widely cultivated in Spain and Italy. Potatoes, on the other hand, did not immediately catch on in Europe; in France they had to be popularized in a propaganda campaign. Tomatoes, or "love-apples," were long believed

The Written Record

THE SLAVE TRADE

The Dutch slave ship *St. Jan* started off for Curaçao in the West Indies in 1659. Its log recorded deaths of slaves aboard, until between June 30 and October 29 a total of 59 men, 47 women, and 4 children had died. They were still 95 slaves aboard when disaster struck, thus matter-of-factly recorded:

Nov. 1. Lost our ship on the Reef of Rocus, and all hands immediately took to the boat, as there was no prospect of saving the slaves, for we must abandon the ship in consequence of the heavy surf. Nov. 4. Arrived with the boat at the island of Curaçao; the Hon'ble Governor . . . ordered two sloops to take the slaves off the wreck, one of which sloops with eighty four slaves on board was captured by a privateer.

And here is the governor's report to his board of directors in Holland:

What causes us most grief here is, that your honors have thereby lost such a fine lot of negroes and such a fast sailing bark which has been our right arm here.

Although I have strained every nerve to overtake the robbers of the negroes and bark, as stated in my last, yet have I not been as successful as I wished. . . .

We regret exceedingly that such rovers should have been the cause of the ill success of the zeal we feel to attract the Spanish traders hither for your honors' benefit . . . for the augmentation of commerce and the sale of the negroes which are to come here more and more in your honors' ships and for your account. . . .

I have witnessed with pleasure your honors' diligence in providing us here from time to time with negroes. That will be the only bait to allure hither the Spanish nation, as well from the Main as from other parts, to carry on trade of any importance. But the more subtly and quietly the trade to and on the island can be carried on, the better will it be for this place and yours.

Documents Illustrative of the History of the Slave Trade to America, ed. Elizabeth Donnan (Washington, D.C.: Government Printing Office, 1930), I, pp. 143, 150–51.

to be poisonous and were cultivated only for their looks. Tea from China, coffee from Arabia, and chocolate from the New World revolutionized taste and social practices. Tea and coffee houses offered an unprecedented environment not simply for the sipping of hot beverages but for public discussion of political issues. Chocolate, along with sugar, introduced an entirely new category of luxury food.

Among Westerners, knowledge of non-European beliefs and institutions eventually penetrated to the level of popular culture, where it was marked by

---

| A Closer Look |

THE IMPORTANCE OF COTTON

Cotton had been known from time immemorial in Egypt, India, and China; it was introduced into Spain in the ninth century, but it was hardly known in England until the fifteenth century. Only in the seventeenth century was it introduced extensively from India, and then into other "divers regions," including the southern colonies of English North America, and, in time, Africa. Empire thus made cotton the world's best known, most important plant fiber.

Eventually cotton would be at the heart of the industrial revolution, would create a revolution in clothing, and would help assure the enslavement of millions of people. But in 1589, when Richard Hakluyt published his collection of *Voyages and Discoveries*, its potential was not yet recognized. Hakluyt's description of the cotton plant combines curiosity, precise observation, and fascination with the new.

This groweth on a certain little tree or briar, not past the height of a man's waist, or little more: the tree hath a slender stalk like unto a briar, or to a carnation gillyflower, with very many branches, bearing on every branch a fruit or rather a cod, growing in round form, containing in it the cotton: and when this bud or cod cometh to the bigness of a walnut, it openeth and showeth forth the cotton, which groweth still in bigness until it be like a fleece of wool as big as a man's fist, and beginneth to be loose, and then they gather it as it were the ripe fruit. The seeds of these trees are as big as peas, and are black, and somewhat flat, and not round; they sow them in plowed ground, where they grow in the fields in great abundance in many countries in Persia, and divers other regions.

In the United States after independence, cotton contributed to the growth and survival of the plantation system and of slavery, since its cultivation was especially amenable to gang labor. The southern states thus became dependent on cotton as an export and failed to keep pace with northern (or "free soil") farming and industry. During the American Civil War the Confederacy hoped to have the support of Britain, since its textile industry relied on American raw cotton. This did not happen, however, because at the outbreak of the war in 1861 Britain had a 50 percent oversupply of cotton and a growing capacity to obtain alternative supplies from Egypt, India, and later Brazil. Thus cotton played a crucial role in economic and political history.

Richard Hakluyt, *Voyages and Discoveries: The Principal Navigations, Voyages, Traffiques and Discoveries of the English Nation*, ed. Jack Beeching (New York: Penguin Books, 1972), pp. 230–31.

---

a host of words—*powwow, kowtow, taboo, totem,* for instance. In religion and ethics, however, the West took little from the new worlds opened after Columbus. The first impression of Westerners, when they met the cultures both of the New World and of the East, was that they had nothing to learn from them. Once the process of interchange had gone further, some Europeans were impressed with the mysticism and otherworldliness of Hindu philosophy and religion and with the ethics of Chinese Confucianism. Others came to admire the dignity and apparent serenity of the lives of many "simple" peoples. But for the most part, what struck the Europeans was the poverty, dirt, and superstition they found among the peoples of India and China.

Scholars dispute even the word to name what happened when Europeans set eyes upon the many diverse and divergent cultures of the Americas and Asia. While "conquest" captures much of the military story, it in no way reflects the impact upon Europeans of the "discoveries." "Discovery" captures something of the very newness of the knowledge, but only by analogy to scientific "discovery" does it reflect anything of the revolution that knowledge occasioned in every realm of European thought. Recently, scholars have preferred "encounter," which is more neutral, but it, too, fails to signal the wonder and wonderment or the violence.

It is perhaps best to begin with the observation: Europeans had no names for many of the flora and fauna they encountered. There was no word in any European language for parrot, for rubber, for coffee, for anteater or opossum. The earliest accounts, those of Columbus, Cortés, and Diaz, use analogy to get at what the Europeans are seeing—something is *like* something known, familiar, but is ultimately not that plant, that animal. Europeans took up classical and medieval tales of giants, pygmies, El Dorado where the streets are paved in gold, plants and animals of fable and fiction to name what they saw. Within the first generation, however, even in Columbus's journals, Europeans sought to describe and then to name, developing with ever increasing precision that language for description that is the fundament still of botany, biology, zoology, astronomy. One of the consequences of those "New World" "encounters" was the conscious creation of a language of description that was then also turned to the "Old World," where it would culminate in the science of phylum and genus.

Another was a kind of rudimentary comparative study of cultures. Early on, travel accounts were collected and collated. Among the earliest of those efforts was the collection in English edited by Richard Hakluyt (c. 1552–1616) in 1589, the year after the Armada. In the different accounts, one sees not only increasingly careful observation, but also early efforts to distinguish among alien cultures, to represent Aztec culture as distinct from, say, Inca culture, with differing levels of technological knowledge, military prowess, or distinctive artistic aesthetics.

The "discovery" of "New Worlds" engendered revolutions in every realm of European thought. In area after area of human knowledge, Europeans discovered that classical Roman and Greek texts, whether Livy or Ptolemy, were in error—that the knowledge they had always privileged as the most authoritative was not simply flawed, but in many instances wrong. Ptolemy's projections were dramatically inadequate, such that they did not allow for entire continents and oceans. Classical historians' descriptions of human civilizations could not account for the cultures Europeans found in the Americas. The "encounter" challenged the authority not simply of Rome or Greece, but of the written text over the human eye, of abstract thesis over observation. Europeans questioned whether Christianity was the only true religion, whether "innocence" did not exist outside of Europe, what it meant to be "human." The most thoughtful among them realized that the pursuit of knowledge itself would never be the same, that reading alone could not ensure certain knowledge. And one, Michel de Montaigne, asked the question "What do I know?" ("¿Que sçay-je?"). With that question, he put his finger on the most shattering consequence of the "discoveries," or, in the words of John Donne, "'Tis all in pieces, all coherence gone."

The great discoveries helped to revolutionize the economy and society of Europe. In the long process of inflation and expansion, some groups gained and others lost. In general, merchants, financiers, and businesspeople enjoyed a rising standard of living. Those on relatively fixed incomes, including landed proprietors, suffered—unless they turned to large-scale capitalist farming. Governments also suffered unless they could find new sources of income. Wage earners, artisans, and peasants usually did not find their incomes keeping pace with the rise in prices. In short, the effects of expansion were unsettling as well as stimulating.

For Spain the vast empire acquired in the New World both helped and hurt. Perhaps alone among the great powers, Spain was permanently put into decline by the so-called general crisis of the seventeenth century. The Catalonian revolt, the Portuguese insurrection of 1640, and the revolt of the Spanish territories in Italy in 1647 made it increasingly difficult for Spain to defend its far-flung empire against other European powers. Britain in particular began to encroach steadily on that empire. By 1670 England and France were negotiating secretly over the future of the Spanish-American colonies.

The death of Philip IV in 1665 brought to the Spanish throne his four-year-old son, and Philip's widow acted as regent; she was preoccupied with religious questions, and the royal armies were being systematically destroyed in an attempt to defend Flanders against Louis XIV of France. In 1670 Spain agreed by treaty with England to admit the English to the New World trade and recognized British conquest of Jamaica; two years earlier the formal independence of Portugal and its colonial possessions had been conceded. Spain's European dominance was ended, and with this collapse went the rapid decline of the empire of Philip II, Spanish mastery of the seas between the New World and Asia, and effective Spanish control over South American colonies.

The transition from medieval to modern history was marked by European expansion. Indeed, the making of one vast new nation in North America—at first a product of European history, then an independent piece of that history, and ultimately a major player within that history—was one of the prime results of the colonial empires and one of the hallmarks of the move from medieval to modern times. Even as Spain declined, the fact that its empire would in part be inherited by another centralizing monarchy meant that the world was drawing more into one.

"There is only one world, and although we speak of the Old World and the New, this is because the latter was lately discovered by us, and not because there are two."* These words were written by a Spaniard in sixteenth-century Peru. By the eighteenth century it was already clear that one system of international politics dominated the world. European wars increasingly tended to be "world wars," fought on the seven seas and on distant continents. Sooner or later, any considerable transfer of territory overseas and any great accession of strength or wealth in any quarter of the globe affected the international balance of power.

The one world of the eighteenth century was not one world of the spirit; the great mass of Europeans were ignorant of other cultures. But already Western goods penetrated almost everywhere. Already an educated minority was appearing, from professional geographers to journalists, diplomats, and businesspeople, who dealt with what were now quite literally the affairs of the world. Perhaps the most powerful act of imperialism was that the history of the world and the history of Western civilization increasingly seemed to overlap, and the history of the non-Western world came to be written in the language of the West, with Western place names imposed upon it.

The conventional date for the end of the great Age of Discovery is 1779—the year in which the English explorer Captain James Cook (1728–1779) was killed on the Sandwich (or Hawaiian) Islands. It was Cook who, in three great voyages, made known the full shape of the Pacific Ocean, from Cape Horn to the Bering Strait, from New Holland (present-day Australia) and New Zealand to Japan, and deep into the Antarctic Ocean. There was, of course, much yet to discover, much fame yet to be won, but from now on it would be more in the interior of the continents and not on the seas.

SUMMARY

In the early modern period explorers representing western European nations crossed vast oceans to discover other civilizations. With superior material and technological strength, especially firearms, Europeans were able to win empires. The motives for European expansion varied from desire to serve God to glory, gold, and strategic need.

Prince Henry directed early Portuguese exploration in order to promote commerce, national power, and Christianity. In 1488 Bartholomeu Dias rounded the Cape of Good Hope, and by 1497 Vasco da Gama had reached India by sea. Soon afterward, Portugal acquired a dominant position in trade with the East.

Europeans were generally contemptuous of Eastern civilization. Taking advantage of military and political disunity in India, western Europeans were able to dominate the subcontinent with relatively few people. In India, Europeans found an entrenched caste system. Further east, in China, they found an ancient civilization that had weathered many changes. The Chinese emperor, with the aid of a bureaucracy run by mandarins, ruled a huge empire that was firmly built on communal villages.

---

*Quoted in J. H. Elliott, *The Old World and the New* (New York: Cambridge University Press, 1970), p. 59.

Portugal established its trading empire on mercantilist principles that held that the mother country should supply manufactured goods in exchange for raw materials from its colony. Other nations were excluded from the trading monopoly the mother country established. Despite their head start, the Portuguese were challenged in the sixteenth century by the French, Dutch, and English, and they eventually lost their dominance in the East.

In 1492 Columbus, an experienced voyager, discovered a "New World" that he claimed for Spain. "Discoveries" multiplied after Columbus, especially as explorers hunted for a northwest or southwest passage around the Americas. Europeans' sense of the breadth and diversity of "the world" multiplied exponentially.

The conquests of Cortés and Pizarro gave Spain a vast empire in the Americas. Spain established a centralized administration in its New World colonies with a viceroy representing the Crown. Indians were converted to Christianity and were protected by the New Laws of 1542. Nevertheless, millions died of European diseases and harsh treatment.

In the seventeenth century England established permanent colonies in North America, overrunning earlier Dutch and Swedish colonies. Although New England was largely settled by Calvinists and the southern colonies by Anglicans, differences among the colonies were influenced by geography and climate as well as by social and economic factors. Unlike the colonies of Spain and France, where royal governors represented centralized bureaucracies, English royal governors lacked extensive bureaucracies.

In the St. Lawrence region explored by Cartier and Champlain, the French established New France. The search for fur led to-exploration of the interior of North America, but the region was not heavily settled by colonists.

Both the Spanish-held West Indies—where sugar, tobacco, fruit, and coffee crops were profitable exports—and the East Indies became battlegrounds for imperialist powers. France, England, and the Netherlands established coastal posts in Africa but did not expand inland. In China and Japan, rulers imposed restrictions on foreigners. By the mid-seventeenth century, Japan had virtually sealed itself off from the West, a self-imposed isolation that lasted until 1853.

At the same time that western European nations expanded overseas, Russia explored and conquered a vast Asian empire that stretched across Siberia to the Pacific.

The age of European expansion resulted in the horrors of the slave trade, the extermination of native populations, and the undermining of social arrangements that had existed for centuries. New products as well as knowledge of other beliefs and institutions created a new world in the West. Expansion revolutionized economies and societies in Europe. As Portugal, Spain, France, Britain, and Russia explored Africa, Asia, and the New World, they set the stage for international politics for centuries to come.

FIVE

The Age of Reformation

"Reformation" is at the very center of Christianity: in Christ's relation to Judaism, in Bernard of Clarivaux's relation to Benedictine monasticism, in St. Francis's relation to the Church, in Wycliffe's relation to the formal doctrine of the Fourth Lateran Council, and in the Conciliar Movement's relation to the papacy. Christianity is a religion of the book, and that book, as Europeans were to discover most dramatically in the sixteenth century, was susceptible to as many readings as there are readers. Generation after generation would return to one or another aspect—to Jesus's life as represented in the four Gospels, to the Acts of the Apostles, to the Pauline epistles' particular delineation of true Christian practice. Generation after generation would find current practices flawed, the conduct of clergy failing to meet the standards embodied by Jesus himself, the increasing wealth and power of the Church at odds with all that Jesus preached.

The question in the sixteenth century was not "Why Reformation?" Martin Luther (1483–1546) did not see himself as founding a new church, but as restoring a church that had been corrupted by medieval inventions. John Calvin's (1509–1564) Church, quickly called "Reformed," again captured that sense that their enterprise was conservative, indeed, restorative of an ancient and true Church. Anabaptists modeled themselves more closely than any other group on the literal descriptions of the Gospels and Acts of the Apostles: Not only did they practice adult baptism, but they also took their "Supper" at a rude table, with simple implements, common bread, and wine. As the martyrologist John Foxe would argue, each of these groups saw themselves as returning to a purer Christianity, not initiating new practices, new doctrine, or new beliefs. Much of what individual reformers called for did indeed have precedents, at least in Wycliffe and Hus, but often much earlier, in Bernard of Clairvaux or nominalist theologians. In sixteenth-century Europe, thousands of pious Christians were seeking to recover the pure Christianity they found described in the Word of God. No, the question that confronts us now is why did the call for Reformation in the sixteenth century result in the fragmentation of "the one True Church" into many "Churches," each with its own claim to be The One True Church?

To understand what distinguished the sixteenth century from earlier reforms, it is best to begin with the text that contributed centrally to the transformation of Christendom into Christians: Erasmus's Greek New Testament. Erasmus (1466–1536) collected and collated fragments of the Greek text of the New Testament, publishing in 1516 a version that Huldrych Zwingli (1484–1531) among others awaited with marked eagerness. His Latin translation, which appeared with the second edition of the Greek text in 1519, brought an immediacy to the words of the Gospel, underlining as the Latin Vulgate, Jerome's third-century translation, had not, Jesus's act of speaking. The Bible came alive, first for those learned in the languages of the text, Latin and Greek, and then quickly thereafter for those who could read the vernacular translations that followed in the 1520s.

In the sixteenth century, the Bible became a revolutionary document, as carpenters, peasants, urban and rural workers, rich and poor all looked to Scripture to tell them how they should live as Christians and what they should do to worship God. Erasmus argued that any reading should be tempered by "tradition," that is, the interpretations of the many different scholars who had read the Bible in the preceding fifteen hundred years. Luther, however, called for a reading based in faith, an immediate relation between the faithful Christian and "God's Word." Editions of the Bible in the languages of the marketplace—the vernacular—proliferated exponentially in the sixteenth century, with new technology, printing with moveable type, and new markets, the literate commercial and artisanal elites of the towns as eager consumers of "the Word of God." Thousands of Christians read the Bible, or had it read to them, hearing often for the first time Jesus speaking—Jesus, not the local parish priest, telling each hearer how he or she might live as a Christian. Bibles brought Jesus into the home, to the hearth, into the workplace, into the daily lives of many different sorts of Europeans.

The Bible gave the laity of the sixteenth century an authority by which they could criticize the Church, in particular, the papacy. Many Christians, lay and clerical, had long been aware that the church needed cleansing. Papal opposition, however, persistently blocked fresh attempts to increase the powers of representative church councils. The great renovation fostered by Queen Isabella and Cardinal Jiménez was restricted to Spanish lands. Meanwhile, a quiet Catholic renewal had been advanced by the activities of the Brethren of the Common Life. Founded in the Low Countries in the 1370s, the Brethren were laypeople, men and women, who pooled their resources in communal living and followed the spiritual discipline of a monastic order without taking religious vows.

Opposed to Scholasticism, the Brethren of the Common Life started schools of their own. Erasmus, who was educated in one of them, complained that the curriculum was too orthodox and rigid, yet he adopted the goals of the Brethren in his own "philosophy of Christ," with its belief that the example of Jesus should be a guide to daily lives. A similar theme, expressed in more mystical terms, ran through the enormously popular *Imitation of Christ*, written by Thomas à Kempis (c. 1379–1471), one of the Brethren.

A more radical and sweeping reform was launched by the Dominican friar Girolamo Savonarola (1452–1498). His eloquent sermons and reputed gift of predicting the future soon made him the most popular preacher in Florence. Sparing no one in his denunciations of what he regarded as un-Christian conduct, he delivered tirades against the Florentine nobles and many of the bishops. In the political confusion following the death of Lorenzo the Magnificent (1492), Savonarola gained power and prestige in Florence, attracting many enthusiastic supporters. By 1494 he was virtual dictator of the Florentine republic and organized troops of children to collect all "vanities"—from cosmetics to pagan books and paintings—and burn them on public bonfires. The zeal for iconoclasm did not last long, and when Pope Alexander VI placed Florence under an interdict and excommunicated Savonarola, his popular following began to disperse. In 1498 Savonarola was condemned for heresy, hanged, and his body burned.

In hindsight we can discern "founders" of different "Churches," men whose ideas would provide the center for new religious identities and communities that sought to institute those ideas: Martin Luther, Huldrych Zwingli, John Calvin foremost. At the time, however, there were many "reformers," hundreds of men and a few women who were actively preaching a call to reform the church, to break with Rome, to live as True Christians. Our second question, then, is How did this handful of men come to found "Churches"—not simply gatherings of men, women, and children in a moment, but institutions, with their own organization, own bureaucracy, own rituals, own doctrine, own creeds, and own religious identity?

The term "Protestant" dates from 1529, when a meeting of the Diet, the legislative and judicial court of the Holy Roman Empire, at Speyer rescinded a grant of toleration to followers of Luther that it had made three years earlier. Lutheran delegates, a minority, then lodged a formal "protest," the name for a specific legal action, with the Diet. Thus they became known as "Protestants." The political context of the term is central to understanding why today there are not as many "Churches" as there are Christians, how it was that a sole Augustinian monk came to "found" a "Church" that the papacy could not suppress as it had suppressed Wycliffe and Hus.

The story of the Reformation is inseparable from the economic, social, and political changes we have been tracing. The transformations of the sixteenth century are unimaginable without the technology of printing, the population density of towns, marketplaces where so many preached the Gospel, the emergence of new social groups who sought a piety as free from feudalism as their social place was, and the emergence of princes and monarchs who pursued with Machiavellian instrumentalism the goals of stability and autonomy. Both Luther and Calvin crafted Churches in dialogue with the political authorities of their respective homes. They shared with medieval reformers the powerful conviction of faith, but they were able to convey that faith more quickly, more widely, to many more and different kinds of Christians. Finally, they spoke of faith as something not simply internal, but something unique to each person, not to be judged by priest or Pope, as something known in an intimate and private relationship between each human being and God.

At the end of the century, there was not one True Church, but the Catholic Church, the Lutheran Church, the Reformed Church, the Anglican Church, the Baptist Church, as well as many smaller groups. All had their roots in medieval Christianity. All accorded the laity greater participation in Christian life than their medieval predecessor. All were "reformed"—in doctrine, in worship, and in ethics. Only one continued to hold that the Pope was the head of the True Church: the Catholic Church. Most powerfully, Europeans no longer thought of themselves as all belonging to one "body of believers," but to the "true body of believers"—thousands of Europeans had acquired a religious identity that separated them from one another: fathers from sons, wives from husbands, and subjects from lords. There was no longer Christendom, but Christians.

Protestant Founders

Martin Luther, 1483–1546

Martin Luther (1483–1546) was a professor of theology at the University of Wittenberg. In 1517 he was undergoing a great religious awakening. Luther's father had sent him to the University of Erfurt, then the most prestigious in Germany, to study law. Luther yearned instead to enter the religious life. On his way back to Erfurt he was terrified by a severe thunderstorm and vowed that he would become a monk. Against his father's opposition, Luther joined the Augustinian friars.

After ordination, however, Luther underwent a prolonged and intense personal crisis. He was convinced that he was lost—literally lost. Nothing could free him of the gnawing feeling that he could not attain God's grace and was destined for hell. Finally a confessor advised the desperate young man to study the Bible and to become a teacher of Scripture. Through his reading in the Epistles of Paul and the writings of Augustine, Luther gradually found an answer to his anxiety: that he should have faith in God and in the possibility of his own salvation.

Luther himself emphasized *faith*, something not visible but inside us all if we could but see it, rather than *works*, the performance of the established conventions of religion. Fortified by his intense conviction of the importance of faith, Luther questioned Catholic practices that in his view were abuses. He cast his questions in the form of his Ninety-five Theses. The specific abuse that the theses sought to prove un-Christian was the "sale" of indulgences, in particular the activities of a Dominican, Johann Tetzel (c. 1465–1519), who was conducting a "drive" for voluntary contributions to rebuild St. Peter's in Rome. One of the German ecclesiastical princes also had a stake in the indulgences; this was Albert, brother of the elector of Brandenburg, who had paid a very large sum to the papacy for a dispensation permitting him to grant indulgences.

"Indulgences" made possible the remission of temporal punishment for sins. Only God can forgive a sin, but repentant sinners also must undergo punishment on earth in the form of penance and after death in purgatory, where they atone by temporary punishment and are prepared for heaven. Indulgences could not assure the forgiveness of sins, but they could remit penance and part or all of the punishment in purgatory. The church claimed the sole authority to grant such remission by drawing on the Treasury of Merit—a kind of storehouse of surplus good works accumulated by the holy activities of Christ, the Virgin, and the saints.

The use of the word *sale* in connection with indulgences became a form of Protestant propaganda. The Catholics insisted that an indulgence was not "sold," that it was "granted" by the priest and any monetary contribution made by the recipient was a freewill offering. However, the highly successful Tetzel had simplified the complex doctrine of indulgences to a slogan: "As soon as coin in coffer rings, the soul from purgatory springs."

At the theological level Luther's quarrel with his ecclesiastical superiors was over one of the oldest and most abiding tensions of Christian thought: the tension between faith and good works. Faith is inward, and good works are the outward demonstration of that belief as expressed by a person's good deeds, partaking of the sacraments, and submitting to the discipline of penance. Indulgences held out the promise that one might secure extra good works by drawing on those stored up in the Treasury of Merit.

In response to Luther's theses, the papacy stiffened its resistance, which in turn drove the Lutherans to further resistance. Moreover, Luther was driven to minimize the importance of works and even to deny their validity altogether. Under pressure of combat, Luther declared that people were saved by faith alone. He went on to deny that priests were necessary intercessors and to affirm the priesthood of all true believers: "every man his own priest."

One part of the puzzle is why it took the Church so long to respond to Luther. Luther posted his theses for debate in 1517. While Tetzel was effectively silenced, his particularly outrageous sales technique having gained him widespread repudiation in German-speaking lands, the Church itself, either in the person of the Archbishop of Mainz or in the person of a papal representative, did not address Luther's protests directly until nearly a year later. The Archbishop's initial correspondence with Rome concerned the financially disastrous consequences of Luther's criticism of Tetzel, not the far more devastating potential of Luther's argument against the entire edifice of good works. In Rome, Pope Leo X (r. 1513–1521), a Medici and a cultivated man of letters, was far more embroiled in Italian politics than attentive to the import of Luther's challenge, responding slowly, even as he gave Luther a more important stage for his position. In 1518 at Augsburg, Luther was summoned before the papal legate and general of the Dominican order and was directed to recant some of his propositions on indulgences. Luther would not. In 1519 at Leipzig, a learned theologian, John Eck, charged Luther in debate with disobeying the authoritative findings of popes and church councils. Luther denied that popes and councils were necessarily authoritative and explicitly declared his adherence to some of Jan Hus's teachings that had been declared heretical by the Council of Constance a century earlier.

A portrait of Martin Luther by Lucas Cranach (1492–1553) in the Uffizi Gallery in Florence, Italy.   (Scala/Art Resource, NY)

Luther did not simply challenge the authority of the papacy to lead Christians; he placed the authority of Scripture over the authority of the papacy, an act not simply of rebellion, but of revolution. He did not accept the Pope's authority over him; he did not accept the jurisdiction of the Church that had its head in Rome. Late in 1520 a papal bull condemned Luther's teachings; Luther burned the bull. In January 1521, he was excommunicated. In April 1521, at an Imperial Diet convened at Worms, he also rejected the authority of the Emperor over things spiritual; the Holy Roman Emperor, Charles V, placed him under the ban of the Empire. By summer 1521, Martin Luther was both an excommunicate and an outlaw.

Although both pope and emperor had condemned him formally, Luther not only survived but prospered. Luther was already gathering a substantial following. He had the protection of the elector Frederick the Wise of Saxony

(r. 1493–1525) and was soon to secure the backing of other princes. Frederick arranged to "kidnap" the outlaw on his way back from Worms, and Luther vanished into seclusion at the castle of the Wartburg, where he began work on his translation of the Bible into vigorous and effective German. In the next year Luther, now a national hero, returned to Wittenberg to begin reshaping the church in Saxony.

Reasons for Luther's Success. If we reflect, is an extraordinary story: A single monk rejects the authority of the two most powerful rulers in Europe, the Holy Roman Emperor, and the Pope, each of whom possessed immeasurable wealth and far-reaching influence—and he does not merely survive, he prospers. How? Part of the answer must lie in Luther's message and its own power: the appeal of faith over works, of inward belief over outward action, of immediate access to the Word of God over clerical mediation, a vision of Christianity in which laymen and women were held to be as capable of profound faith as any priest, and a Christianity in the language of the marketplace, not of the clerical elite. The printing press carried his ideas to a far wider readership than might have been possible a century earlier. And Luther benefited from the protection of the Saxon Elector, a man of considerable power in his own right. Luther also benefited from the miscalculation of Pope Leo X, who saw no reason to turn his personal attention to this rebellious monk, and from the particular political landscape of the Holy Roman Empire.

Far more than theology was at issue in Luther's success. The papacy, triumphant over the councils, had become embroiled in Italian politics. The Rome Luther visited as a young man was to him a shocking spectacle of intrigue and luxury. One reason for Luther's success was his attack on practices already abhorrent to many; another was his specific attack on the exploitation of Germans by Italians. In *To the Christian Nobility*, he claimed:

> For Rome is the greatest thief and robber that has ever appeared on earth, or ever will. . . . Poor Germans that we are—we have been deceived. . . . It is time the glorious Teutonic people should cease to be the puppet of the Roman pontiff.*

He wrote *To the Christian Nobility* in German to reach the largest possible number of readers; that his expectations were fulfilled further demonstrates the combined power of the vernacular and the printing press, as well as nascent national identity. Luther's defiance of the pope was well known among Germans, giving voice to a more general sense in the Empire of the distance of the papacy from them. His marriage to a former nun and their rearing of a large family dramatized the break with Rome. His translation of the Scriptures and the hymns he composed became part of German culture; indeed,

---

*Martin Luther, *To the Christian Nobility*, in *Documents of the Christian Church*, ed. H. S. Bettenson, 2nd ed. (Oxford: Oxford University Press, 1963), p. 196.

The Written Record

LUTHER ON CHRISTIAN LIBERTY

In 1520 Martin Luther wrote *On Christian Liberty*. Considered to be "the most beautiful" of Luther's writings, the *Treatise on the Liberty of a Christian Man* (its correct formal title) was an affirmation rather than a protest. Luther said he was sending his long essay as a gift to Pope Leo X.

Many have thought Christian faith to be an easy thing, and not a few have given it a place among the virtues. This they do because they have had no experience of it, and have never tasted what great virtue there is in faith. For it is impossible that anyone should write well of it or well understand what is correctly written of it, unless he has at some time tasted the courage faith gives a man when trials oppress him. But he who has had even a faint taste of it can never write, speak, meditate, or hear enough concerning it. For it is a living fountain springing up into life everlasting, as Christ calls it in John 4. For my part, although I can have wealth of faith to boast of and know how scant my store is, yet I hope that, driven about by great and various temptations, I have attained to a little faith, and that I can speak of it, if not more elegantly, certainly more to the point, than those literalists and all too subtle disputants have hitherto done, who have not even understood what they have written.

That I may make the way easier for the unlearned—for only such do I serve—I set down first these two propositions concerning the liberty and the bondage of the spirit:

A Christian man is a perfectly free lord of all, subject to none.
A Christian man is a perfectly dutiful servant of all, subject to all.

Although these two theses seem to contradict each other, yet, if they should be found to fit together they would serve our purpose beautifully. For they are both Paul's own, who says, in I Corinthians 9, "Whereas I was free, I made myself the servant of all," and Romans 8, "Owe no man anything, but to love one another." Now love by its very nature is ready to serve and to be subject to him who is loved. So Christ, although Lord of all, was made of a woman, made under the law, and hence was at the same time free and a servant, at the same time in the form of God and in the form of a servant. . . .

Martin Luther, *Christian Liberty*, trans. W. A. Lambert (Philadelphia: Muhlenberg Press, 1943), pp. 5–6. Used by permission of Fortress Press.

Luther's German became the standard of what would become modern German.

Yet another reason for Luther's success was the relative disorganization of the forces opposing him. Religious opposition centered in the top levels of the Catholic bureaucracy. There were many moderate Catholics anxious to compromise and avert a schism. The great Catholic historian Lord Acton

(1834–1902) claimed that if the Catholic church had been headed by a pope willing to reform to preserve the unity of the church, even Luther might have been reconciled. Luther's ablest associate, Philip Melanchthon (1497–1560), was a moderate and a humanist. Yet once Luther had been excommunicated and outlawed and had gained powerful political backing, compromise was unlikely.

Political opposition to Luther was centered in the young Habsburg, Charles, who became the Holy Roman Emperor Charles V in 1519. Charles was perhaps the greatest beneficiary of the medieval dynastic practice of primogeniture, in which the eldest son inherited both the title and the land of the family. When he became Emperor he had already inherited the crowns of Aragon and Castile, that is, of his maternal grandparents, as well as their conquests in the Americas; and at his grandfather's death, he inherited directly from him the Habsburg lands of Tyrol, Styria, Austria, and Hungary, from his paternal grandmother, Burgundy, where he had been raised, as well as various footholds in Italy. Those diverse lands would be both a source of unparalleled wealth for Charles and an ongoing distraction, as he sought to rule each according to its own indigenous customs of government. Over the course of his reign, he was confronted with rebellion from his nobles in Spain, his subjects in the Netherlands, his princes in the Empire, and Protestants throughout his lands. Those, however, did not capture his attention nearly as much as the presence of the Ottoman Turks at his eastern borders. We may think that Luther was his most important adversary, but for Charles, the real enemy was the Turk. Again and again, in pursuit of funding for his war against the Turk, Charles would reach compromises with the German princes, turning to crush them only in the interstices of his war with the Ottoman Empire.

Charles ruled largely through representatives. In 1522, he named his brother Ferdinand his representative in the German lands of the Empire, entrusting to him the daily and regular governance of the hundreds of principalities and Imperial Free Cities. Ferdinand formed alliances with Bavaria and Mainz, among others, building a network of Catholic political alliances to oppose the Lutheran princes.

The military arm of the Protestant princes and cities was the League of Schmalkalden (named for the town where it was founded in 1531), led by Philip landgrave of Hesse (1504–1567). When Charles finally crushed the League in 1547, his victory was short-lived because it threatened to upset the balance of power and alarmed both the papacy and the German princes, Catholic as well as Protestant. In 1555, in the twilight of his reign, Charles was forced to accept the Peace of Augsburg, a religious settlement negotiated by the German Diet.

The peace formally recognized the Lutherans in the German states where they already held power. Its guiding principle was expressed in the Latin phrase *cuius regio, eius religio* (he who rules, his religion), which meant in practice that since the elector of Saxony was Lutheran, all his subjects were supposed to be, too; and since the duke of Bavaria was Catholic, all Bavari-

The emperor Charles V, by Titian.   *(Erich Lessing/Art Resource, NY)*

ans were to be Catholic. No provision was made for Catholic minorities in Lutheran states or Lutheran minorities in Catholic states. The settlement also failed to recognize any Protestants except Lutherans; the growing numbers of Calvinists and still more radical Protestants had no legal status in the Empire. More trouble was also bound to arise from the failure to deal with the question of "ecclesiastical reservations," that is, what should be done with church property in a German state headed by a prelate who had turned Protestant. Yet with all these deficiencies, the Peace of Augsburg did make possible the permanent establishment of Protestantism on a peaceful basis in Germany.

A Conservative Revolutionary.   Luther did not push his doctrines of justification by faith and the priesthood of all believers to their logical conclusion, namely, that if religion is wholly a matter between "man and God," an organized church would be unnecessary. When radical reformers attempted to apply these concepts to the churches of Saxony in the early 1520s, there was immense confusion, then iconoclasm and religious revolution. Luther, who had no sympathy with such experiments, left his sanctuary in the Wartburg and returned to Wittenberg to drive out the radicals. He and his followers then organized a Saxon church that permitted its clergy to marry and put increased emphasis on sermons, but that also included ordained clergymen, ritual, dogma, and three sacraments: baptism, confession, and the Last Supper.

The Lutherans did not found their separate Church as an alternative to the Catholic, but as the one true Church. Where a Lutheran Church was founded, a Catholic Church ceased to be; the Lutherans usually just took over the church building. Stimulated by Luther and his clerical and academic disciples, this process at first went on among the people of Germany without the intervention of political leaders. In 1525, the head of the Teutonic Knights turned Lutheran, dissolved the order, and became the first duke of Prussia. Meantime, many of the free cities also opted for Lutheranism.

A major debate among historians recently centers on the role of the cities in the growth of Protestantism. Some have argued that the free imperial cities of the Holy Roman Empire tended to find Lutheran teachings attractive because their civic institutions already emphasized those elements of Christianity that Luther found most important. There was a clear drift toward Protestantism in those regimes—whether city-state or emerging centralized monarchy—which were developing a limited centralism, for the idea of a transcendental God was compatible with emphasis on a single approach to God, as opposed to a complex and trinitarian one. Furthermore, centralizing governments, and perhaps especially those in which guild representatives were most important, found it easier to identify with religious thought that taught that humanity was essentially corrupt. Luther's view of the depravity of human nature supported the burghers' fear of an undisciplined mob, "a great beast." Thus Luther's success was greatest in areas already politically predisposed toward his view of humanity.

Other scholars contest this view, which gives political or social structure precedence over ideas, for they argue that even structure develops from and reflects a pattern of beliefs. Virtually all agree, however, that the cities played a vital role. Since population was concentrated in them, the new power of the printing press could be effective more quickly in an urban setting.

Other social groups also took up the Lutheran revolt to assert themselves. Just beneath the lay and ecclesiastical princes in the German social pyramid were the knights—the lesser nobility. Some of them held a castle and a few square miles from the emperor and were in theory as sovereign as the elector of Saxony or Brandenburg; others were simply minor feudal lords. Many knights were younger sons, gentlemen without land, whose only career could be that of arms. Luther's challenge to the established order and the opportunity it gave to take over ecclesiastical holdings was too good a chance to be missed.

The most bitter social conflict of the early German Reformation, however, was the Revolution of the Common Man in 1524–1525. In some ways it resembled the peasant revolts of the fourteenth century in England and France: A number of the grievances were rural, directed against lords. In other ways, the Revolution was a break with medieval agrarian revolts: Among both the leadership and the rank and file were artisans, some poor, but many prosperous and responsible citizens. By contemporary accounts, it was unprecedented in geographic reach and sheer numbers: Perhaps upwards of 100,000 "common men" participated, storming monasteries, manors, and towns. Their grievances, moreover, were a striking mix of economic and religious. The Twelve Articles, the most widely distributed of the formal grievance petitions, asked first for the right to choose their own priest, and only further down listed the more traditional demands of the right to take wood and game from the forests.

Perhaps most important, among the leadership of the Revolution were theologians. They called for all social, political, and economic practices to be held to the norm of Godly Law. They did not ask for the abolition of the tithe, but for its just use. A number called for a kind of Christian utopia on earth. Their vision was the most "radical" of all those in the early years of the Reformation, going back, as it did, to the roots (*radix*) of Christianity and seeking to model human life on the communalism and egalitarianism of the apostles.

Luther, along with hundreds of townsmen across the Empire, was horrified by this particular kind of biblicism. He did not simply repudiate their particular reading of the Bible, but called for the righteous extermination of "the Murdering, Thieving Hordes of Peasants," the title of a pamphlet he published in the midst of the Revolution. Luther's alliance with political authority was set then. He supported the necessity of secular authority to govern the sinning nature of humanity and the cooperation between secular and spiritual authority in the governing of all human beings' conduct—the doctrine of the "two swords." Politically conservative, by 1525, Luther had made clear to all Christians he would not support the use of the Bible to reorder social or political hierarchies. Divine justice was not social justice. And Lutheranism would become a "state religion" in German principalities, in Denmark, and in Sweden, serving the political goals of various dynasties.

Luther's conservatism in social, economic, and political matters was by no means inconsistent with his fundamental spiritual position. To Luther, if the visible external world was really wholly subordinate to the invisible spiritual world, the most one could hope for in the world of politics was that the visible, external world be kept in as good order as possible, so that the spiritual could thrive. Authority, custom, law, and existing institutions combined to provide this orderliness.

Luther's refusal to acknowledge the revolutionary potential of the Bible cost him a broad peasant and artisanal base. His appeal remained largely urban and princely. In places that had traditions of more communal forms of government—in particular Switzerland, Swabia, Imperial Free Cities, and the Low Countries—Luther's conservatism led to an early disenchantment. In these places, the visions of the Swiss theologian Huldrych Zwingli and the French humanist John Calvin were more compelling, their efforts to organize Churches that were not so rigidly hierarchical and that were closer to the ancient apostolic church than the Lutheran episcopal Church in far deeper harmony with traditions of guild government and extensive citizenship. Zwingli, in particular, would take up, even as he transformed its resonance, the Revolutionaries' call for the standard of "brotherly love" to organize all of society. Until his death in 1531, Zwingli was far more popular among artisans and peasants in the southern Empire than was Luther.

Huldrych Zwingli, 1484–1531

The sixteenth century was distinguished not by criticisms of clerical abuses, or even by criticism of the papacy. What distinguished sixteenth-century Protestant reformers, both from their medieval predecessors and from Catholic reformers of the sixteenth century, was their rejection of "the Church of Rome." That phrase is new to the sixteenth century, signaling both a widespread sense that the church hierarchy had become detached from the spiritual needs of laymen and laywomen and an increasing sense of linguistic and national identity: The papacy was Italian, not, for them, the leader of a universal Church. Indeed, John Calvin would call his church "Catholic," adopting the ancient term for the universal church to which all true believers belonged. It was one of the victories of "the Church in Rome" that we now call that church "Catholic": Protestant reformers did not share that perception.

So, too, the sixteenth century was unparalleled in the sheer numbers of charismatic and passionate preachers and theologians. No two agreed completely with one another; all found in the text of Scripture "true Christianity," but they found it in different places, according to different voices in the text. For Luther, the Pauline Epistles held the key. Thomas Müntzer (c. 1470–1525), one of the theologians who helped shape the agenda of the Revolutionaries of 1525, found in Scripture an egalitarian community of believers. While hundreds of these preachers have subsequently disappeared, two in particular shaped the third great tradition that would emerge in the sixteenth century: the Reformed Tradition. Of the two, Huldrych Zwingli (1484–1531) comes first in time, but John Calvin (1509–1564) proved the most influential.

Huldrych Zwingli came from a very different background from that of Luther. The son of a Swiss peasant, he grew up in the mountains of German-speaking Switzerland, in a village whose tradition of self-governance was strong. He was first distinguished for his voice: At an early age he was sent to study singing, which meant a clerical career. His education was more eclectic than Luther's, guided by Swiss humanists and by his own fascination with biblical languages. He came to the study of theology through philology and language.

In 1519, he was called to the Swiss city of Zurich, which lay on major north-south trade routes and was itself pursuing an expansionist policy over its surrounding countryside. He was, by all accounts, a gifted preacher, accessible and dramatically persuasive. With his first sermon, he departed from the medieval practice, reading instead the opening text of the Gospel of Matthew and then explicating the passage. He continued this biblical exegesis in his sermons, working through Matthew methodically. It electrified the people of Zurich.

Like Calvin in Geneva, Zwingli worked to realize the "true Church" within his own community. He worked with the political authority in Zurich, instituting his reformed liturgy, no longer the "Mass," as Luther continued to call his liturgy until later, but "das Abendmahl," the Supper, in which lay men and women were offered both the cup and the bread, in direct contravention of medieval practice. That communion was intended to approximate much more accurately the original Passover seder, complete with simple bread and wine, offered at a table, not an altar, and to all Christians. The Zurich Town Council reformed poor relief, established a marriage court, and created a morals court. It assumed jurisdictions that had previously belonged to the Church, not making them secular, but arguing for all daily life to come under moral and religious supervision.

Zurich was the first community in which Reformation was fully legislated, the liturgy defined in law passed by the Town Council, the definition and regulation of Christian morals also legislated by the Town Council. In Zurich, the ancient line between *saeculum*, the world, and *spiritus*, the spirit, was fundamentally reconceived. Zwingli's conception of human nature called for all Christians to live in the world as true Christians, for government to participate actively in the disciplining and shaping of Christian conduct, and for the transformative power of the Word of God to be allowed to work over time. In Zurich, he founded the first group whose sole function was the study of Scripture in its three languages—Hebrew, Greek, and Latin: the *Prophezei*. There the most learned of theologians in Zurich, Zwingli, his fellow minister Leo Jud, as well as humanists, worked through the text of Scripture together. While they did so, young men were to be seated around them, learning the languages of Scripture and the discipline of interpretation.

Luther broke with Zwingli over the doctrine of the Eucharist. Luther held a complex position, called consubstantiation, in which he argued that the substance of the bread and wine is present in, around, and with the substance of the body and blood of Christ. It was a difficult conceptualization of the central mystery of the Eucharist—so difficult, in fact, that a number of his own followers broke with him. Zwingli conceived the Eucharist differently. Sharing the humanists' attention to human psychology and imagination,

Zwingli called for the reenactment of the historic event, that believers might feel themselves present at that moment in Christ's life. He had a horror of the Catholic doctrine of transubstantiation—in which the words of the priest transform the substance of the bread and wine into the substance of the body and blood of Christ. He descried the very idea, as he put it, of grinding Christ's flesh between our teeth. Luther caricatured Zwingli's position as "mere commemoration," but Zwingli was making a complex cultural argument about the relation between matter and faith. For him, Christ was indeed "present," in ways that Calvin would take up. Zwingli's position helped to shape not only Calvin's understanding of the Eucharist but also the Anglican tradition, although neither are purely "Zwinglian" in their formulation.

John Calvin, 1509–1564

Although Zwingli and Calvin both worked to realize the True Church within specific human communities, with their distinctive political traditions, and devotional practices, Zwingli came to Zurich as a local, someone who had grown up in familiar territory. Calvin came to Geneva as a French refugee who had spent much of his adult life in exile. In Geneva, Calvin would forge a concept of "the Church" that refugees throughout Europe would find powerfully addressed their sense of homelessness and dislocation. Calvin's Church required no particular place, not even a church structure, in order to be realized. It could be—and was—built among minorities in hostile states, lived clandestinely, providing the single most powerful religious identity in all of early modern Europe. Literally thousands of Calvin's followers would be persecuted in France, the Netherlands, Scotland, and England, as well as in parts of the Empire and Bohemia. And yet, Calvin's formulation of "the Church" provided every believer with structure, discipline both inner and external, and a sense that the elect might be called to suffer as witness to their faith. More than any other church, it invoked the experience of the earliest Christians, who worshiped out of public scrutiny, vulnerable to the whims of a powerful state, whose "faith" had to be certain, even as it was intimately a part of their identity.

Calvin's career had many parallels with Luther's. Both men had ambitious fathers who had made their way up the economic and social ladder; both gave their sons superior educations; the young Calvin studied theology and, to please his father, law. Both young men experienced spiritual crises, Calvin's resulting in his conversion to Protestantism in his early twenties. In temperament, however, the two men differed markedly. In contrast to the emotional, outgoing Luther, Calvin was a very private man, an intellectual, austere, very certain of his convictions and of his vocation to convert others to them, yet filled with anxieties over the formlessness of any life that would be attempted without doctrine.

In 1536 Calvin published in Basel his *Institutes of the Christian Religion,* which laid the doctrinal foundation for a Protestantism that, like Zwingli's, broke completely with Catholic church organization and ritual. Calvin's system had a logical rigor and completeness that gave it great conviction. Also

A portrait of John Calvin, attributed to Hans Holbein.   *(Hekman Digital Library, Calvin College)*

in 1536 Calvin passed through Geneva and was invited to remain. There he set about organizing his City of God and made Geneva a magnet for Protestant refugees from many parts of Europe who were trained in Calvin's faith and then returned to promote his teachings in their own countries. Within a generation or two Calvinism had spread to Scotland, where it was led by a great preacher and organizer, John Knox (c. 1510–1572); then to England, whence it was brought to Plymouth in New England; to parts of the Rhineland; to the Low Countries, where it was to play a major role in the Dutch revolt against Spanish rule; and to Bohemia, Hungary, and Poland.

In France, where concern over the worldliness of the Catholic Church was very great, Calvin's ideas also found ready acceptance. Soon there were organized Calvinist churches, called Huguenot, especially in the southwest. But King Francis I was not eager to challenge Rome. In 1516 he had signed with the pope the Concordat of Bologna, which increased royal authority over the Gallican church in exchange for certain revenues that went to Rome. In the mid-sixteenth century few people could conceive of the possibility of subjects of the same ruler professing and practicing differing religious faiths. In France, therefore, Protestantism had to fight not for toleration, but to succeed Catholicism as the established faith. The attempt failed, but only after wars of religion lasting for a generation in the later 1500s (see Chapter 6) and after Calvinism had left its mark on French thought.

Henry VIII, 1509–1547

In England, legal Reformation followed from the desire of King Henry VIII (b. 1491; r. 1509–1547) to put aside his wife, Catherine of Aragon (1485–1536) who was the aunt of the Holy Roman Emperor, Charles V, because she had not given him a male heir. In 1533 Henry married Anne Boleyn (1507–1536), whom he had made pregnant; Thomas Cranmer (1489–1556), the archbishop of Canterbury, annulled the marriage with Catherine. In the wake of the sack of Rome in 1527, the pope excommunicated Henry and declared the annulment invalid. Henry's answer was the Act of Supremacy of 1534, which made the king supreme head of the church in England.

Much more than the private life of Henry VIII was involved in the English Reformation, however. Henry could not have secured the Act of Supremacy and other Protestant legislation from Parliament if there had not been a considerable body of opinion favorable to the break with Rome. Many English scholars were in touch with reformers on the Continent, and one of them, William Tyndale (1494–1536), was taken with the work of Luther and published an English translation of the New Testament. Anticlericalism went back to the days of Wycliffe; under Henry VIII it was aimed particularly at the monasteries. In the eyes of many in England, the monasteries had outlived their purpose and needed to be reformed or abolished.

Between 1535 and 1540 Henry VIII closed the monasteries and confiscated their property; during the 1540s the Crown sold much of the land. The principal purchasers were members of the rising merchant class, of the nobility, and above all, of the country gentry, or squirearchy. By greatly increasing the wealth of the landed gentry, the dissolution of the monasteries amounted to a social and economic revolution.

Henry VIII did not consider himself a Protestant. The Church of England set up by the Act of Supremacy was in his eyes a Catholic body. Henry hoped to retain Catholic doctrines and ritual, doing no more than abolish monasteries and deny the pope's position as head of the Church in England. Inevitably, his policies aroused opposition, in part from English Roman Catholics who opposed the break with Rome, and still more from militant Protestants, who began to introduce within the Church of England such Protestant practices as marriage of the clergy, use of English instead of Latin in the liturgy, and abolition of confession to priests and the invocation of saints.

Henry used force against the Catholic opposition and executed some of its leaders. He then tried to stem the Protestant tide by appealing to Parliament. In 1539, at Henry's behest, Parliament passed the statute of the Six Articles, reaffirming transubstantiation, celibacy of the priesthood, confession to priests, and other Catholic doctrines and ritual, and making their denial heresy. But there were now far too many heretics to be repressed. England was to become a great center of religious variation and experimentation; the Anglican Church, much more Protestant than Henry had intended, became a kind of central national core. Although he most likely thought of himself as the preserver of the Catholic Church, Henry was really the founder of the Church of England, the first national church.

*Henry VIII, king of England, displays determination and strength in this portrait done in
1540 by Hans Holbein the Younger.   (Royal Collection © 2002, Her Majesty Queen Elizabeth II)*

Anabaptists and Other Radicals, 1521–1604

Socially and intellectually less "respectable" than the established Lutheran
and Anglican churches or the sober Calvinists was a range of radical sects, the
left wing of the Protestant revolution. In the sixteenth century most of these
were known as Anabaptists (from the Greek for "baptizing again"). A number of Christians throughout Europe had come to hold that the Catholic
sacrament of baptism of infants had no validity, since the infant was too
young to "believe" or "understand." At first, the Anabaptists baptized members again when the believer voluntarily joined the company of the elect.
Later generations were never baptized until they came of age, so the prefix
ana- was dropped, leading to the Baptists of modern times.

The Anabaptists split under the pressure of persecution and as a result of
the spread of private reading and interpretation of the Bible. Some observers
saw the increasing number of Protestant sects as the inevitable result of the
Protestant practice of seeking in the Bible for an authority they refused to find
in the dogmas of Catholic authority. The Bible contains an extraordinary variety of religious experience, from rigorous ritual to intense emotional commitment and mystical surrender. The Bible is also deceptively simple, open

to multiple, often conflicting interpretation. Many of the leaders of these new sects were seeking to bring heaven to earth immediately.

In 1534–1535 a group of Anabaptists led by John Bockelson of Leiden, a Dutch tailor, took control of the city of Münster in northwest Germany, expelled its prince-bishop, and tried to set up a biblical utopia. The Anabaptists pushed the Lutheran doctrine of justification by faith to its logical extreme, in theological language, *antinomianism* (from the Greek "against law"): Each person was to find God's universal law within the private conscience, not in written law and tradition. They did not believe in class distinctions or in the customary forms of private property. The established order—an alliance between the Catholic bishop of Münster and the Lutheran landgrave of Hesse—put them down by force; their leaders were executed, and the troops hunted the members of the sect down to the last man and woman.

The great majority of Anabaptists were far removed from the fanaticism of Münster. Many sought to bring the Christian life to earth in quieter and more constructive ways. They established communities in accordance with their beliefs about how the primitive Christians had lived—in brotherhood, working, sharing, and praying together. This sober majority of Anabaptists also met violent persecution in the sixteenth century but survived, thanks to the discipline and submissiveness insisted upon by their gifted leader, Menno Simons (c. 1496–1561), a Dutch ex-priest whose followers became Mennonites.

Two other radical strains in Protestantism were the mystical and the Unitarian. The first was exemplified by Caspar von Schwenkfeld (1489–1561), a former Teutonic Knight and convert to Lutheranism who believed that the true church was to be found solely in the inner spirit of the individual. His stress on the spiritual and the mystical and his antagonism toward formalistic religion contributed later to the development of German pietism in reaction against the established Lutheran church.

Unitarianism is usually identified with rejection of the Trinity as an irrational concept and the view that Christ was simply an inspired human being. In the sixteenth century, the man credited with founding Unitarianism, Michael Servetus (1511–1553), a Spanish physician, held different views. Modelling his theology on what he knew of the circulation of blood, he argued for a *unitary* God and denied Christ's salvific role. While Servetus hoped that it would be possible to reconcile the Jewish and Muslim traditions of Spain with the Christian, his teachings and the uncompromising way he presented them were judged heretical by many Protestants and Catholics. Servetus was prosecuted for heresy by Calvin himself, and burned at the stake in 1553 in Geneva.

Protestant Beliefs and Practices

Common Denominators

There were certain common beliefs and practices that linked all Protestant sects and set them apart from Catholicism. The first of these common denominators was repudiation of Rome's claim to be the one true faith. The difficulty here was that each Protestant sect initially considered itself to be the one true faith, the legitimate successor to Christ and his apostles. Some early Protestants were confident that their particular belief would eventually prevail through the slow process of education and conversion. Others, however, could not wait, and though they had once been persecuted themselves, they did not hesitate to persecute in their turn when they rose to power.

The humanist Sebastian Castellio (1515–1563) attacked Calvin's action against Servetus in *Concerning Heretics* (1554), which asserted that force should not be used to change religious ideas. This, however, was a minority opinion. In the sixteenth and seventeenth centuries few Europeans accepted the separation of church and state and the coexistence of many creeds tolerated by an impartial government.

A second common denominator of Protestantism was that all its churches placed less emphasis on organization, ritual, and other religious externals than the Catholic Church did. All the sects relaxed the requirement of clerical celibacy and either banned or sharply curtailed monasticism. All reduced the sacraments, retaining only baptism and communion. Veneration of saints declined and pilgrimages and the use of rosaries and amulets disappeared among all Protestants. The more radical also banished musical instruments, sculpture, painting, and stained glass as distracting attention from the contemplation of God.

The Conservative Churches

The divergent beliefs and practices that separated the Protestant churches one from another may be arranged most conveniently in order of their theological distance from Catholicism. The Church of England managed to contain almost the whole Protestant range, from High Church to extreme Low Church. Yet it retained a form of the Catholic hierarchy, with archbishops and bishops, although without acknowledging the authority of the pope. Perhaps the central core of Anglicanism became a tempered belief in hierarchy and authority from above, a simplified ritualism, and a realistic acceptance of an imperfect world.

But there has also been a strong puritanical current in Anglicanism. Puritanism, which may be defined as a combination of plain living and high thinking with earnest piety, was an important variant of the Low Church attitude. While some Puritans reluctantly left the Anglican communion in the late sixteenth and early seventeenth century, many others remained within it.

The Church of England assumed its definitive form during the reign of Elizabeth I (1558–1603), daughter of Henry VIII and Anne Boleyn. The Thirty-nine Articles enacted by Parliament in 1563 were a kind of constitution for the church. The Articles rejected the more obvious forms of Romanism: the use of Latin, confession to a priest, clerical celibacy, the allegiance to the pope. They also affirmed the Protestant stand on one of the great symbolic issues of the day—the Eucharist—by giving both the bread and the

Woodcut by Lucas Cranach the Elder. One of thirteen pairs published as the pamphlet Passional Christi und Antichristi, *in Wittenberg in 1521. Each of the pairs contrasted Christ's life as described in the Gospels with the current practices of the papacy. Here, on the left, Christ is shown driving the usurers out of the Temple; on the right, the pope is collecting profits he has forced ordinary Christians to pay under penalty of Papal Bull or Bann.* (Beinecke Rare Book and Manuscript Library, Yale University)

wine to communicants, as the reformers had long demanded, in contrast to the Catholic custom of giving only the wafer. Finally, the Thirty-nine Articles sought to avoid the anarchistic dangers implicit in the doctrines of justification by faith and the priesthood of the believer.

The Church of England has always seemed *Erastian,* so called after Thomas Erastus (1524–1583), a Swiss theologian and a disciple of Zwingli who objected to the theocratic practices of the Calvinists. Erastus wanted to increase the power of the political authorities to check abuses by the religious authorities. The term *Erastianism,* however, has come to imply that the state is all-powerful against the church and that the clergy should be simply a moral police force. While Anglicanism seldom went this far in practice, a modified Erastianism does remain in the Church of England.

To outsiders the Lutheran church has appeared even more Erastian than the Anglican. As the state church in much of northern Germany and in Scandinavia, it was often a docile instrument of its political masters. And in its close association with the rise of Prussia it was brought under the rule of the strongly bureaucratic Prussian state.

Luther was at heart a conservative. He wanted the forms of Lutheran worship to recall the forms he was used to. Once it had become established, Lutheranism preserved many practices that seem Catholic in origin but that to Luther presented a return to early Christianity before the corruption by Rome. Lutheranism preserved the Eucharist, now interpreted by the doctrine of consubstantiation. The tradition of good music in the church was not only preserved but greatly fortified. The Lutheran church, however, had a strong evangelical party as well as a conservative high church party.

Calvinism and Predestination

If Luther preserved much of the medieval Church in his Reformation, Calvin cut the Gordian knot. One of the most ancient of tensions in Christianity is between an omnipotent God and human free will: If God is omnipotent, how can human choice be truly free? If human choice is free, how can God be truly all-powerful? At the center of that debate was Augustine's question: Whence evil? If it is the creation of humanity, then God is not omnipotent. If it is not the creation of humanity, how could God create evil? Who is responsible for sin?

Augustine was not the first to confront the conundrum, nor the last. Medieval theologians struggled with this question, arriving at subtle and nuanced answers. Augustine pointed one way out, arguing that God existed out of time, simultaneously foreknowing all that humanity would do, but preserving, within the context of human action, freedom. In that particular solution is the prospect of God's great distance from humanity, a distance that Thomas Aquinas, among others, would consider to be the true nature of sin: Those who sin are alienated from God.

For Calvin, God's omnipotence was preeminent: All other questions fell before the fact of God's glory, God's power, and God's singular role as Creator. God chooses to save whom he will; God chooses to damn whom he will. Human beings have no power over their own salvation—good works have no effect in human salvation. And God's choice of whom he saves— the "elect"—is inscrutable to human beings. God's design is rational, but human beings cannot discern it; their powers of reason are flawed. Someone who seems to number among the damned may, because of God's wisdom, prove to be among the elect, and no one will be able to determine. With Luther, he shared the conviction that human beings sin by their nature. Faith, for Calvin, was a far more complex experience. Faith did not give one certainty that one was saved, but gratitude for God's mercy that some are saved. Faith brought one to recognize one's sinful nature and the magnificence of God's mercy that a single human being was saved. Faith, moreover, was also a gift from God, not a psychological state one could choose on one's own, but the free gift of a merciful God.

Calvin's doctrine of predestination does not sit well with modern traditions of liberalism and individualism. At the time, however, it was received differently, as liberating pious Christians from the overwhelming burden of trying to please God, even as they acknowledged their essential imperfection. All human beings were flawed, according to Calvin. What distinguishes the elect is not perfection, but humility and gratitude. In keeping with that doctrine, Calvin constructed a Church that was intended first to supervise their private lives as well as their public—through the institution of the Consistory—and to strengthen its members through frequent sermon attendance and the discipline of conduct both private and public. Calvin understood Christian life as a process, of movement from the acceptance of one's own imperfection to the desire to worship God through the smallest of daily activities, as well as prayer and liturgy. A Christian sought "sanctification" through a lifelong process of self-examination, humility, self-criticism, and devotion to a wondrously merciful God, whose magnificence and glory contrasted utterly with human frailty and weakness.

Calvin did not intend many of the consequences of this doctrine, such as the particular self-righteousness of Puritans and the intolerance of many Reformed communities. He called for humility in the face of one's imperfection and he himself doubted throughout his life that he could be so blessed as to be saved. Certainty, for Calvin, was no sign of salvation. Quite the contrary, doubt was a more certain sign of salvation, because it signaled the inner understanding of human inadequacy and divine omnipotence. The Consistory he helped found in Geneva served as a model, more or less closely followed, for Reformed communities on both sides of the Atlantic, an organ not only of supervision and admonishment, as it was largely in Geneva, but of rigid regulation and strict enforcement, as it became in other communities.

The Consistory Calvin fashioned functioned pastorally, admonishing and exhorting the citizens of Geneva to cleave more closely and consistently to a standard of conduct: to dress modestly; to speak without rancor; to avoid frivolous or seductive activities, such as dancing, card-playing, or excessive drinking. By the end of the sixteenth century, Dutch paintings were recording a new aesthetic: Laity dressed somberly, in black, with stark collars, unadorned by the elaborate lace of the Renaissance or the pearls imported from southeast Asia. Calvinist communities were industrious, somber, eschewing all forms of display, such as jewelry or luxury goods, and thereby accumulating extraordinary capital for the investment in overseas development. Reformed Scotland, Puritan England and New England, as well as Geneva presented to the world the outward manifestation of souls seeking sanctification through the discipline of their daily lives. God was worshiped not simply on Sundays in church, but seven days a week in all the waking hours, in every aspect of human activity, from the most quotidian to the most elevated. Calvin and his followers did not separate "the world" from "the spirit," but held that the spirit was manifested in how one lived in the world.

Calvinism appeared in some form in many sects: Presbyterian and Congregational in Britain, Reformed on the Continent. It influenced even the Anglicans and the Lutherans. Theologically its main opponent was a system of ideas called *Arminianism*, from Jacobus Arminius (1560–1609), a Dutch professor at Leiden. Arminius held that election and damnation were conditional in God's mind—not absolute as Calvin had maintained—and that therefore what a person did on earth could change that person's fate.

Where it became the established state church—in Geneva, in the England of the 1650s, in Massachusetts, for instance—the Calvinist church ran or tried to run the state. However, this theocracy was never fully realized, even in

Geneva, where the city council refused to surrender its authority. Where Calvinism had to fight to exist, it preached and practiced an ardent denial of the domination of the state over the individual. Later generations turned these affirmations of popular rights to the uses of their own struggles against both kings and churchmen.

The Radicals

Among the radicals, preaching was even more important than in other forms of Protestantism, and more emotionally charged with hopes of heaven and fears of hell. Many sects expected an immediate Second Coming of Christ and an end of the material world. Many were economic equalitarians, communists of a sort; they did not share wealth, however, so much as they shared the poverty that seemed to them an essential part of the Christian way.

What is most striking about these sects is the extraordinary range of their ideals and behavior. John of Leiden—crowned at Münster as "King David," with two golden jeweled crowns, one royal, one imperial, with his "Queen Diavara" and many women in attendance—seems a mad parody of the Protestant appeal to the Bible. Yet most Anabaptists were shocked by what went on at Münster and were for the most part pious and earnest pacifist Christians, living simply and productively.

These sects often displayed a remarkable combination of pacifist principles with readiness to fight (as long as the weapons were not ones to inflict bodily injury). Such men were also martyrs, and they were persecuted by more moderate reformers with as much violence as that which Protestant tradition attributes to the Catholic Inquisition. But not all sectarians were as insistently nonviolent. An even stronger and more lasting note is that sounded by the English John Bunyan (1628–1688), whose *Pilgrim's Progress* is an allegory of life seen as a pilgrimage, which, while full of trials, leads toward a happy end.

The Catholic Reformation

While Protestantism often is accorded dramatic center in the religious transformations of the sixteenth century, it remained a minority religion—as it does to this day. The Church that had its head in the pope shared with Protestantism medieval origins. Unlike Protestantism, however, that Church embraced its medieval roots, claiming that its "tradition" went uninterruptedly back to St. Peter. Those who called themselves "Catholic" did not reject reform, but sought to reform from within that tradition, eliminating "abuses" as they preserved practices that had their origin in the early Middle Ages and were affirmed at the Fourth Lateran Council of 1215. All reform shared an increased attention to the spiritual needs of the laity. Indeed, what distinguishes the Catholic Reformation foremost is the reform of the training and discipline of parish priests and the creation of new religious orders whose primary responsibility was ministering to the laity.

The Catholic church achieved a large measure of reform from within. By winning back areas in Germany, Bohemia, Hungary, the Netherlands, and

The only authentic portrait of Ignatius Loyola, by the Spanish artist Claudio Coello (c. 1630–1693). (Credit TK)

Poland, it limited the spread of Protestantism in the West. While many have characterized Catholic reform as the "Counter-Reformation," the successful recatholicization of lands in Europe was a more far positive spiritual renewal that reinvigorated fundamental Catholic beliefs and practices.

They could not have been preserved, however, without secular aid. The powerful house of Habsburg, both in its Spanish and its Austrian branches, was the active head of political Catholicism in the next generations. The French monarchs, although their support was often more political than religious, acted to keep France Catholic. In southern Germany and in Italy the reigning princes were powerful supporters of Catholicism.

New orders of clergy essentially aided Catholic renewal. During Leo's pontificate one group formed at Rome the Oratory of Divine Love, dedicated to the deepening of spiritual experience through special services and religious exercises. In the 1520s the Oratory inspired the founding of the Theatines, an order aimed particularly at the education of the clergy. A revived branch of the Franciscans, the Capuchins, sought to lead the order back to Francis's own ideals of poverty and preaching to the poor. During the next decade a half dozen other new orders were established, among them the Ursuline nuns, pioneers in the education of young women.

The Jesuits and the Inquisition

In 1540, Pope Paul III confirmed The Society of Jesus with the Bull, Regimini Militantis Eccelsiae. The new order's purpose: "to fight for God under the standard of the cross and to serve the Lord and the Roman Pontiff, his Vicar on Earth." The members of the new order were to take the customary three vows—poverty, celibacy, and obedience—and a fourth: "to obey without hesitation or excuse every command given by the Pope for the salvation of souls and the spread of the faith." It was the first order founded specifically for the spread of the faith. It was an order answerable only to the Pope—no bishops or archbishops had any authority over the Jesuits, as the members were called.

The order had begun nearly twenty years earlier, at Pamplona, when a Basque nobleman, Iñigo López de Loyola (1491–1556), was wounded in battle and forced to rest. He began reading the lives of saints, seeking to imitate the lives of Saints Francis and Dominic—significantly the founders of two mendicant orders of preachers. Within a couple of years, Ignatius, as his name is now known, had been joined by "companions," who also wished to live by begging and to preach. Ignatius experienced visions, which brought him to the attention of the Inquisition in Spain, but those visions ultimately helped to convince both the Inquisition and the Pope that he was indeed blessed.

The Formula of Institution underlined three key elements of the Society. The members were to be "Soldiers of God," themselves embodying a militant, disciplined piety. Their order was organized according to a military hierarchy: The head was the "General" and elected for life; beneath him were "provincials," who governed "provinces"; and then "rectors" who supervised individual houses.

The second key element was the education of children: The Jesuits were the first order to take the education of children as a centerpiece of their mission. With this they did not simply create heirs for a celibate order, but shaped the character, the will, and the minds of generations of Catholics. These schools were central to the recatholicization of Poland. The Jesuits also founded colleges, beginning with the College in Rome (Collegium Romanum) in 1551; by 1556, they had founded twenty-six colleges, which had a total of fifty-seven hundred students.

The third key element was the particular understanding of confession. The Jesuits practiced "casuistry," a notion that has been skeptically received by their critics. Casuistry, or the study of cases of conscience, took as its point of departure that questions of culpability and morality are contingent; it sought to bring moral absolutes from the realm of abstraction to the specific "times, places, and circumstances"—to the specificities of human experience. The Jesuits became confessors par excellence, serving as confessors to monarchs, princes, and figures of singular power. They were considered incorruptible, discrete, and themselves above reproach.

The order expanded exponentially in its first years, both in sheer numbers and in geographic reach. When Loyola died in 1556, there were already a thousand members in twelve provinces; by 1565, there were thirty-five hundred members in eighteen provinces; and during a time when Catholicism seemed under assault in so many quarters, the Society of Jesus had a waiting list for novitiates and still had to turn away more than it could accept. Even more dramatic than its growth in membership was its immediate spread across the globe. At Loyola's death there were twelve provinces: Italy (except for Rome), Sicily, Upper Germany, Lower Germany (Jesuits concentrated on the recatholicization of the Empire), France, Aragon, Castile, Andalusia, Portugal, Brazil, India, and Ethiopia.

The Jesuits formed a "Society" not through cloister, enclosing themselves within a wall: "We are not monks. . . . The world is our house." They forged a "union of hearts" through a network of letters that were shared, read aloud, copied, and passed on. Often a single Jesuit would travel to a remote place: for example, the rain forests of modern-day Paraguay. The first Jesuit set foot in China in 1555. They were a "Society" without fixed place of ministry. What bound them together, from the most remote and isolated corners of the globe, was a book, *The Spiritual Exercises*, which Loyola first drafted in the 1520s. In it, Loyola outlined an "exercise" for the soul, to be done with a superior during one's novitiate, and then throughout one's life, an inner disciplining of the will to concentrate on certain images and themes. The book, like so much of the Jesuits' work, was a blend of medieval and utterly original practices.

Perhaps most important, the *Spiritual Exercises* were portable. Once mastered, they could be carried to the reaches farthest from Europe, carried by a solitary Jesuit, into cultures, languages, and religions utterly unfamiliar to him. The Jesuits embodied a very different understanding of what it meant to be "Catholic": no longer attached to a physical place, whether it were the parish or Europe, but a "union of hearts"—a spirituality that depends not upon walls or church, but upon a disciplined will and a psychological identity.

Jesuits carried Catholicism into the rain forests of South and Central America, to India, briefly to Japan, and without success to China. They were instrumental in the recatholicization of Hungary and Poland, as well as the intensification of Catholic piety in Bavaria. They did not preach "the Word," but a Christianity of mystical visions, of Christ's Passion and physical suffering, in which dancing was to serve deportment, in which music was to speak to the souls of those who did not understand Latin, and in which the next generation of Jesuits learned Latin through plays. Even as they embodied austerity and severity of discipline, the Catholicism they offered embraced art, music, dancing, and even plays in the service of that "union of hearts."

While the Society of Jesus was the chief new instrument of the Catholic Reformation, an old instrument of the church was also employed—the Inquisition. This special ecclesiastical court in its papal form had been instituted in the thirteenth century to put down the Albigensian heresy, and in its Spanish form in the fifteenth century to bolster the efforts of the new Spanish monarchy to force religious uniformity on its subjects. Both papal and Spanish inquisitions were medieval courts that used torture as a method of truth-finding, and both were employed against the Protestants in the sixteenth century.

Protestant tradition sometimes makes both the Inquisition and the Jesuits appear as the promoters of a widespread reign of terror. Certainly the Jesuits and their allies made full use of the many pressures and persuasions any highly organized society can bring to bear on nonconformists. And the Inquisition did perpetrate horrors against former Muslims and Conversos in Spain

---

The Written Record

THE INQUISITION

In the sixteenth century the Inquisition inquired into the faith and correctness of view of many people who considered themselves to be Christians. In 1583 Domenico Scandella, called Menocchio (1532–1599), was denounced for heresy. Menocchio had been asked about the relationship of God to chaos, and he had answered "that they were never separated, that is, neither chaos without God, nor God without chaos." This led to further efforts to clarify Menocchio's views. This selection ends with the exact moment when Menocchio commits heresy.

INQUISITOR: It appears that you contradicted yourself in the previous examinations speaking about God, because in one instance you said God was eternal with the chaos, and in another you said that he was made from the chaos: therefore clarify this circumstance and your belief.

MENOCCHIO: My opinion is that God was eternal with chaos, but he did not know himself nor was he alive, but later he became aware of himself, and this is what I mean that he was made from chaos.

INQUISITOR: You said previously that God had intelligence; how can it be then that originally he did not know himself, and what was the cause that afterwards he knew himself? Relate also what occurred in God that made it possible for God who was not alive to become alive.

MENOCCHIO: I believe that it was with God as with the things of this world that proceed from imperfect to perfect, as an infant who while he is in his mother's womb neither understands nor lives, but outside the womb begins to live, and in growing begins to understand. Thus, God was imperfect while he was with the chaos, he neither comprehended nor lived, but later expanding in this chaos he began to live and understand.

INQUISITOR: Did this divine intellect know everything distinctly and in particular in the beginning?

MENOCCHIO: He knew all the things that there were to be made, he knew about men, and also that from them others were to be born; but he did not know all those who were to be born, for example, those who attend herds, who know that from these, others will be born, but they do not know specifically all those that will be born. Thus, God saw everything, but he did not see all the particular things that were to come.

INQUISITOR: This divine intellect in the beginning had knowledge of all things: where did he acquire this information, was it from his own essence or by another way?

MENOCCHIO: The intellect received knowledge from the chaos, in which all things were confused together: and then it [chaos] gave order and comprehension to the intellect, just as we know earth, water, air, and fire and then distinguish among them. . . . I believe that it is impossible to make anything without matter, and even God could not have made anything without matter. . . . The Holy Spirit is not as powerful as God, and Christ is not as powerful as God and the Holy Spirit.

INQUISITOR: Is what you call God made and produced by someone else?

MENOCCHIO: He is not produced by others but receives his movement within the shifting of the chaos, and proceeds from imperfect to perfect.

INQUISITOR: Who moves the chaos?

MENOCCHIO: It moves by itself.

Quoted in Carlo Ginsburg. *The Cheese and the Worms: The Cosmos of a Sixteenth-Century Miller,* trans. John and Anne Tedeschi (New York: Penguin Books, 1982), pp. 54–56. Reprinted by permission of The Johns Hopkins University Press. English translation copyright © 1980 by the Johns Hopkins University Press and Routledge & Kegan Paul Ltd.

and against Protestants in the Low Countries. But it was most active in countries of southern Europe—Italy, Spain, Portugal—where Protestantism was never a real threat. And where the Catholic Reformation succeeded in winning back large numbers to the Roman faith—in Germany and eastern Europe—persecution was not the decisive factor, education and lay piety were.

The Council of Trent, 1545–1564

If anything, revulsion against the Protestant tendency toward the "priesthood of the believer" hardened Catholic doctrines into a firmer insistence on the miraculous power of the priesthood. Protestant variation promoted Catholic uniformity. Not even on indulgences did the church yield; interpreted as a spiritual rather than a monetary transaction, indulgences were reaffirmed by the Council of Trent.

The council met in Trent on the Alpine border of Italy in 1545 at the call of Paul III (1534–1549), the first of a line of reforming popes. Along with many Catholics, Paul saw the necessity of reforming the Church root and branch. To other Catholics, however, the Council of Trent seemed an instrument in the hands of the popes and the Jesuits. In theory it was meant to provide at least a chance for reconciliation with the Protestants, and leading conservative Protestants were invited but did not attend. The French clergy did not cooperate freely, and part of the work of the Council of Trent was not accepted in France for fifty years. The council was caught in a web of religious wars and political intrigues, and its work was several times interrupted. Nevertheless, it continued to meet off and on for twenty years until it completed its work of reaffirming and codifying doctrine in 1564.

The Council of Trent reaffirmed the essential role of the priesthood, all seven sacraments, and the importance of both faith and works. It maintained

A session of the Council of Trent, meeting in 1555.   *(Réunion des Musées Nationaux/Art Resource, NY)*

that both the Scriptures and the spokesmen of the church were authorities on theology. It insisted on the strict observance of clerical vows and on the end of such abuses as absentee bishops and the sale of church offices. It imposed censorship on a large scale to promote discipline among the laity, issuing the *Index*—a list of books that Catholics were not to read because of the peril to their faith, including the works of such anticlericals as Boccaccio, Machiavelli, and Erasmus and the writings of heretics and Protestants.

The strength of the Catholic Reformation is shown by the fact that, once it was well launched, the Protestants made few further territorial gains. Within a century of Luther's revolt, the broad lines of the territorial division between areas dominantly Roman Catholic and areas dominantly Protestant were established. No significant part of Europe turned Protestant after 1580—when the United Netherlands was created—and much of central Europe had changed from Protestant to Catholic by 1650, either by persuasion (as in Poland) or by direct force (as in Bohemia). England, Scotland, Holland, northern and eastern Germany (with a southward projection toward Switzerland), and Scandinavia thereafter were predominantly Protestant. Ireland, Belgium, France, southern Germany (with a northern projection in the Rhine valley), the Habsburg lands, Poland, Italy, Spain, and Portugal were predominantly Catholic. There were strong Catholic minorities in England, Scotland, and Holland, and the two faiths mingled confusedly in Germany. There were Protestant minorities in Ireland, France, and some of the Habsburg lands, notably Hungary, that the Jesuits had won back.

Protestantism and the Idea of Progress

How "Modern" Was Protestantism?

The Reformation has often been interpreted, especially by Protestants, as peculiarly modern, forward-looking, and democratic—as distinguished from the stagnant and class-conscious Middle Ages. This view seems to gain support from the fact that those parts of the West that in the last three centuries have been most prosperous, that have seemed to have worked out democratic government most successfully, and that have often made the most striking contributions to science, technology, and culture were predominantly Protestant. Moreover, the states that since the decline of Spain after 1600 rose to power and prestige in the West—France, the British Empire, Germany, and the United States—were, with one exception, predominantly Protestant. And the exception, France, had since the eighteenth century a strong element that, although not in the main Protestant, was strongly anticlerical.

The contention that Protestantism is a cause or at least an accompaniment of political and cultural leadership in the modern West needs to be examined carefully. Protestantism in the sixteenth century was in many ways quite different from Protestantism in the nineteenth and twentieth centuries. First, sixteenth-century Protestants were not rationalists. They were almost as "superstitious" as the Catholics; it is said that Luther threw his ink bottle at the devil, and Calvinists hanged witches. The Protestants for the most part shared with their Catholic opponents fundamental Christian concepts of original sin, the direct divine governance of the universe, the reality of heaven and hell. Most important, they did not have, any more than the Catholics did, a general conception of life on this earth as capable of progressing toward a better life for future generations, since the point of life was not to improve the temporal world but to prepare for the spiritual one.

Second, the early Protestants were by no means tolerant and did not believe in the separation of church and state. When they could, they used governmental power to prevent public worship in any form other than their own. Many of them persecuted those who disagreed with them, both Protestants of other sects and Catholics.

Third, the early Protestants were not democratic. Logically, the Protestant change from the authority of the pope, backed by Catholic tradition, to the conscience of the individual believer and a reading of the Bible fits in with developing ideas about individualism, the rights of man, and liberty. But most early Protestant reformers did not hold that all men are created equal. Rather, they believed in an order of rank, a society of status. In this sense, Lutheranism and Anglicanism were clearly conservative in their political and social doctrines. Calvinism can be made to look very undemocratic indeed if a critic concentrates on its conception of an elect few chosen by God for sal-

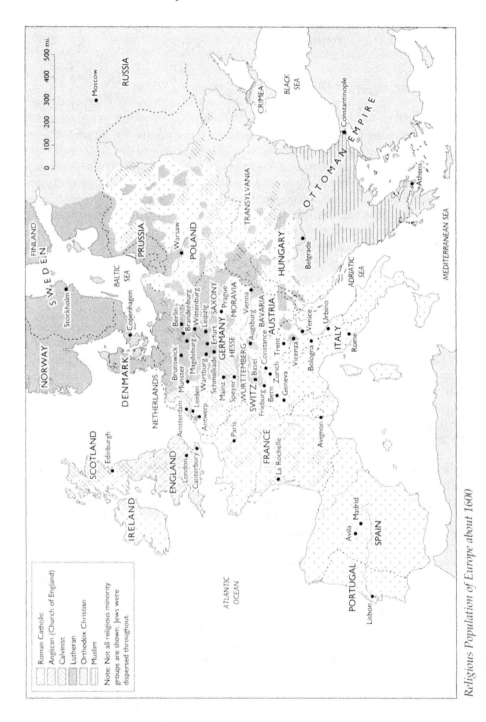

Religious Population of Europe about 1600

vation and a majority condemned to eternal damnation. In its early years in Geneva and in New England, Calvinism came close to being a theocracy.

In the long run, however, Calvinism favored domination by a fairly numerous and prosperous middle class, especially in the cities. The most persuasive argument for a causal relationship between Protestantism and modern Western democratic life proceeds less from the ideas of the early Protestants about society than from the way in which Protestant moral ideals strengthened a commercial and industrial middle class.

The impact of the Reformation for women was thought originally to be good: The Reformation introduced the possibility of divorce. That conclusion, however, has largely been overthrown. While "divorce" was forbidden in medieval Europe, people did effectively end marriages, through a number of legal and illegal practices. Divorce, moreover, was not necessarily a good in the sixteenth century. Then, as now, many women had few economic protections and considerably less personal wealth than their husbands. Marriage remained preferable for most women, providing a home, a measure of financial protection, and certain legal rights.

In one way, the Protestant Reformation had a direct and crystalline impact on the lives of women: the closing of the convents. For noblewomen in particular, the convents had been one of the few venues where they might live freer—but not utterly free—from male supervision. Often noblewomen resisted leaving their convents, having found there a good environment for the practice of their faith and a place where they might read, even take up philosophy or classical texts. While convents represented a very small portion of the overall population of women, in some places they functioned as a kind of island. Moreover, as the life of Teresa of Avila testifies, they were ruled by abbesses, who were themselves subject to masculine supervision, but who had a real measure of autonomy within the cloister walls. Catholicism continued to offer women that significant form for the expression of their faith, as well as a model of a life lived apart, in a community of women, which was otherwise rare.

The effects of the century of Reformation are difficult to demonstrate. Some scholars have called attention to Luther's language, not only his insistence on the father's singular role as governor within his home and household, but also his representation of "God the Father." Few would disagree that certain kinds of paternalism permeate his writings, although we still do not know how extensively he influenced real households and their arrangements of authority. Certainly it was true for all the major Churches into last century that women could not serve as priests or ministers. Women are still not permitted ordination in the Catholic Church, and only very recently have they been ordained in the Anglican Church. Women and men were divided in Protestant Churches, both being permitted to approach the altar, but women to one side, men to the other. Equally significant, the Society of Jesus, that dramatic new order, remained strictly male in its membership, resisting even the implementation of female tertiaries, as some medieval orders had. In no Protestant Church was divorce easy, and breaking a marriage was never easier for women, Catholic or Protestant, than men. All Churches sought to preserve marriage as an orderly microcosm of the state.

The printing press made more copies of all sorts of texts more available, and we even have evidence of women publishing pamphlets. Literacy of any kind, whether male or female, remains largely the stuff of speculation: There are no devices for measuring it accurately. All Reformations emphasized the importance of preaching, which could bring certain kinds of textual literacy to broad numbers of people, and more families were reading the Bible than before.

When we turn to the more "radical" forms of Protestantism, the picture changes. Women numbered among Anabaptist preachers as well as martyrs. Some sects were founded by women, the Shakers, for example, while others held an egalitarianism of gender as well as social place. Although most were wiped out, the very fact of the experiment had powerful consequences: It could be imagined. Women such as Marguerite de Navarre and Elizabeth I were pivotal patrons of nascent Churches, providing sanctuary and financial resources to minority and often persecuted Churches.

Perhaps more important in understanding the Reformation's significance for women are two shifts that seem in some ways tangential. The first was Protestantism's embrace of the people of cities and, especially with Calvinism, its promotion of an ethic and an aesthetic that were particularly attuned to commercial culture. Women of different social strata had very different sorts of access and freedoms, but no Protestant Church was feudal, embracing a society of warriors and peasants, in which "power" was a sword. All the Protestant Churches emerged in a society in which commercial wealth was coming to play an increasingly central role, and in which social relations were felt to be more fluid.

Second, in the clash between Jesuits and Dominicans and the conquistadores in the New World arose a question of immeasurable reverberations: What is it to be human? The model of humanity, based in that classical tradition, had been male—women's bodies were even understood as the "negative" of masculine bodies. As Europeans tried to make sense of the peoples they had encountered across the Atlantic, they framed questions that would resonate well into the eighteenth century, when Mary Wollstonecraft spoke of the "Rights of Women." Those debates, which arose in direct reference to indigenous peoples of the Americas, would also come to penetrate the debates on the morality of slavery—if a person is human, an entire range of conduct toward him or her becomes immoral by any Christian standard, Catholic or Protestant. Slavery throve throughout the Reformation, but some of the seeds of its destruction were laid in the agonized debates of Catholics and Protestants.

Contesting Views

The German sociologist Max Weber explored this question in *The Protestant Ethic and the Spirit of Capitalism*, first published in 1904. What started Weber's exploration was evidence suggesting that in his own day German Protestants had a proportionately greater interest in the world of business, and German Catholics a proportionately smaller interest, than their ratio in the German population would lead one to expect. Why was this so? Weber's answer may be summarized as follows: The accumulation of capital requires some sacrifice of immediate consumption; true capitalists must plow some of their profits back into their businesses so that they can produce more and make higher profits, with a higher potential for future capital; to achieve this, they must not only curb expenditures but also work very hard, spending most of their time making money.

Protestantism, especially in its Calvinist form, encouraged this sort of life. It encouraged hard work because work keeps one from sexual temptation, from playing silly games, from drinking, or acting in other ways displeasing to God. Moreover, work is a positive good, a kind of tribute paid to the Lord.

Protestantism, and in particular Calvinism, discouraged many kinds of consumption that took energies away from the large-scale production that became the essence of the modern economic system. The Calvinists discouraged the fine arts, the theater, the dance, expensive clothes. But they encouraged the satisfaction of the simple needs of solid, substantial food, adequate shelter, clothing, and the like—needs most readily supplied by large-scale industry serving a mass demand. A society with many Calvinists tended to produce much, to consume solidly but without waste or ostentation. Therefore, under competitive conditions, its business leaders accumulated capital, which they could invest in the methods of production that enriched the West. Much work and little play made Calvinist society prosperous. Merchants in government tended to emphasize economic growth, prudence, and a desire for predictable (that is, steady) work conditions.

The Scots, Dutch, Swiss, the Yankees of New England—all Calvinistic peoples—acquired a popular reputation for thrift, diligence, and driving hard bargains. The Protestant societies at once cut down the number of holy days—*holidays* without work. With Sunday rigorously observed as a day without work, the other six were all the more clearly work days.

Many Protestant theologians rejected the medieval Catholic doctrine that regarded interest on investments beyond a low or "just" rate as usury, and they also rejected most of the medieval attitudes suggested by the term "just price" in favor of something much closer to the ideas of free competition in the market. In the marketplace, God would take care of his own. Wealth became a sign of the good life—that is, the moral life—well lived.

Weber's thesis must not be taken as the sole or sufficient explanation of capitalism in early modern times. Indeed, the stirrings of modern economic life began long before Luther and Calvin and were first evident in regions that were never won over to Protestantism: Italy, southern Germany, Belgium. Banking began in Florence and other northern Italian cities under Catholic rulers. Almost certainly rules against usury would have been relaxed by the Catholic church even if there had been no Protestant Reformation. Moreover, there is no perfect correlation between Protestantism and industrial development, on the one hand, and Catholicism and slower development, on the other. Belgium, the German Rhineland, and northern Italy are productive and prosperous Catholic regions. Finally, no sensible explanation for the rise of a modern industrial economy can neglect the simple facts of geography and natural resources. Even if Italy had turned Calvinist, it would still have lacked the coal and iron deposits that contributed to Protestant Britain's industrial head start.

Can we so easily separate one ethic as "Protestant" and accord that singular efficacy, when there was simultaneously European expansion overseas? What is the relationship, if any, of that "ethic" to the natural resources of northern and western Europe, the damp, temperate northern climate conductive to hard labor and longer hours, especially indoors in contrast to the milder Mediterranean climate; What of the Catholic thinkers Galileo and René Descartes?

Nationalism, Modernity, and the Reformation

After the great break of the sixteenth century, both Protestantism and Catholicism became important elements in the formation of modern nationalism. Neither Protestants nor Catholics were always patriots. French Protestants sought help from the English enemy, and French Catholics from the Spanish enemy. But where a specific religion became identified with a given political unit, religious feeling and patriotic feeling reinforced each other. This is most evident where a political unit had to struggle for its independence. Protestantism heightened Dutch resistance to the Spanish; Catholicism heightened Irish resistance to the English. But even in states already independent in the sixteenth century, religion strengthened patriotism. Despite the existence of a Catholic minority, England from Elizabeth I on proudly held itself up as a Protestant nation; with equal pride Spain identified itself as a Catholic nation. In the wars of early modern Europe, religion and politics were inextricably combined.

As scholars look more and more closely into the local aspects of religious change during the Reformation, they find the differences between Catholics and Protestants on purely doctrinal matters less great than at first appearance. Both believed in witchcraft and persecuted witches. Both drew a distinction between a crime and a sin, that is between civil law (increasingly applied to the marketplace and public matters) and church law (applied to private, and by the seventeenth century more specifically sexual, matters). Both recognized the necessity to work within the temporal world. And both were compatible, although to different degrees and for different reasons, with capitalism. The Protestants emphasized education and the control of morals, but so did the Jesuits in the Catholic Reformation. Both originally defined madness in individuals as "a different form of reason" and set those deemed mad apart because of a presumption that they possessed a special kind of spirituality; and both experienced a shift in attitudes toward madness in the seventeenth century, seeing the "mad" as ill, no longer to be kept at a "sacred" distance by which they might reach salvation but instead to be confined in order to protect society. In matters of charity (which was taken increasingly from the hands of monasteries), of religious practice, of marriage, the family, and sex—in short, in a vast range of changes in human attitudes and practices—Protestants and Catholics differed, but those differences generally appear more minor now than scholars once supposed.

Thus the question of the "modernity" of the Reformation is being asked differently. In many matters both Protestants and Catholics appear quite "modern," in the sense that their views were, by the early seventeenth century, often much like those of today. Yet there were significant exceptions, as in witchcraft trials, that appear to place great distance between the beliefs of the Reformation and those of the twenty-first century. Indeed, historians no longer find the debate over modernity very productive, for today they are more interested in exploring the connections between political and religious experience, the concept of an exchange between spheres of human experience that were often analyzed separately by earlier historians.

SUMMARY

In 1517 Martin Luther drew up Ninety-five Theses for debate. In them he questioned church practices, specifically the practice of granting indulgences—popularly believed to grant forgiveness of sin and remission of punishment. Luther himself had come to believe in the primacy of faith over good works and in the priesthood of individual believers.

Luther's challenge unleashed a storm within the Church that eventually drove him to reject some Catholic doctrine and organize his own Church. Excommunicated in 1521, Luther became a national hero under the protection of the elector of Saxony, and soon other German princes joined the revolt.

Luther owed his success partly to religious sentiment and partly to political issues. Luther's doctrine of justification by faith had widespread appeal. Moreover, many Catholics sympathized with the need for reform.

Although the Holy Roman Emperor Charles V fought Protestantism, he was distracted by the many other concerns of his huge empire. In 1555 he had to accept the Peace of Augsburg that recognized the right of each prince to determine whether his lands would be Catholic or Lutheran. The Peace did not, however, recognize any other Protestant groups.

Ulrich Zwingli led a quiet reform in Switzerland. He shared with Luther the rejection of works theology, the doctrine of Sola fideism. Far more than Luther, he rejected the medieval liturgy, calling for a return to the simple Supper of the early church. John Calvin shaped the Protestant movement as a way of life and was instrumental in its spread across Europe to France, Scotland, and England.

The English Reformation was carried out by royal authority. By the Act of Supremacy in 1534, Henry VIII became head of the English Church. He retained Catholic doctrine and ritual but ended the authority of Rome. Henry enjoyed the support of the middle class in his action. His seizure of monastic lands and dissolution of monasteries fostered an economic and social revolution.

Although beliefs differed among Protestants, they shared a repudiation of Rome, relaxation of ritual and organization, a limit on the number of sacraments, and their rebel origins.

Calvinists rejected the Catholic emphasis on salvation and emphasized instead the belief that only a very few had been chosen by God to be saved. Although Calvinism was not originally democratic, its preaching set the individual above the state and may have contributed to modern democratic thought.

At first the Catholic Church responded to the Protestant challenge by trying to suppress the revolt. Then it rallied to reform itself from within, an effort known today as the Catholic Reformation. Habsburg rulers in Spain and Germany actively led the Catholic Reformation. The Jesuits, founded by Ignatius Loyola and organized on military discipline, won back some lands from Protestantism and made new converts overseas.

The Council of Trent, convened in 1545, brought about reform but also reaffirmed Catholic doctrine, ending the hope of some Catholics for compromise with Protestants. The Catholic Reformation succeeded in stemming the tide of Protestantism. Thus, by 1580 the lines of Catholic and Protestant lands in Europe were drawn.

Interpretations vary as to the causal relationship between Protestantism and the rise of modern Western democracy. Most historians agree that Protestant moral ideas strengthened the commercial and industrial middle class and led people to reexamine old ideas and institutions. In 1904, the German sociologist Max Weber advanced the much-debated thesis that Protestantism, especially Calvinism, established precepts and values that created a society predisposed to hard work, an essential of modern economic life. A more widely accepted generalization is that the Protestant and Catholic Reformations, along with other currents, were important elements in the rise of modern nationalism.

SIX

The Great Powers in Conflict

There is no general agreement on which date, or even which development, best divides the medieval from the modern. Some make a strong case for a date associated with the emergence of the great, ambitious monarchs: Louis XI in France in 1461; or Ferdinand of Aragon and Isabella of Castile, who were married in 1469; or the advent of Henry VII and the Tudors in England in 1485. Scholars who value international relations tend to choose 1494, when Charles VIII of France began what is often called "the first modern war" by leading his army over the Alps to Italy. Other historians find 1492 a convenient date, for the discovery of America began the great age of European expansion overseas. Still others would emphasize 1517, when Martin Luther opened his attack on the Roman Catholic church. All such dates are arbitrary, for, as our discussion of the Renaissance has shown, the dividing line between medieval and modern culture cannot be placed in a single country or a single year. Moreover, it can be argued that what really makes the modern world modern is the combination of rationalism, natural science, technology, and economic organization that has given us new power over natural resources. By this standard, the great change came in the eighteenth century, and the sixteenth and seventeenth were but preparation.

A Long Durée

In the long struggle between the European nations for hegemony, there was an enduring theme—a "long sixteenth century," or *long durée*, of population growth and price inflation during which the Mediterranean basin largely remained the economic and military heart of Europe. In the past a steady increase in population tended to exceed the capacity of a society to feed the new mouths. This was true until the eighteenth century in Europe and remains true in certain parts of the world today. The great population rise between 1450 and 1650 was followed by regression, while that after 1750 was not, for society had changed in ways that made it possible to feed the

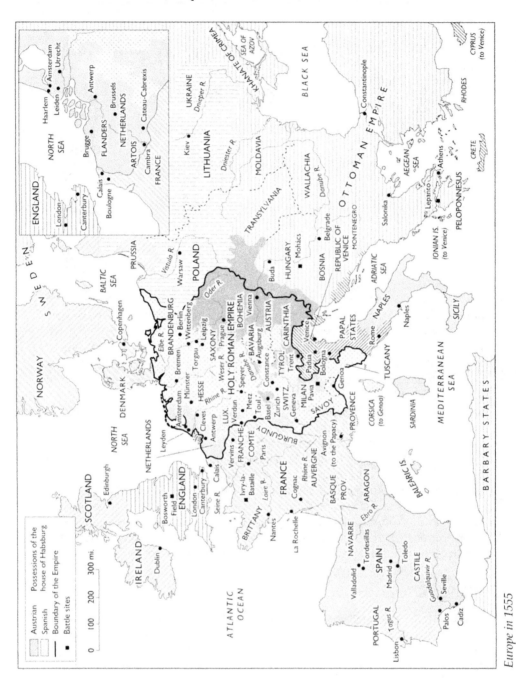

Europe in 1555

increase. These changes—in political, social, family, and economic structure—were in progress during the long durée, but their impact was not felt for over a century.

However, since the first genuine census was not taken until 1801, and then only in England, all population figures are guesswork for the sixteenth century. The lowest estimate of world population for 1300 is 250 million people, and the highest estimate for 1780 is 1,380 million people. Conservatively, historians accept that from the fifteenth to the eighteenth centuries world population at least doubled, despite economic and physical disasters. Europeans expanded during this time into vast new lands that had not been systematically tilled by their native populations. While the specific interpretations remain controversial, historians today generally agree that this systematic extension of agriculture and industry into new areas was made possible by a combination of social and technological changes, as well as by rhythms of climate variation.

Renaissance Monarchies, 1450–1650

In early modern times, Europe comprised a group of states, each striving to grow, usually by annexing other states or at least bringing them under some sort of control. At any given moment some states were on the offensive, trying to gain land, power, and wealth; others were on the defensive, trying to preserve what they had. The units in this competitive system are usually termed *sovereign states,* which means in practice that their rulers had armed forces to carry out their policies and could take initiatives independently of other states.

By the end of the Middle Ages, most smaller feudal units had been absorbed into bigger states over much of the West, with the exceptions of Germany and Italy. As the modern state system began to take shape in the fifteenth and sixteenth centuries, the three well-organized monarchies of Spain, France, and England dominated western Europe; Scotland, Portugal, and the Scandinavian states generally played subordinate roles. In central Europe, the Holy Roman Empire, with its many semi-sovereign member states, did not have the kind of internal unity enjoyed by the Atlantic powers. Yet under the leadership of the Austrian Habsburgs, the Empire was a leading international competitor. Between France and the Empire lay a zone of small sovereign states where the fifteenth-century dukes of Burgundy had tried to build a revived middle kingdom. Out of this phantom kingdom would eventually come Holland, Belgium, Luxembourg, Switzerland, and parts of both France and Italy. In southeastern Europe the new and expanding Ottoman Empire extended to the central Danube valley. To the east, Muscovite Russia was beginning to become a great state, and Poland-Lithuania was already great in size if not in power.

Many political units made up the competitive state system: dynastic states to about the end of the eighteenth century, and nation-states thereafter. Some early modern states were groupings of formerly independent units that might be separated from each other by foreign territory, that sometimes spoke different languages, and that were tied together almost solely by the ruling dynasty. Early modern wars were not total wars, and, except in their disastrous effects on government finances and on taxes, they scarcely touched the lives of the common people if those people were not in the way of contending armies trying to live off the land. In the peace settlements, no one worried greatly about transferring areas and populations from one dynasty to another.

However, the distinction between dynastic states and nation-states must not be overdrawn. Especially in the great Atlantic monarchies, a degree of national identity existed in the sixteenth century, and in England and France it had already been evident during the Hundred Years' War. At the time of the great Spanish Armada (1588) the English showed a dramatic sense of national identity, hating and fearing the Spanish both as foreigners and as Catholics. Even in divided Germany, Luther could count on Germans to dislike Italians. In the sixteenth century national identity was increasingly reinforced by religious identity.

The Instruments of Foreign Policy

By 1500 almost all European sovereign states possessed, at least in rudimentary form, most of the social and political organs of a modern state. They had two essential instruments: a professional diplomatic service and a professional army. The fifteenth and sixteenth centuries saw the steady development of modern diplomatic agencies and methods. Governments established central foreign offices or ministries, sent diplomats and regular missions to foreign courts, and organized espionage under cover of open diplomacy. Formal peace conferences were held and formal treaties were signed. To govern these formal relations a set of rules or expectations began to take shape.

The apparatus of interstate politics was developed most elaborately in Renaissance Italy, especially in the diplomatic service of the Republic of Venice. The detailed reports Venetian ambassadors sent back to the councils from their residences abroad are careful political and social studies of the personalities and lands involved, in which the relative merit of gossip and rumor—the latter often used by diplomats to further their ends—was weighed. The diplomat was often an important maker of policy in his own right. With travel very slow, his government could not communicate with him in time to direct him in detail, and he often had to make important decisions on his own. Good or bad diplomacy, good or bad intelligence about foreign lands, made a vital difference in a state's success or failure in the struggle for power.

The armed forces made still more difference. Freed from the restrictions of feudal warfare, the officer class could plan, drill, and campaign on a fairly large yet manageable scale. The common soldiers for the most part were mercenaries. (The word *soldier* comes from *solidus*, Latin for "piece of money.") Some of these mercenaries were recruited at home, usually among the poor and dispossessed, sometimes by impressment. Others were foreigners who made a career of soldiering, particularly the Swiss and Germans; thousands of them served in the armies of Francis I of France, together with contingents of Englishmen, Scots, Poles, Italians, Albanians, and Greeks.

Early modern armies showed many feudal survivals in organization and equipment. The officer class continued to preserve many of its old habits of chivalry, such as the duel. If the feudal lord no longer brought his own knights, his descendant as regimental colonel often raised his own regiment and financed it himself. Desertion was common, as was whipping as punishment. Each regiment might wear a prescribed uniform, but entire armies did not, so that in battle it was difficult to tell friend from foe. Weapons were of a great variety. Reminders of hand-to-hand fighting survived in the sword and in the pike, a long shaft used by foot soldiers against the armored knight and his mount. Hand firearms—arquebus, musket, pistol, and many others—were slow-loading and slow-firing and could seldom be accurately aimed. The cannon, unstandardized as to parts and caliber and hard to move, fired solid balls rather than exploding shells. Armies on the march lived mostly off the land, even when they were in home territory. But they were beginning to organize their supply and to use engineers.

Both the growth of military technology and the differences of national temperament were reflected in the shift of military predominance from Spain to France about 1600. Spain excelled in infantry, where the pike was a major weapon. France excelled in artillery, engineering, and fortification. By the sixteenth-century France was overpopulated in relation to its resources, and Spain and England were not, so that many Frenchmen sought to be mercenaries and were content to learn the less romantic military tasks.

Meanwhile, the first modern navies were also being developed. In the Renaissance, Venice took the lead with its arsenal and its detailed code of maritime regulations. Naval organization, naval supply, the dispatch and handling of ships, all required more orderly centralized methods than did an army; navies could not tolerate lack of discipline and planning. As in the armies, the officer class was predominantly aristocratic.

During the sixteenth century, naval supremacy passed from the Mediterranean to the Atlantic, where it rested briefly with Spain and then passed in the seventeenth century to the northern maritime powers of Holland, France, and England. These shifts were the result of changes in marine architecture, maritime technology and knowledge, and alterations in both the balance of power and the organization of centralized states. Of course, these instruments of foreign policy were both shaped by, and helped to shape, the economic developments of the "long sixteenth century." The upswing in population, trade, and prices made war more likely. New commercial trends that first appeared in port cities, where new money entered the European economy, gave the municipal governments of these cities greater say in the affairs of state and made the ports increasingly attractive targets of diplomacy or battle.

Still, failures in diplomacy and in military strategy were most important in the decline of the Hanseatic League, in the disruption of trade between Italy and the Levant, in the rise of English competition in the Mediterranean cloth trade, and in the reshaping of the political and religious map of Europe. After midcentury it was apparent that the Dutch and English were moving into a dominant position at the expense of the Spanish, French, and Habsburg (or Holy Roman) Empires.

A Complexity of Wars

The Italian Wars of Charles VIII and Louis XII, 1483–1515

Charles VIII of France (r. 1483–1498) continued Louis XI's policy of extending the royal domain by marrying the heiress of the duchy of Brittany. Apparently secure on the home front, Charles decided to expand abroad. As the remote heir of the Angevins, Charles disputed the right of the Aragonese, then led by Ferdinand (1458–1494), to hold the throne of Naples. He chose to invade Italy, however, not only because of his family claim but also because Renaissance Italy was rich and was divided into small rival political units. It looked, in short, easy to conquer. And so it was at first, for in the winter of 1494–1495 Charles marched his army through Italy to Naples in triumph. But his acquisition of Brittany had disturbed his neighbors, and his possession of Naples threatened the balance of power in Italy.

The French intrusion provoked the first of the great modern coalitions, the so-called Holy League composed of the papacy (as an Italian territorial state), the Holy Roman Empire, Venice, Milan, Spain, and soon England. This coalition forced the French armies out of Italy in 1495. Thereafter, various changing coalitions would seek to prevent the domination of Italy by any one power.

Charles was followed on the French throne by his cousin, Louis XII (r. 1498–1515). Louis married Charles's widow to make sure of Brittany, and then tried again in Italy, reinforced by another family claim, this time to Milan. Louis drove Ludovico Sforza from Milan in 1499. In this second French invasion the play of alliances was much more complicated. Louis tried to ensure himself against the isolation that had ruined Charles by allying in 1500 with Ferdinand of Aragon, with whom he agreed to partition Naples. Then in 1508 Louis helped form the League of Cambrai, in which Louis, Ferdinand, Pope Julius II, and the emperor Maximilian joined to divide up the lands held in the lower Po valley by the rich Republic of Venice.

All went well for the allies until Ferdinand, having taken the Neapolitan towns he wanted, decided to desert Louis. The pope, frightened at the prospect that France and the Empire might squeeze him out entirely, in 1511 formed another Holy League against France with Venice and Ferdinand, joined later by Henry VIII of England and the emperor Maximilian. The French could not hold out against such a coalition, for they now faced war on two fronts. Henry VIII attacked the north of France, and Louis XII, like Charles VIII, was checkmated.

Francis I versus Charles VI, 1515–1559

There were now two aggressors: the French house of Valois, still bent on expansion, and the house of Habsburg. When the Habsburg Charles I in Spain succeeded his grandfather Maximilian as Emperor Charles V in 1519, he had inherited Spain and lands in Spanish America from his mother, the Low Countries and the Habsburg lands in central Europe from his father, and a new preponderance in Italy. He purchased the imperial Crown with his singular personal wealth. He apparently had France squeezed in a vise. Louis XII's successor, Francis I (r. 1515–1547), was badly defeated by the largely Spanish Habsburg forces at Pavia in 1525 and was himself taken prisoner and held in Madrid until he signed a treaty giving up all the Valois Italian claims and ceding the duchy of Burgundy. He repudiated this treaty the moment he was safely back in France.

One of the imperial commanders at the battle of Pavia was the constable de Bourbon (1490–1527), a French noble at odds with his king. The same Bourbon next commanded the emperor's Spanish and German mercenaries in the sack of Rome in 1527. Pope Clement VII (1523–1534), a Medici, had turned against Charles V after Pavia. In the League of Cognac (1526) he had allied himself with the other main Italian powers and with Francis. Charles had besieged Rome, but he did not intend the sack, which took place when his mercenaries became infuriated by delays in pay and supplies. By the end of the decade Charles had made peace with the pope and with Francis, and in 1530 he was crowned by the pope as emperor and as king of Italy.

France was still in the vise between the Spanish, the German, and the Netherlands holdings of Charles. Francis I was not one to accept so precarious a position. He used the death of the Sforza ruler of Milan in 1535 to reopen the old claim to Milan and to begin the struggle once more. Neither side secured a decisive military victory. In 1559 the Treaty of Cateau-Cambrésis confirmed Habsburg control of Milan and Naples. France failed to acquire a real foothold in Italy, but the Habsburgs also failed to reduce the real strength of France. The Habsburg vise had not closed, primarily because France proved militarily, economically, and politically strong enough to resist the pressure.

The last phase of the personal duel between the aging rivals, Charles and Francis, shows how many variables affected the balance of power. To gain allies, Francis did not hesitate to turn to Charles's rebellious German subjects. Although head of a Catholic country, he allied himself with the Protestant duke of Cleves and even concluded an alliance with the Muslim Ottoman emperor, Suleiman the Magnificent, who attacked Charles from the east in Hungary.

One other participant in the complex struggles of the first half of the sixteenth century was England. England had on its northern border an independent Scotland, which tended to side with France, the hereditary English enemy. Yet the English were quite capable of supporting France if they thought Charles V too strong. After Charles had won at Pavia and taken

Francis I of France.   *(Réunion des Musées Nationaux/Art Resource, NY)*

Rome, the English minister Cardinal Wolsey worked out an alliance with France in 1527. The English were also capable of reversing themselves. In 1543, when Charles was beset by Protestants and Turks, Henry VIII came to his aid against France.

The Wars of Philip II and the Dutch Revolt, 1556–1598

In 1556 Charles V abdicated both his Spanish and imperial crowns and retired to a monastery, where he died two years later. His brother, who became Emperor Ferdinand I (r. 1556–1564), secured the Austrian Habsburg territories; his son, Philip II of Spain (r. 1556–1598), added the Spanish lands overseas (Mexico, Peru, and in the Caribbean), the Burgundian inheritance of the Netherlands, and Milan and Naples in Italy. Even without Germany, Philip's realm was a supranational state, drawing much gold and silver from the New World and threatening France, England, and the whole balance of power. Aware of the potential of such power, contemporary Italians were saying that "God has turned into a Spaniard."

Like his father, Philip II found Protestantism intolerable. His attempt to invade England and restore Catholicism would make him one of the villains of Anglo-Saxon and Protestant tradition. In fact, he was no lover of war for its own sake, but was a serious, hard-working administrator who was both the most powerful monarch and the greatest civil servant of the age.

Charles V had come to count heavily on the wealth of the Netherlands to finance his constant wars. But he joined into a unified state the seventeen provinces of the Netherlands, which were jealous of their traditional autonomy. Each province had its own medieval Estates or assembly, dominated by the nobility and wealthy merchants, which raised taxes and armies. In the mid-sixteenth century the area was still overwhelmingly Catholic.

Whereas Charles V had liked the Netherlands, Philip II was thoroughly Spanish in outlook. Not only did Philip's temperament antagonize his subjects in the Low Countries, but so did his ideas about centralized efficient rule, which led him to curtail their political and economic privileges. The inhabitants were intent on conducting business without the restrictions imposed on trade and industry by Spanish regulations. The Protestants among them resented and feared Philip's use of the Inquisition in the Netherlands.

Philip sent Spanish garrisons to the Netherlands and attempted to enforce edicts against heretics. Opposition, which centered at first in the privileged classes, soon spread downward. In 1566, when two hundred nobles petitioned Philip's regent to adopt a more moderate policy, an official sneeringly referred to "these beggars." The name stuck and was proudly adopted by the rebels. The political restlessness, combined with an economic slump and the growing success of the Calvinists in winning converts, touched off riots in August 1566 that resulted in severe destruction of Catholic churches in Ghent, Antwerp, and Amsterdam.

Philip responded by dispatching to the Netherlands an army of ten thousand Spaniards headed by the unyielding, politically clumsy duke of Alva. Alva set up a Council of Troubles—later dubbed the Council of Blood—which resorted to large-scale executions, confiscations, and fines. The number of victims executed under the Council of Blood totaled about fifteen hundred, yet repression only heightened the opposition to Spanish policy. In 1573 Alva was recalled to Spain.

Meantime, the rebel "Beggars" turned to naval guerrilla warfare, gaining control of the ports of the populous northern province of Holland, which became a refuge for Protestants from other provinces. A split was developing between a largely Catholic south and a mainly Protestant north—to use modern terminology, between Belgium and Holland. North and south had much to unite them, and union of all seventeen provinces was the goal of the rebel leader, Prince William of Orange.

William's goal of unification seemed almost assured in the wake of widespread revulsion at the "Spanish Fury" of 1576, when Spanish troops sacked Antwerp and massacred several thousand inhabitants. But in 1578, when the duke of Parma arrived to govern the Netherlands, Philip at last appeared willing to compromise. The cost of the war was becoming intolerable, and

Spanish executions had made the Dutch resolve to fight to the last man. By restoring old privileges of self-rule, Parma won back the ten southern provinces, which remained largely Catholic; it was too late to win back the northern provinces.

In 1581 the Dutch took the decisive step of declaring themselves independent of the Spanish Crown. They made good that declaration by courageous use of their now much better-organized land forces. Moreover, Philip faced grave internal economic problems just when he was being drawn into fighting on other fronts. He had to cope with the Turks, the French Protestants, and the anti-Spanish moderate wing of French Catholics. In 1585 the English queen, Elizabeth I, came out on the side of the Dutch and sent an army to their aid. The great armada of unwieldy men-of-war that Philip sent out to invade England was defeated in the English Channel in July 1588 by a skillfully deployed lighter English fleet and was further battered afterward by a great storm. This battle was the beginning of the end of Spanish preponderance, the start of English greatness in international politics, and the decisive step toward Dutch independence. These portentous results were not as evident in 1588 as they became later, but even at the time the defeat of the Spanish Armada was viewed as a great event, and the storm that finished its destruction was christened the "Protestant wind."

In 1598 Philip II died. Save for the seven northern provinces of the Netherlands, the great possessions that had been his when he began his reign were intact. In 1580 he had added Portugal by conquest and brought the whole Iberian peninsula under a single rule. Yet after over forty years of rule he had left his kingdom worn out, drained of men and money, only sluggishly able to attend to the needs of a vast empire.

Between Feudal Kingdom and Nation-State: Absolutism

Before 1648, most of Europe was governed by families whose blood, whose lineage, was perceived as "royal"—whose ability and right to govern were seen as "natural." Dynasties dominated the political map of Europe: the Valois, then Bourbon in France; the Tudor, then Stuart in England; the Habsburg in Spain, Austria, and the Holy Roman Empire. Venice's particular form of republican government outlasted Florence's experiment in republicanism, but both were subject to French and Imperial, sometimes papal, interference.

It is within the context of those diverse dynasties that we speak of "absolutism." Confusingly, the term "absolutism" has been used to refer both to a political ideology and to the practice of kingship in early modern Europe. Today most scholars no longer hold that it names a historical reality. Most agree, on the other hand, that the term "absolutism" accurately captures the nature of political power that early modern monarchs pursued through various strategies. Absolutism is best understood in terms of the ruler's will: Its goal was to eliminate any constraints on a monarch's ability to execute his will. No early modern monarch achieved the perfect freedom of his political will, but individual monarchs sought over three centuries to reduce those local and personal privileges and rights, inherited from medieval feudalism, that inhibited the monarch's ability to create laws, to define and execute justice, and to control all violence and turn it, in the form of military and police force, to serving the will of the Crown.

In some ways, absolutism can be seen as a logical extension of the medieval practice of personal rule, individual monarchs' pursuit of greater personal authority, and their use of clients and vassals to "represent" their authority where they could not themselves be. In pursuing "absolutist" policies, however, early modern monarchs sought to eliminate the wide variety of particular privileges and the spectrum of exemptions their subjects had inherited. They sought to make their authority uniform and to level all differences among their subjects within the realm. In this way, absolutism looks toward the modern sense of the "state" as a uniform unity. An extension of Renaissance monarch's pursuit of personal power, absolutist policies had as their consequence the severing of the reciprocal ties of vassalage, their replacement with ties of clientage, the development of the court as a site for the display of power, the introduction of instrumentality—very much in keeping with Machiavelli's advice in *The Prince*—and the emergence of a kind of political power that was no longer charismatic, but more abstract: represented in the bureaucrats who served the Crown and centered in the Crown more than the person of the king.

Early modern monarchs all sought in one way or another to "centralize"— another term of scholarship—authority in their person, to be not simply the final court of appeal or the most powerful lord, but the *source*, the origin, *in their persons* for the legitimacy of law, of the definition and enactment of justice, and of the sole form of legitimate violence, whether police or military. In seeking to expand the fiscal base of the Crown, they both negotiated with and sought to curb legislative bodies, whose traditional rights included the right of setting and collecting taxes. The Stuart kings of England and the Bourbon kings of France suspended their respective parliamentary bodies for long periods of time in the seventeenth and eighteenth centuries, respectively, ruling without the formally constituted legislative bodies. Each monarch pursued the means to maintain a standing army, seeking military power autonomous of their vassals, both through new forms of taxation and through the institution of new forms of military. Monarchs pursued new systems of taxation and its collection, new methods of military organization, and unparalleled displays of royal wealth and dominance.

Medieval kings were itinerant, their "courts" mobile, consisting of retainers and others bound to the monarch through reciprocal oaths of fealty and protection. They relied upon such personal connections, whether it was to expand geographically the boundaries of their domain or to raise armies. In pursuing absolutist policies, early modern monarchs all sought to make the ruler the *center* of all branches of government—legislative, judicial, and executive. Philip II of Spain, the Valois, and the Tudors each chose a city to make the capital of the realm—Madrid, Paris, London—fixing geographically "centers" of government, in which royal bureaucracies increasingly had "offices" that were filled by men not of rank, but of talent and skill. In these capital cities, the monarchs built courts that were no longer itinerant, but foci for elaborate displays of power: the power of wealth and status, the singular power of royalty, the unique political power of the Crown. Each royal house, in part through the display and the theater of royal courts, but also in part through laws and the withdrawal of privileges, sought to alter the relations of status between the Crown and the nobility, from a position as first among peers to one in which the king was "peerless": unique, not simply above all the nobility, but remote, of a different status entirely. Louis XIV's Versailles was the culmination of this particular pursuit: It featured long halls of mirrors in which courtiers could observe themselves paying elaborate homage to the king.

For each monarch, however, those pursuits were circumscribed by custom, existing institutions, nobility, merchants, commercial entrepreneurs, and, ultimately, peasants, artisans, "the middling sort," or "the people." In the Empire, princes and parliaments resisted the efforts of the Habsburgs to institute their will in matters both religious and constitutional. In England, as we shall see, an alliance of gentry, landed nobility of middle rank, and successful merchants tried and condemned for treason the Stuart king. In France, some 150 years later, the Third Estate, "the people," an alliance of bourgeois, lawyers, artisans, and peasants, also overthrew a monarchy they perceived as remote, indifferent, and transgressive of traditional rights. The challenges to absolutism lie largely beyond this chapter, but as early as 1641, English gentry and London merchants effectively blocked Stuart claims to absolute authority in any realm of governance, and, as we shall see, in 1648, an alliance of German princes with shifting foreign allies broke Habsburg dominance in central Europe.

The Catholic Monarchies: Spain and France

The early modern monarchies had many characteristics in common: splendid courts, representative assemblies of some kind, complex diplomatic policies and foreign services to pursue those policies, expensive armies, and, above all, growing bureaucracies. For Spain, efficiency in government turned upon the bureaucracy nurtured by Philip II. For France, torn by religious and civil wars, bureaucracy depended more upon the personal popularity of the monarch. For England, the Tudor monarchs achieved a new balance between the reality and the appearance of royal and parliamentary powers. Localism remained strong, and true national patriotism had not yet developed. But a growing emphasis on the structure of government that flowed outward from the monarch and the assemblies meant that a divided Europe sought security and stability in the concept of the state.

Spanish Absolutism, 1516–1659

Spain in its Golden Age, 1516–1659, offers a case study of the clash between the ideal of absolutism and the persistence of the varied groups on which the monarchy sought to impose its centralized, standardizing rules. The reigns of its two hard-working monarchs, Charles I (r. 1516–1556) and Philip II, span almost the entire century. Brought up in the Low Countries, Charles came to

Spain a stranger. Charles's election to the imperial throne in 1519 made him further suspect in Spain; the aristocrats were restless in the face of the distractions of his Habsburg responsibilities, and the municipalities disliked the growth of imperial fiscal controls. In 1520 a league of Spanish cities led by Toledo rose up in the revolt of the *Comuneros*, which was put down in 1521. Charles had been frightened, and in the future he did his best not to offend his Spanish subjects openly.

Unlike his father, Philip II grew up as a Spaniard and was much more willing to build a professional, centralized regime in Spain. He devised a system of councils, topped by a council of state, which were staffed by great nobles but had only advisory powers; final decisions rested with Philip. Philip also greatly reduced the power of the Cortes, or representative assemblies. In Castile nobles and priests, because they did not pay direct taxes, no longer attended the sessions of the Cortes. The Cortes of Aragon, while retaining more power, was seldom convoked by Philip. Above all, Philip began with assured sources of income: his tax of a fifth of the value of the precious cargoes from America; direct taxes from the states of his realm; revenues from the royal estates and from the sale of offices and patents of nobility; and revenues from the authorized sale, at royal profit, of dispensations allowed by the pope, such as permission to eat meat on Fridays and during Lent.

Even in this matter of revenue, the limitations of the absolute monarch were clear. Except by borrowing and hand-to-mouth expedients like the sale of offices, he could not notably increase his income at home; he could not summon any representative group together and get them to vote new monies. In the first place, the constituent parts of his realm each had to be dealt with as a separate entity, and the slowness of communication with his far-flung domains further delayed the process of decision making. For the most part the nobility and clergy were tax-exempt and could not be called upon for unusual financial sacrifices. The difficulty of collection, the opportunities for graft, and the lack of administrative and financial experience were additional reasons why Philip could not introduce more systematic general taxation.

Outside the financial sphere, the obstacles to effective centralization were even more serious. The union of the crowns of Aragon and Castile, achieved by the marriage of Ferdinand and Isabella, had by no means made a unified Spain. In the sixteenth century, some of the provinces would not even extradite criminals within the peninsula, and many of them levied customs dues on goods from the others. The northern regions preserved many ancient privileges known as *fueros*, and Aragon still kept the office of *justicia mayor*, a judge nominated by the Crown for life and entrusted with enormous public authority.

What the Habsburg dynasty might have accomplished had it been able to expend its full energies on uniting and developing its Spanish lands can never be known. What actually happened was that it exhausted the peninsula and weakened its lands overseas in trying to secure hegemony over Europe and to subdue the Protestant heresy. This was the great age of Spain, when Spain seemed to be the richest of states, destined to rule over both the

Americas; it was also the Golden Age of Spanish religion, literature, and art. And yet it was a brief flowering, for Spanish greatness largely vanished in the seventeenth century.

The Spanish Economy

The Iberian peninsula is mountainous, and its central tableland is subject to droughts, but its agricultural potential is considerable and it has mineral resources, notably iron. Spain was the first major European state to secure lands overseas and to develop a navy and merchant marine to integrate the vast resources of the New World with a base in the Old World. Yet all this wealth slipped through Spain's fingers in a few generations. An important factor here was the immense cost of the wars of Charles V and Philip II.

Sixteenth-century Spain drew from the New World immense amounts of silver and many commodities—sugar, indigo, tobacco, cocoa, hides. But all this revenue was not enough to pay for world dominion. The bullion passed through Spanish hands into those of bankers and merchants in other European countries, partly to pay for the Spanish armies and navies and partly to pay for the manufactured goods sent to the New World. These goods, which the colonies were forbidden to make for themselves, Spain could not supply from its own meager industrial production. Although a royal decree gave Spanish merchants a monopoly on trade with the Indies, as the century wore on they became mere middlemen, sending to the Indies items imported from the rest of Europe. Thus Spain's governmental expenditures primed foreign economies, and by 1600 Spain's home industry was declining.

Sixteenth-century Spain was certainly moving toward the economic policy of mercantilism. Although Spain lacked the true mercantilist passion for building national wealth under government auspices, it used many mercantilist techniques: close regulation in general, and narrow channeling of colonial trade in particular. In Castile a single institution, the *Casa de Contratación* (House of Trade) in Seville, controlled every transaction with the Indies and licensed every export and import. The paperwork was staggering, slowing the flow of trade and encouraging smuggling to avoid frustrating delays and high taxes.

The vast riches of the New World were not an unmixed blessing. Competition for gold and silver bullion increased the probability of war with other European powers. The flow of bullion in unprecedented quantity may well have stimulated a rate of inflation that Philip's sluggish bureaucracy could not control. Certainly inflation was a persistent problem throughout the sixteenth century, and unabated inflation usually revolutionizes economic life. Castilian prices more than doubled in the first half of the century in sharp spurts, and doubled again in a steady rise in the second half of the century; such a rate of increase was unheard of before then.

Sometime between 1600 and 1620 Spain moved from an expansionist to a stagnant economy. Furthermore, climatic changes severely affected Spain during the sixteenth century. While neither the New World nor the policies of Philip could be blamed for the vagaries of nature, the inability to adjust to the change from a dry and sunny climate at the beginning of the century to a cycle of wet, cold years marked by exceptionally harsh winters reflected the conservative nature of Spanish agriculture.

In any case, the story of Spanish inflation is more complicated and not yet fully understood. The crucial precious metal from the New World was not gold, but silver, which became more plentiful than gold in the 1530s. The actual movement of the silver cannot be fully known; much of it apparently went to buy Asian luxury goods, and most of it may not have entered the Spanish monetary system. Any direct relationship between the influx of silver and the movement of prices is impossible to demonstrate. What can be said is that the New World Trade, and the conventional belief at the time that bullion was the best form of wealth, no doubt did attract men (and some women) of enterprise who saw the silver of the New World as a windfall by which they might change their individual fortunes.

Still, it was Philip's imperial wars that brought Spain nearer to destruction. The cost of the lost armada alone was 10 million ducats; the war in the Netherlands was eating up another 2 million ducats annually, while 3 million were sent as subsidies to French Catholic leaders. In 1589 the Cortes voted a new, expedient tax, the *millones*, which brought in 8 million ducats over a decade. Even before this, it is estimated that peasant farmers in Castile were surrendering half their income in taxes, tithes, and feudal dues.

Yet all this income was still insufficient. Philip II had to borrow heavily, quadrupling the public debt. Eventually debt interest absorbed at least half the Crown's income, so that funds were not sufficient to meet military needs, thus leading to a vicious circle of more borrowings. Furthermore, the outlay of public money did not remain in Spain, for the wages of those in military service were spent where the soldiers were: in Italy, France, or the Netherlands. By the 1590s Spain was in the midst of an acute crisis, made worse by a series of harvest failures across all of western Europe. In 1598–1599 the great plague struck an undernourished population, killing perhaps 600,000 in Castile alone; in some areas half the population died.

Still Philip had not retreated from his wars, for he felt that the religious issue was paramount. After 1596 Philip was often ill, and his pleasure at the *auto de fé* (public burning of heretics) and his anti-Semitism were unabated. Worse was to come for the Spanish economy after Philip's death, however, for while his policies may have started the downward slide, his attention to detail, his ability to get through mountains of work, and the fact that, except for the Netherlands, he had held the Empire together until his death, had prevented the general decline from becoming fully evident. When Philip IV came to the throne in 1621, it was too late to turn the tide.

"The Spanish Century"

The sixteenth century was known as the Golden Age of Spain. The wealth of the Americas, the dominance of the Atlantic, and the military might that wealth enabled, all contributed to Spain's preeminence among states in the sixteenth century. A corps of extraordinarily skilled diplomats and statesmen carried Spanish sensibilities, Spanish court culture, and a Spanish aesthetic to much of Europe. That aesthetic was rendered in many forms: in the dramatically shadowed paintings of Velásquez, painter to the Habsburg court; in the particular courtliness of Miguel de Cervantes's (1547–1616) character, the knight Don Quixote; and in the religious orders for which Spain was the wellspring: for example, the Jesuits and the Reformed Discalced Nuns of St. Teresa. Italians and Frenchmen remarked on the singular bearing—a distinctive combination of arrogance and austerity—of Spanish nobles. So, too, Europeans associated the Jesuits, with their austere black robes and striking scarlet sash, with their own bearing, itself a commanding dignity and reserve, with Spain, the Jesuit presence in England, the Low Countries, and Germany provoking xenophobia even more than the fear of recatholicization.

Spain was fertile ground for Baroque Catholicism. Three of the most influential saints of the "Counter-Reformation" (the Reformation the Catholic Church mounted self-consciously to counteract Protestantism) were Spanish: Ignatius Loyola, Teresa of Avila (1515–1582), and St. John of the Cross (1542–1591). Each embodied the renewed Catholicism of the sixteenth century: led by mystical visions, experiencing moments of mystical transformation throughout their lives, physically expressive of their piety, in both dramatic gestures of devotion and in the sheer energy of their activity. Ignatius and Teresa were rendered in Baroque sculpture, St. Teresa by the great Baroque sculptor Gian Lorenzo Bernini. Bernini's sculpture captures the moment of ecstasy when Teresa saw the radiant face of an angel and was transported to a higher spiritual realm. Her feet, her hands, her face, even her torso give material expression to her spiritual life. She, along with St. John of the Cross, reformed the cloistered life in Spain, bringing their particular combination of prayer, contemplation, and mystical visions to reform.

Cervantes's *Don Quixote* captured something of the paradox of Spain. Don Quixote is a knight led by ideals of chivalry to their most extreme expression—to a multitude of moments of what readers, for centuries, have taken as madness. Sancho Panza, his squire, is his antithesis: a peasant, "realistic," and, as he himself acknowledges, unlikely ever to have taken on any quest, let alone the "irrational" quest of his master. Throughout the novel, Sancho Panza provides a commentary on what is "rational," "realistic," "common sensical." But Don Quixote is both the "hero" of the story and the main character. Most commentators have not identified with Don Quixote, but they have been enchanted or frustrated, provoked by him as Sancho Panza could never be. Don Quixote's "chivalry" is unrealistic, but it also captivates the imagination and brings to his life its narrative force. "Reason" and visions are set in tension, common sense seems the valued position to readers, but the fantasy, the visions, make *Don Quixote* a singularly unforgettable book. Spain captivated European imaginations, even as they thought the manner excessively formal, the dominance of black austere, and the visions of Loyola and Teresa possibly "diabolical."

Extreme pride—pride of status, of faith, of nation—was often the mark of Spain. Five hundred years before, El Cid (c. 1040–1099), the legendary hero of the reconquest from the Muslims, was fatalistic and proud. The same tone was representative of the writers of the Golden Age of Spain, although perhaps the painter El Greco best expressed what was important to the Spanish leaders of the time. El Greco (1541–1614) was born on Crete. After studying in Venice, he settled in the 1570s in Toledo. His work showed the influence of other cultures; Titian and Tintoretto in particular were of great importance to his early development. Yet he also developed his own independent voice. He was an intellectual who developed the arguments of the Catholic Reformation explicitly in his art. The famous picture of St. Peter in tears, painted between 1580 and 1585, emphasized the importance of penitence, even for the founder of the church, precisely because the Protestants had disparaged penitence. He personalized the saints, encouraging a personal attachment to a specific saint, and he glorified the Virgin Mary in his work. To bring the church fathers and the saints closer to the people, he depicted them in sixteenth-century dress.

Historians loosely speak of great world powers as having possessed, or being dominant in, a particular century: The twentieth century has often been referred to as "the American century"; certainly the nineteenth was "the British" and the seventeenth century the "French." The sixteenth century, the Golden Age of Spain, was distinctively marked by the Spanish sense of style and by Spain's initiatives in western European affairs.

France: Toward Absolutism, 1547–1588

The long-established French monarchy began to move toward more efficient absolutism after the Hundred Years' War, particularly under Louis XI. In this development, France had certain advantages. None of its provinces showed quite the intense regionalism that could be found in Catalonia or among the Spanish Basques. Moreover, unlike the Iberian peninsula, most of France is not cut up by mountain ranges into compartments isolated by problems of transport and communications. Yet despite these assets, France was still only loosely tied together under Francis I. Many provinces retained their own local Estates, their own local courts (*parlements*), and many other privileges.

Nonetheless, the kingdom of Francis I had been strong enough to counter the threat of encirclement by Charles V. The king himself was not another Louis XI, however. Self-indulgence weakened his health and distracted him from the business of government; his extravagant court and frequent wars drained French finances. Francis lived in the grand manner. It is reported that it took eighteen thousand horses and pack animals to move the king and his court on their frequent journeys. He built the châteaux of Chambord and Fontainebleau, and in Paris he remodeled the great palace of the Louvre and founded the Collège de France. He patronized Leonardo, Cellini, and other artists and men of letters.

At the beginning of his reign he had extended the royal gains first made in 1438 at papal expense in the Pragmatic Sanction of Bourges; through the Concordat of Bologna in 1516 the pope had granted the king increased control over the Gallican Church, including the important right to choose bishops and abbots. But Francis was the last strong monarch of the house of Valois.

El Greco, the great artist of Spain's Golden Age, depicted the city of Toledo with a heightened sense of drama, just as he would reveal the tension, asceticism, and bigotry in those who sat for portraits by him. A View of Toledo *is not only the first Spanish landscape painting of note, it is one of the most famous paintings in the world. Its elongated structures, the ectoplasmic clouds that fill the nighttime sky and reflect the lightening, and its rearrangement of the city's landmarks in accordance with the artist's sense of composition and drama (a dramatic rearrangement of which contemporary viewers were well aware) give the painting a sense of eerieness and foreboding.　(The Metropolitan Museum of Art, Bequest of Mrs. H. O. Havemeyer, 1929, the H. O. Havemeyer Collection)*

The second half of the sixteenth century was the age of French civil and religious wars, a time of crisis that almost undid the centralizing work of Louis XI and his successors.

The religious map of France in the 1550s showed a division by class as well as by territory. While Protestantism scarcely touched the French peasantry except in parts of the south, the Huguenots were strong among the nobility and among the rising classes of capitalists and artisans. Paris, Brittany, most of Normandy, and the northeast remained ardently Catholic. Protestantism was gaining in the southwest. Even in these regions, however, the employer class was more likely to be Protestant, the workers to be Catholic.

Sporadic warfare began soon after the death of Henry II in 1559. Thereafter, the crown passed in succession to Henry's three sons—Francis II (r. 1559–1560), Charles IX (r. 1560–1574), and Henry III (r. 1574–1589). Since Charles IX was a boy of ten at his accession, authority was exercised by his mother, Catherine de' Medici, who had no particular religious convictions. Catherine was determined to preserve intact the magnificent royal inheritance of her sons, however, which seemed threatened by the rapid growth of the Huguenots. What especially worried Catherine was the apparent polarization of the high nobility by the religious issue; the great family of Guise was passionately dedicated to the Catholic cause, and the powerful families of Bourbon and Montmorency to the Huguenot.

Success in scattered fighting during the 1560s netted the Huguenots some gains. Their ambitious leader, Gaspard de Coligny (1519–1572), gained great influence over the unstable Charles IX and hoped to control the government. Panicky at the danger to the prospects for her sons and to her own position, Catherine threw in her lot with the Guises and persuaded Charles to follow suit. The result was a massacre of Huguenots on St. Bartholomew's Day (August 24, 1572). Six thousand Protestants were killed in Paris; the Huguenots remained strong. As warfare continued, the Catholic nobles organized a threatening league headed by the Guises, and both sides negotiated with foreigners for help—the Catholics with Spain and the Protestants with England.

French civil and religious strife culminated in the War of the Three Henrys (1585–1589)—named for Henry III, the Valois king and the last surviving grandson of Francis I; Henry, duke of Guise, head of the Catholic League; and the Bourbon Henry of Navarre, Protestant cousin and heir-presumptive of the childless king. The threat that a Protestant might succeed to the throne pushed the Catholic League to propose violating the rules of succession by making an uncle of Henry of Navarre king. But this attempt to alter the succession alienated moderate French opinion, already disturbed by the extreme positions taken by both Catholics and Protestants.

Paris was strongly Catholic, and a popular insurrection there (May 1588) frightened Henry III out of his capital, which triumphantly acclaimed Henry, duke of Guise, as king. Henry III responded by conniving in the assassination of the two great leaders of the Catholic League, Henry of Guise and his brother Louis. Infuriated, the Catholic League rose in full revolt, and Henry

III fled to refuge in the camp of Henry of Navarre, but on the way he was assassinated by a monk.

The First Bourbon King: Henry IV, 1589–1610

Henry of Navarre was now by law Henry IV (r. 1589–1610), the first king of the house of Bourbon. In the decisive battle of Ivry in March 1590, he defeated the Catholics, who had set up the aged cardinal of Bourbon as "King Charles X." But Henry's efforts to besiege Paris were repeatedly frustrated by Spanish troops sent down from Flanders by Philip II. Philip planned to have the French Estates General put Henry aside and bestow the crown on Isabella, daughter of Philip II and his third wife, Elizabeth of Valois, who was the child of Henry II and Catherine de' Medici. In the face of this new threat, Henry was persuaded that if he would formally reject his Protestant faith, he could rally the moderate Catholics and secure at least toleration for the Protestants. He turned Catholic in 1593 and Paris surrendered to him, giving rise to the tale that he had remarked, "Paris is well worth a Mass." Henry thereupon declared war against Spain and brought it to a successful conclusion with the Treaty of Vervins (1598).

Within France the Edict of Nantes, also in 1598, endeavored to achieve a lasting religious settlement. While it did not bring complete religious freedom, it did provide for a large measure of toleration. The Huguenots were granted substantial civil liberties and were allowed to exercise their religion in certain towns and in the households of great Huguenot nobles. Public worship by Huguenots was forbidden in cities that were the seats of bishops, and most particularly in Paris. In the two hundred towns where Huguenots could worship, they were free to fortify and garrison one hundred soldiers at government expense as symbols of their right to their own safeguard.

The intellectual preparation for the Edict of Nantes and for the revival of the French monarchy under Henry IV had been in large part the work of a group of men known as *politiques*, a term that comes closer to meaning political moralist than politician. The greatest of them was Jean Bodin (1530–1596). He and his colleagues stressed the need for political unity to maintain law and order; yet they were moderates who by no means preached that the king must be obeyed blindly. The politiques were convinced that under the supremacy of the French state, French citizens should be allowed to practice different forms of the Christian religion.

Henry IV was fortunate in arriving on the French scene when the passions of civil war were nearing exhaustion and the nation was ready for peace. The casualty rate in war had become catastrophic; commonly a third of those engaged in battle died. Slowly a general revulsion against the excessive destructiveness of war offset the fanaticism displayed on both sides. Henry balanced concessions to the Huguenots with generous subsidies to the Catholic League for disbanding its troops, and he declined to summon the Estates General because of its potential for proving troublesome. He was the most human king the French had had for a long time and the best-liked

The Written Record

THE EDICT OF NANTES

By this edict Henry IV granted religious freedom to the Huguenots. Its key provisions follow:

We have by this perpetual and irrevocable Edict pronounced, declared, and ordained and we pronounce, declare and ordain:

I. Firstly, that the memory of everything done on both sides from the beginning of the month of March, 1585, until our accession to the Crown and during the other previous troubles, and at the outbreak of them, shall remain extinct and suppressed, as if it were something which had never occurred.

II. We forbid all our subjects, of whatever rank and quality they may be, to renew the memory of these matters, to attack, be hostile to, injure or provoke each other in revenge for the past, whatever may be the reason and pretext . . . but let them restrain themselves and live peaceably together as brothers, friends, and fellow-citizens.

III. We ordain that the Catholic, Apostolic, and Roman religion shall be restored and re-established in all places and districts of this our kingdom and the countries under our rule, where its practice has been interrupted.

IV. And we permit those of the so-called Reformed religion to live and dwell in all the towns and districts of this our kingdom and the countries under our rule, without being annoyed, disturbed, molested, or constrained to do anything against their conscience, or for this cause to be sought out in their houses and districts where they wish to live, provided that they conduct themselves in other respects to the provisions of our present Edict.

XXII. We ordain that there shall be no difference or distinction, because of the aforesaid religion, in the reception of students to be instructed in Universities, Colleges, and schools, or of the sick and poor into hospitals, infirmaries, and public charitable institutions.

XXVII. In order to reunite more effectively the wills of our subjects, as is our intention, and to remove all future complaints, we declare that all those who profess or shall profess the aforesaid so-called Reformed religion are capable of holding and exercising all public positions, honours, offices, and duties whatsoever . . . in the towns of our kingdom . . . notwithstanding all contrary oaths.

The Edict of Nantes, in *Church and State through the Centuries: A Collection of Historic Documents*, ed. and trans. S. Z. Ehler and John B. Morrall (New York: Biblo and Tannen, 1967), pp. 185–87.

monarch in their history, for he convinced his subjects that he was truly concerned for their welfare.

The range of efforts to improve the economy was extensive and innovative. Henry's economic advisers reclaimed marshes for farmland, encouraged luxury crafts in Paris, and planted thousands of mulberry trees to foster the manufacture of silk. They extended canals and built roads and bridges that eventually gave France the best highways in Europe. Faced with a heavy deficit when he took office, Henry's chief minister, the Huguenot Maximilien Sully (1560–1641), systematically lowered it until he balanced government income and expenditure. His search for new revenues had some unhappy consequences, however. He not only continued the old custom of selling government offices, but permitted the beneficiary to transmit the office to his heir on payment of an annual fee—a lucrative new source of royal income but an even greater source of future difficulty. And the distribution of taxation remained lopsided, with some provinces much more heavily burdened than others, and with the poor paying much more than their share.

The Protestant States: Tudor England and the Dutch Republic

Henry VIII, 1509–1547

Critics have often accused European royalty of ruinous expenditures on palaces, retinues, pensions, mistresses, and high living in general, and yet such expenditures were usually a relatively small part of government outlays. War was really the major cause of disastrous financial difficulties for modern governments. Henry VIII's six wives, his court, his frequent royal journeys did not beggar England; the wars of Charles V and Philip II did beggar Spain.

Henry VIII made war prudently, never really risking large English armies on the Continent. He used the English Reformation to add to royal revenues by confiscating monastic property and rewarding his loyal followers with the lands so confiscated. Henry thus followed in the footsteps of his father in helping create a new upper class, which soon became a titled or noble class. The result was a "balanced monarchy," with substantial power to which there were, nonetheless, limits.

Under Henry VIII and his successors the newly rich continued to thrive, and many others also prospered. But Tudor England also had a class of the newly poor as a result of the enclosing of land for sheep farming. These small farmers, who lost their right to pasture animals on former common lands now enclosed in private estates, lost the margin that had permitted them to make ends meet.

Lacking the patience to attend to administrative details, Henry relied heavily on members of the new Tudor nobility as his chief assistants—and above all, Thomas Cromwell (c. 1485–1540). Cromwell was a master administrator who endeavored to make the royal administration more loyal, professional, and efficient, and less tied to the king's household and to special interests. In achieving much he antagonized other ambitious royal servants. Discredited by his enemies in the eyes of the king, Cromwell was executed for treason in 1540.

Henry could be ruthless, yet he could be tactful and diplomatic, as in his handling of Parliament to get everything he wanted, including statutes separating the English church from Rome and grants for his wars and conferences. Henry's parliaments were far from being elected legislatures based on wide suffrage. The House of Lords had a safe majority who were of Tudor creation or allegiance. The evolving and complex House of Commons was composed of the knights of the shire, chosen by the freeholders of the shires, and of the burgesses, representatives of incorporated towns or boroughs (not by any means all towns). In most boroughs a very narrow electorate chose these members of Parliament. Since most of the people of the shires were agricultural workers or tenants, rather than freeholders of land, the county franchise was also limited.

Still, even the Tudor parliaments were nearer a modern legislative assembly than the assemblies on the Continent. The great difference lay in the composition of the House of Commons, which had emerged from the Middle Ages not as a body representing an urban bourgeoisie, but as a blend of the rural landed gentry and the ruling groups in the towns. On the Continent the assemblies corresponding to the English Parliament usually sat in three distinct houses: one representing the clergy, another all the nobles, great and small, and a third the commoners.

By the beginning of the Tudor era, Parliament had already obtained much more than advisory powers. Parliament emerged from the Middle Ages with the power to make laws or statutes, although these did require royal consent. Yet, although the Tudor monarchs had their difficulties with Parliament, they usually got what they wanted without serious constitutional crises. This was particularly true of Henry VIII and Elizabeth I, who succeeded in part because their parliaments were generally recruited from men indebted to the Crown for their good fortune. But the Tudors also succeeded because they were skillful rulers, willing to use their prestige and gifts of persuasion to win the consent of Parliament.

Edward VI and Mary, r. 1547–1558

The death of Henry VIII in 1547 marked the beginning of a period of extraordinary religious shifts. Henry was succeeded by his only son, the ten-year-old Edward VI (r. 1547–1553), borne by his third wife, Jane Seymour. Led by the young king's uncle, the duke of Somerset, as lord protector, Edward's government pushed on into Protestant ways. The Six Articles, by which Henry had sought to preserve the essentials of Roman Catholic theology, worship, and even church organization, were repealed in 1547. In the brief reign of Edward VI an effort was made to prescribe uniformity of religious worship through a prayer book and articles of faith imposed by Parliament.

In 1553 the young king, always a frail boy, died. Protestant intriguers vainly attempted to secure the crown for a Protestant, Lady Jane Grey, a quiet, scholarly great-granddaughter of Henry VII. But Edward VI was followed by his older sister Mary (r. 1553–1558), daughter of Catherine of Aragon, whom Henry VIII had divorced. Mary had been brought up a Catholic and began at once to restore the old ways. Rebellion flared into the open when Mary announced her marriage to Philip II of Spain. Mary prevailed against the rebels, and Lady Jane Grey was executed for a plot in which she had never really participated.

Catholic forms of worship came back to the parishes, although, significantly, the church land settlement of Henry VIII remained undisturbed. In 1554 three statutes of heresy were reenacted, and vigorous persecution of Protestants followed; nearly three hundred people were burned. The queen was given the lasting name of "Bloody Mary," and the foundations of the English Protestant hatred and suspicions of Catholicism, traces of which still survive today, were laid.

Elizabeth I, r. 1558–1603

When Mary died in 1558, Henry VIII's last surviving child was Elizabeth, daughter of Anne Boleyn. She had been declared illegitimate by Parliament in 1536 at her father's request; Henry's last will, however, had rehabilitated her and she now succeeded as Elizabeth I (r. 1558–1603). She had been brought up a Protestant, and so once more the English churchgoer was required to switch faith. This time the Anglican Church was firmly established; the prayer book and Thirty-nine Articles of 1563 issued under Elizabeth have remained to this day the essential documents of the Anglican faith.

The Elizabethan settlement, moderate though it was, did not fully solve the religious problem. England still had a large Catholic minority, Catholic Spain was a serious enemy, and independent Scotland could always be counted on to take the anti-English side. The new queen of Scotland was Mary Stuart (r. 1542–1567), granddaughter of Henry VIII's sister Margaret, and therefore heir to the English throne should Elizabeth die without issue. Mary, who was Catholic, did not wait for Elizabeth's death to press her claim. On the ground that Elizabeth was illegitimate, she assumed the title to queen of England as well as Scotland.

Meantime, numerous Protestant groups not satisfied with the Thirty-nine Articles were coming to the fore. Collectively, they were called nonconformists or Puritans, since they wished to purify the Anglican Church of what they considered papist survivals in belief, ritual, and church government. In practice, their proposals ranged from moderate to radical. The moderates would have settled for a simpler ritual and retained the office of bishop. The Presbyterians would have replaced bishops with councils (synods) of elders, or *presbyters*, and adopted the full Calvinist theology. The Brownists, named for their leader Robert Browne (c. 1550–1633), would have gone still further

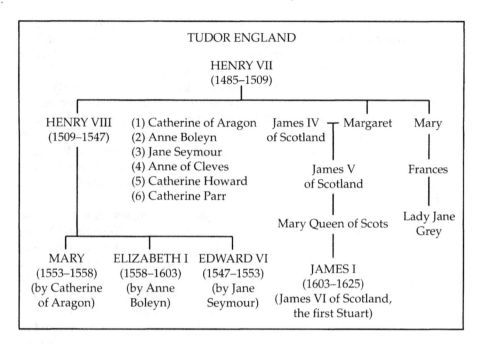

TUDOR ENGLAND

HENRY VII
(1485–1509)

HENRY VIII
(1509–1547)

(1) Catherine of Aragon
(2) Anne Boleyn
(3) Jane Seymour
(4) Anne of Cleves
(5) Catherine Howard
(6) Catherine Parr

James IV ⊤ Margaret
of Scotland

Mary

James V
of Scotland

Frances

Mary Queen of Scots

Lady Jane
Grey

MARY
(1553–1558)
(by Catherine
of Aragon)

ELIZABETH I
(1558–1603)
(by Anne
Boleyn)

EDWARD VI
(1547–1553)
(by Jane
Seymour)

JAMES I
(1603–1625)
(James VI of Scotland,
the first Stuart)

and made each congregation an independent body; from this group would emerge the Congregationalists.

Thus Elizabeth had a religiously divided kingdom at the start of her reign. Dissension seemed all around her, yet she was to reign for nearly fifty years. She was a Renaissance realist who personally set English policy, while accepting that it would be widely discussed. She was loved by her people, if not by her intimates. She never married, but played off foreign and domestic suitors one against another with excellent results for her foreign policy. She sought to avoid the expense and danger of war, always trying to get something for nothing. Most important, she realized that engaging in open war with Spain to protect the Netherlands, an ally that might soon no longer exist, could be disastrous.

Mistrusting the great English aristocrats, Elizabeth picked most of her ministers from the ranks just below the nobility, talented men who put her government in splendid order. Thanks to skillful diplomacy that made full use of the French and Dutch opposition to Spain, the final confrontation with Philip was postponed until 1588, when the kingdom was ready for it. Mary, as queen of Scots, proved no match for her gifted cousin. Mary was Catholic, and Scotland under the leadership of John Knox was on its way to becoming one of the great centers of Calvinism. The Scots revolted, and Mary was forced to take refuge in England, where Elizabeth had her put in confinement. Mary alive was a constant temptation to all who wanted to overthrow

Elizabeth. Letters, which Mary declared were forged, involved her in a conspiracy against Elizabeth. She was tried, convicted, and executed in 1587.

The dramatic crisis of Elizabeth's reign was the war with Spain, resolved in the defeat of the Armada in 1588. This victory arose from an unprecedented commitment of resources, especially on the Continent, where forty-eight thousand English soldiers fought. Forced to turn frequently to Parliament for approval of financial measures, Elizabeth met mounting criticism of her religious policy from Puritan members of the House of Commons. She got her money by grudgingly conceding more rights to the Commons. But the Commons responded with bolder criticism of the queen's policy. The stage was being set for the seventeenth-century confrontation between the Crown and Parliament.

During Elizabeth's final years the stage was also being set for a drama that was to have an even longer run—the Irish question. The half-English (Anglo-Irish) ruling class was out of touch with the local population, mostly peasants. In 1542 Ireland had been made a kingdom, but hardly an independent one, since the crowns of England and Ireland were to be held by the same person. Earlier, in 1495, a statute had put the Irish Parliament firmly under English control and had made laws enacted by the English Parliament applicable to Ireland as well. Attempts to enforce Protestant legislation passed by the English Parliament outraged the native Irish, who had remained faithful Catholics. In 1597 the Irish revolted under the earl of Tyrone. The favorite of Elizabeth's old age, the earl of Essex, lost influence by his failure to cope with the Irish rebels; Essex then became involved in a plot against the queen and was executed. The rebellion was put down bloodily in 1601, but the Irish issue remained unresolved. Elizabeth's successor, James I, sought to further the conversion of the Catholic Irish by planting Protestant settlers in the northern part of the island, known as Ulster.

The English Renaissance

Elizabeth's reign was marked by intrigue, war, rebellion, and personal and party strife. Yet there were solid foundations under the state and society that produced the wealth and victories of the Elizabethan Age and its attainments in literature, music, architecture, and science. The economy prospered in an era of unbridled individual enterprise. The solid administrative system was based on national unity. A common sentiment kept the English together and set limits beyond which most of them would not carry disagreement. Elizabeth herself played a large part in holding her subjects together. Her religious policy, for example, was directed at stretching the already broad principles and practices of the Church of England so that they would cover near-Catholicism at one extreme and near-Congregationalism at the other.

The age of Elizabeth was marked by a remarkable flowering of culture. This was the English Renaissance, when ladies and gentlemen played the lute, sang madrigals, admired painting, and sought to dress as did their counterparts in Italy. The high glory in the English Renaissance lay in its literature, in the works of William Shakespeare (1564–1616), Francis Bacon (1561–1626), Edmund Spenser (1552–1599), and many others who shaped the English language for generations to come.

These Elizabethans and Jacobeans were exuberant even in their refinement, full-blooded even in their learning. To a later generation they were uncouth, undisciplined, too full of the gusto of life. The love of excess is obvious in much Elizabethan writing: in the interminable, allusion-packed, allegory-made stanzas of the *Faerie Queene*; in the piling up of quotations from the ancient Greeks and Romans; in Shakespeare's fondness for puns and rhetorical devices; in the extraordinarily bloody tragedies and exuberant comedies that made Elizabethan drama second only to that of the ancient Greeks.

Shakespeare is the most quoted author of all time. The son of a glove manufacturer in Stratford-on-Avon, Shakespeare began his career on the London stage, where he was well recognized before he was thirty. He became part owner of the Globe Theatre, which from 1603 presented his plays to raucous London audiences. Ever since that time he has been recognized as the genius of Elizabethan literature and a supreme example of Renaissance views on individualism. He wrote classical dramas such as *Julius Caesar* and *Antony and Cleopatra*; famed comedies such as *The Tempest* and *Much Ado About Nothing*, stirring histories that gave the English a strong sense of pride, as in *Richard II* and *Henry IV*; and above all, the greatest tragedies since the days of the ancient Greeks—*Othello, Macbeth, Hamlet,* and *King Lear*. He took up literature's great themes: sin, revenge, love, honor.

Contemporaries of Shakespeare's contributed importantly to the Elizabethan Renaissance. Edmund Spenser's *The Faerie Queene* is recognized as perhaps the finest moral epic of Western writing. Sir Thomas More's *Utopia*, the product of an earlier time, became a revolutionary argument much debated in Shakespeare's time, as it described an ideal community on an island off the New World and argued that crime and violence did not come from the inherently corrupt nature of men and women, as had been argued in earlier centuries, but were the product of society. This view is commonplace today—it is widely believed that education, the environment, the laws of society, the nature of punishment, the workplace, and the family shape a person's behavior—but in the sixteenth and seventeenth centuries it was revolutionary.

The Elizabethan Renaissance, which ended with Queen Elizabeth's death in 1601, merged into the Jacobean period, in which Shakespeare produced some of his finest work. One other important product of this period was the King James Version of the Bible. In 1604 Puritan theologians asked James I to support a new translation of the Scripture, and the committee of scholars to whom he committed the assignment completed the Bible in the form we know it today, divided into chapters and verses, in 1611. Because it was in English, and hence accessible to lay readers, it increased literacy and profoundly influenced the development of the English language and an English self-consciousness.

Queen Elizabeth, the most consistently successful ruler of the sixteenth century, gave her name to an entire age. Here she appears before Parliament. This engraving is taken from Nobilitas Politica vel Civilis, *published in London in 1608. The book depicted the major dignitaries and nobles of England.* (By permission of the Folger Shakespeare Library)

Historians today emphasize that the political differences between England and the Continent reflected differences in social structure. England had its nobility or aristocracy ranging from barons to dukes. These nobles, plus Anglican bishops, composed the House of Lords. But in England, the younger sons of nobles were not themselves titled nobles, as they were on the Continent. Still, they were members, usually top members, of a complex social and political group that also included the squires and rich bankers and merchants, who almost always acquired landed estates and became squires themselves. This group comprised, in addition, leading lawyers and civil servants, the Anglican clergy, professors at Oxford and Cambridge (who at first were usually Anglican clergymen), officers in the army and navy, and a scattering of others in the liberal professions. This large and diverse group was never a closed caste and remained open to the socially mobile from the lower classes. The imprecise terms *gentry* and *gentlemen* are sometimes applied to this group, although the former is too exclusively rural in connotation and the latter is not always accurate in its implication that gentlemen invariably own enough property or capital so that they do not have to work for a living. Perhaps "ruling elite" or "establishment" would be as good names as any for this uniquely English class.

The Dutch Republic, 1602–1672

The United Provinces of the Northern Netherlands gained independence from Spain before the death of Philip II, although formal recognition of that independence came only in 1648. The Dutch state was an aristocratic merchant society, the first significant middle-class state in Europe with virtually no landed aristocracy. Despite its small size, it was a great power, colonizing in Asia, Africa, and the Americas, trading everywhere, and supporting an active and efficient navy.

Dutch ships played a predominant role in the international carrying trade; in the mid-seventeenth century the Dutch probably operated between half and three quarters of the world's merchant vessels. The Dutch also controlled the very lucrative North Sea herring fisheries. Their East India Company, founded in 1602, assembled and exploited a commercial empire. It paid large regular dividends and was a pioneer instance of the joint-stock company, sponsored by the state and pooling the resources of many businessmen who could not have risked such a formidable undertaking on an individual basis. The Bank of Amsterdam, founded in 1609, was also a model, minting its own florins and so innovative in its services to depositors that it made Amsterdam the financial capital of Europe.

The Dutch instituted life insurance and perfected the actuarial calculations on which it is based. Specialized industries flourished in particular cities and towns: diamond cutting, printing, and bookbinding at Amsterdam; shipbuilding at Zaandam; gin distilling at Schiedam; ceramics at Delft; woolens at Leiden; and linens at Haarlem. The Dutch were in the forefront of European agricultural progress; they created new farm plots called *polders* by diking and draining lands formerly under the sea, and they experimented with new techniques of scientific farming and with new crops. Among the latter were tulips, imported from the Ottoman Empire; the growing of tulip bulbs in the fields around Haarlem set off a wild financial speculation—the Tulipomania of the 1630s.

In government, the Dutch republic was no model of efficiency, for the United Provinces were united in name only. The seven provinces sent delegates to the Estates General, which functioned like a diplomatic congress rather than a central legislature. Each province did have a chief executive, the *stadholder*. Most of the provinces chose as stadholder the incumbent prince of the house of Orange, which made him a symbol of national unity. Twice in the seventeenth century, however, the preponderance of the Orange stadholder was challenged by the ranking local official of the most important province, the grand pensionary of Holland. In the first quarter of the century the grand pensionary, Jan van Olden Barneveldt (1547–1619), dominated Dutch politics until he was executed because of his support for Arminian doctrines of free will against Calvinist predestination. The grand pensionary Jan De Witt (1625–1672) ran the republic until he was lynched by a mob when the soldiers of Louis XIV overran an ill-prepared Holland in the 1670s.

The liberal Calvinists in Holland felt that religious fanaticism retarded the growth of commerce and of the state. Although there was a marked decline of tolerance by the end of the seventeenth century, the United Provinces generally remained relatively benign toward the Dutch Catholic minority. In particular, Johannes Althusius (1557–1638), a Westphalian who was a chief magistrate in the United Provinces from 1604, set forth clear arguments for permitting relatively free selection of religious worship. He would not tolerate atheists, but he extended his arguments to embrace Jews. Althusius's thoughts on religious freedom were advanced by Baruch Spinoza (1632–1677), a Dutch Jew, who began with the premise that personal liberty was the foundation of civil peace, obedience, and stability in the state, and that on matters of religion all persons must have absolute freedom of conscience. Under the influence of such theorists on the relationship of church and state, Amsterdam in particular became a haven for religious dissenters.

In the Netherlands, the beneficiaries of religious toleration were the large Catholic minority; Jewish refugees from Spain, Portugal, Poland, and Lithuania; and various Protestant dissidents escaping from Calvinist orthodoxy elsewhere on the Continent: Lutherans, Anabaptists, and in time even Arminians. As the southern Netherlands (present-day Belgium) became rigorously Catholic, Calvinist refugees from the south also added to the vigor and commercial growth of the north.

The style of Dutch civilization in this great age was solid, reasonable, sober, but far from colorless. This republic, through intelligence, hard work, hard trading, and adventurous exploration, won a high place in the world. But by 1700 the great days of the Dutch republic were ending, as it was eclipsed by its larger and more powerful neighbors. Although at times competitors with the English, Dutch fate was inked to Tudor policy, and the interchange between the countries—in trade, in technology, in manpower, even in artists—was close.

The Holy Roman Empire and the Thirty Years' War

Like the great wars of the sixteenth century, the Thirty Years' War of 1618–1648 was in part a conflict over religions. This time, however, most of the fighting took place in the Holy Roman Empire. The Habsburg Emperor, Ferdinand II (r. 1619–1637), made the last serious political and military effort to unify the Empire under Catholic rule. The Thirty Years' War began as a conflict between Catholics and Protestants; it ended as a struggle to reduce the power of the Habsburgs. The war finally involved most of the European powers and their colonies. It was, in the context of the times, the first "world war."

By the opening of the seventeenth century, the religious situation in the Empire was becoming increasingly unsettled. Calvinism had spread rapidly since 1555; Calvinist princes sponsored missions and banded together in the Protestant Union (1608). This led Catholic states to form the rival Catholic League (1609). Both the Union and the League also had political ambitions, representing the interests of German particularism—that is, of the individual states—against those of the Holy Roman Empire.

The religious situation concerned the Spanish Habsburgs as well as the Austrians. After the Dutch revolt, the Spaniards wanted to stabilize a line of communications between their Belgian and Italian lands traversing the Rhine valley and the Alps. The Dutch and the French both wanted to thwart Spanish plans for securing this overland route.

The Struggle over Bohemia and the Palatinate, 1618–1625

A major physical obstacle blocking Spanish communications was the Palatinate, a rich area in the Rhineland ruled by a Calvinist prince, the Elector Palatine. In 1618 the Elector Palatine, Frederick V, also headed the Protestant Union. Frederick hoped to break the Catholic hold on the office of emperor upon the death of the emperor Matthias (r. 1612–1619), who was old and childless. The electors of Saxony and Brandenburg were also Protestants. If there could be four Protestant electors instead of three when the emperor died, the majority could then install a Protestant. Because three electors were Catholic archbishops, the only way to add an additional Protestant was to oust the one lay Catholic elector, the king of Bohemia—a position filled in name by the emperor and in practice by his heir, Ferdinand, who was styled "king-elect."

Bohemia, today a part of the Czech Republic, was then a Habsburg crown land; its Czech inhabitants wanted local independence from the rule of German-speaking imperial governors and also of Vienna. Some Czechs expressed their defiance by following the faith that Jan Hus had taught them two centuries earlier, called *Utraquism* (from the Latin for "both") because it gave the laity communion in both bread and wine. While Ultraquists, Lutherans, and Calvinists were all tolerated in Bohemia, Catholicism was the official state religion. The prospect of Ferdinand becoming king of Bohemia and then emperor, with the added obligations of religious orthodoxy this would force upon him, alarmed Czech Protestants. When Protestant leaders opposing the erosion of Czech religious liberties were arrested, a revolt broke out, beginning with the "defenestration of Prague" (May 23, 1618), in which two Catholic imperial governors were thrown out of a window into a court-yard seventy feet below. Landing on a pile of dung, they escaped with their lives.

The Czech rebels offered the crown of Bohemia to Frederick of the Palati-nate. Frederick went off to Prague without ensuring the defense of his home territories in the Rhineland, which the Spaniards occupied in 1620. Mean-while, Catholics in Bohemia, Spain, and Flanders rallied against the Czech rebels. On the death of the emperor Matthias in 1619, the imperial electors duly chose the Catholic Habsburg Ferdinand II as his successor. Maximilian of Bavaria, head of the Catholic League, supported Ferdinand's cause in Bohemia in return for a promise of receiving his electoral vote. The Lutheran elector of Saxony also supported Ferdinand.

In Bohemia, Maximilian and the Catholic forces won the battle of the White Mountain (1620). Frederick now fled, and Ferdinand made the Bohemian throne hereditary in his own family. He also abolished toleration of Czech Utraquists and Calvinists, but granted it temporarily to Lutherans because of his obligations to the elector of Saxony. He executed the leaders of the rebel-lion, confiscated their lands, and sanctioned destruction of Protestantism in Bohemia.

The continued presence of Spanish forces in the Palatinate, however, had upset the balance of power. The Lutheran king of Denmark, Christian IV (r. 1588–1648), feared that the Habsburgs would move north toward the Baltic; the French faced a new Habsburg encirclement; the Dutch were threatened by an immediate Spanish attack. The Dutch therefore made an alliance with Christian IV, and another with the fugitive Frederick, agreeing to subsidize his attempt to reconquer the Palatinate. When fighting resumed, Frederick was defeated again, whereupon the emperor Ferdinand transferred the Pala-tine electorate to Maximilian of Bavaria (1625).

Intervention by Denmark and Sweden, 1625–1635

A vigorous and ambitious monarch, King Christian IV sought to extend Dan-ish political and economic power over northern Germany. To check the Dan-ish invasion, the German Catholics enlisted the help of the private army of Albert of Wallenstein (1583–1634). Wallenstein recruited and paid an army that lived off the land. He had bought huge tracts of Bohemian real estate confiscated from Czech rebels and was in essence a private citizen seeking to become a ruling prince. Although he never came close to success, his army was a major factor in the war at its most critical period. Together with the forces of the Catholic League, Wallenstein's army defeated the Danes and invaded Denmark.

The Hanging, *by Jacques Callot (1592–1635), who developed etching to virtuoso heights, is taken from his series* The Miseries of War, *which emphasized the savagery of the Thirty Years' War.* (The Art Museum, Princeton University. Gift of Junius S. Morgan, Class of 1888.)

Then, at the height of success, the emperor Ferdinand and his advisers overreached themselves. In the Edict of Restitution (1629) they demanded the restoration of all clerical estates that had passed from Catholic to Lutheran hands since 1551. The Edict also affirmed the Augsburg exclusion of Calvinists and radical Protestants from toleration. The Treaty of Lübeck, two months later, allowed Christian IV to recover his Danish lands but exacted from him a promise not to intervene again in Germany.

Ferdinand's heavy-handedness contrasted with Cardinal Richelieu's handling of the Huguenots at the siege of La Rochelle, which ended in 1628. There, despite the unprecedented length and ferocity of the siege and the wide agreement that fallen cities could be sacked, the royal army was kept under absolute discipline and food was provided to the starving inhabitants of the city. Richelieu acted with magnanimity, making it clear that while La Rochelle must abandon its political independence, and every church be returned to the Catholics, the price of heresy need not be paid in blood. What concerned Richelieu was maintaining a balance of power. The Habsburgs were now pressing into the Baltic, well beyond their spheres of influence, and although fellow Catholics, they were trespassers who ought to be forced to withdraw.

The more the emperor Ferdinand became indebted to the ambitious Wallenstein, the less he could control him. Wallenstein planned to found a new Baltic trading company with the remnants of the Hanseatic League, and by opening the Baltic to the Spaniards make possible a complete victory over the Dutch. Thus, when Ferdinand asked him for troops to use in Italy against the French, Wallenstein, intent on his northern plans, refused. Ferdinand dismissed Wallenstein, leaving the imperial forces under the command of the count von Tilly and of Maximilian of Bavaria, who had been alarmed by Wallenstein's activities and was placated by his departure. If Ferdinand had also placated the Protestants by revoking the Edict of Restitution, peace might have been possible. But he failed to do so, and the war was resumed with Gustavus Adolphus as the Protestant champion.

Called the "Lion of the North," Gustavus Adolphus (r. 1611–1632) was a much stronger champion than Christian of Denmark had been. Like Christian, he had ambitions for political control over northern Germany, and he hoped that Sweden might assume the old Hanseatic economic leadership. Gustavus brought a large well-disciplined army and added to it all the recruits, even prisoners, that he could induce to join him. Sharing the hardships of his troops, he usually restrained them from plunder. Richelieu agreed to subsidize his forces, and Gustavus agreed not to fight against Maximilian and to guarantee freedom of worship for Catholics. The Protestant electors of Brandenburg and Saxony mobilized, both to revive the Protestant cause and to protect the Germans against the Swedes.

German Protestant hesitation ended after a Catholic victory that probably did more to harm the Catholic cause than a defeat—the fall and sack of Magdeburg, a great symbol of the Protestant cause. Stormed by the imperialists in May 1631, it was almost wholly destroyed by fire and pillage. Each side sought to blame the sack on the other and sued the printing press to enlist public opinion in its cause throughout Europe. The Protestants accused the imperial commander-in-chief, Tilly, of planning the destruction of the city and its inhabitants—an accusation from which most historians absolve him, for the imperial troops clearly got out of hand. The Catholics countered by accusing the Protestants of setting the fires themselves. But in the long run, as the outpourings of the press took effect, the Protestant cause was strengthened.

The Protestant electors of Brandenburg and Saxony now allied themselves with Gustavus. In September 1631 Gustavus defeated Tilly. Combined with a defeat of the Spaniards off the Dutch coast, this turned the tide against the Habsburgs. The Saxons invaded Bohemia and recaptured Prague in the name of Frederick of the Palatinate, while Gustavus invaded the Catholic lands of south-central Germany, achieving an alliance of many princes and free cities. In the crisis, Ferdinand turned again to Wallenstein.

Gustavus was planning to reorganize all Germany, to unite the Lutheran and Calvinist Churches, and to become emperor—aims opposed by all the German princes, Catholic and Protestant alike. In the face of his ambitions, his allies proved untrustworthy, and his enemies, Maximilian and Wallenstein, drew together. In November 1632 the Swedes defeated Wallenstein at Lützen, but Gustavus Adolphus was killed.

Peace might now have been possible, yet the fighting continued. Richelieu preferred war to further advance French aims in the Rhineland; the Swedes needed to protect their heavy investment and come out of the fighting with some territory; the Spaniards hoped that Gustavus's death meant that the Habsburg cause could be saved and the Dutch at least defeated. As Wallenstein negotiated with the enemies of the Empire, hoping the French would recognize him as king of Bohemia, his army began to fade away, and he was again dismissed by the emperor Ferdinand. In February 1634 an English mercenary in the imperial service murdered Wallenstein and won an imperial reward. In September 1634 the forces of Ferdinand defeated the Protestants.

The Habsburg-Bourbon Conflict, 1635–1648

The remainder of the Thirty Years' War was a Habsburg-Bourbon conflict. The Protestant commander had to promise future toleration for Catholicism in Germany and to undertake to fight on indefinitely in exchange for a guarantee of French men and money. The war became transformed into a struggle between emerging national identities. The armies on both sides were a mixture of men from every nationality in Europe; they fought as professional soldiers, changing sides frequently. As these armies ranged across central Europe, the land was laid waste in their wake.

In 1635 the emperor Ferdinand at last relinquished the Edict of Restitution and made a compromise peace with the Protestant elector of Saxony. Most of the other Lutheran princes signed also. Alarmed by the imperial gains and by renewed Spanish activity in the Low Countries, Richelieu made new arrangements with Germany and a new alliance with the Dutch and openly declared war on Spain.

A Dutch victory in 1639 ended the power of the Spanish navy, which had been declining for years. Spanish strength was further sapped by the unrest in Catalonia and by a revolt in Portugal. Preoccupied by Catalonia, the Spanish allowed the election to the Portuguese throne of John IV, of Braganza (r. 1640–1656), a dynasty that would reign until 1910. Nor did the death of Richelieu (1642) and of Louis XIII (1643) alter French policy. A few days after the death of Louis, the French defeated the Spaniards so thoroughly at Rocroi that Spain was permanently removed from effective competition for European hegemony. Another factor making for a negotiated settlement of the war was the accession of the peace-loving Christina, daughter of Gustavus Adolphus, as Swedish queen in 1644.

Peace conferences were already underway in Westphalia—between Habsburgs and Swedes at Osnabrück and between Habsburgs and French nearby at Münster. The differences between the allies that had been unimportant during open warfare proved critical when it came to negotiating a religious settlement. The conferences dragged on for several years while fighting continued. The Dutch made a separate peace with the Spaniards and pulled out of the French alliance after they learned of secret French negotiations with Spain. French victories forced the wavering emperor Ferdinand III (r. 1637–1657) to agree to the terms that had been so painstakingly hammered out, and on October 24, 1648, the Peace of Westphalia put an end to the Thirty Years' War.

The Peace of Westphalia, 1648

The terms of the peace extended the Augsburg settlement to Calvinists as well as to Lutherans and Catholics. Princes would still "determine" the faith

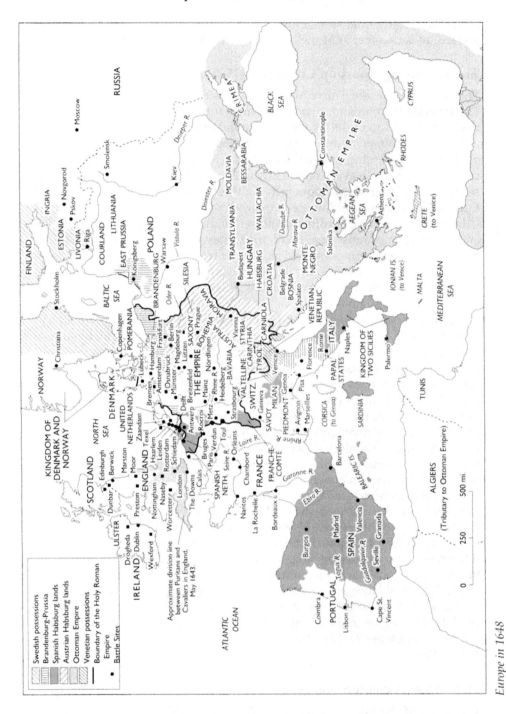

Europe in 1648

of their subjects, but the right of dissidents to emigrate was recognized. In most of Protestant Germany, multiplicity of sects was in fact accepted. On the question of ecclesiastical reservation, 1624 was designated as the base year for establishing the status of church property. For Protestants this was a great advance over the Edict of Restitution since states forcibly converted to Catholicism during the war won the right to revert to Protestantism. For Protestants in Habsburg territories, however, there was no toleration.

Although some of the separate German states came out well, the Empire itself was a victim. France secured part of Alsace and sovereignty over the bishoprics of Metz, Toul, and Verdun. Sweden received much of Pomerania plus three votes in the Imperial Diet and a large cash indemnity. As recompense for the loss of Pomerania, Brandenburg received the archbishopric of Magdeburg and several other bishoprics. The family of Maximilian of Bavaria kept the electoral vote of the Palatinate and a part of its territory; the rest was returned to the son of Frederick, who was restored as an elector, thus raising the total number of electors to eight.

The individual German states secured the right to conduct their own foreign affairs, making treaties among themselves and with foreign powers if these were not directed against the emperor. This principle of *Landeshoheit* was a face-saver for the Habsburgs, for the fact that the constituent states now had their own foreign services, their own armies, their own finances showed that the Holy Roman Empire was no longer a viable political entity. The Westphalian settlement also formally recognized the independence of the Dutch republic, already independent for over half a century, and of the Swiss Confederation, the nucleus of which had broken away from Habsburg control during the later Middle Ages.

The final outcome of the war raised almost as many problems as it solved. It did not end hostilities between two of the chief belligerents, France and Spain, who continued to fight for another eleven years, until the Treaty of the Pyrenees in 1659. The Peace of Westphalia satisfied neither the pope, who denounced it, nor many Protestants, who felt betrayed by it. Politically, the fresh successes of German particularism limited the Habsburgs' direct power in Germany to their family lands and enabled such states as Bavaria, Saxony, and, above all, Brandenburg-Prussia to move to the fore in German affairs.

One can appreciate why several modern historians have pronounced the Thirty Years' War a crucial event in the development of a "crisis" in seventeenth-century Europe. Whether the problems stemming from the Thirty Years' War induced, prolonged, or merely revealed a crisis in European societies, there can be no question that it made Europeans aware of the need for stability in matters of state and concerned with issues that could create the stability and security they lacked.

Absolutism and Slavery

Among the most difficult questions confronting modern historians is the expansion of slavery in the early modern period. In the wake of Renaissance discussions of the "dignity" of humankind, the traffic in human chattel seems the cruelest of hypocrisies. While the story of early modern slavery cannot but be deeply troubling, it is important to capture some of the complexity of that story.

The story begins with the Portuguese, both their exploration of the coast of Africa and their particular form of farming. Along the coast of Africa, over the course of the fifteenth century, the Portuguese established contacts with African slavers, who were willing to sell the enslaved enemies of various tribes to a wider market. For the Portuguese, those slaves were a valuable commodity: exotic, to decorate the homes of prosperous merchants as household slaves, and a durable form of labor for agricultural products the Portuguese were seeking to promote in European markets, sugar foremost.

Slavery has existed in most cultures and at most times. The Portuguese were not the first to deal in slave labor: It was customary in classical Greece and Rome, common as a form of revenge against one's enemies in warfare in and around Europe for most of the Middle Ages. By the time the Portuguese began massive export of African slaves, however, serfdom—analogous to, but not identical with, slavery—had been abolished in western Europe, although not in eastern Europe or Russia. The ownership of *labor* remained very much a part of the fabric of the European economy, but labor's relation to the individual was changing. Indentured servants, for example, of which there were thousands in early modern England and North America, owed a specified period of labor to another person, were therefore bound to remain with that person, but were not legally the "property" of that person in the same way that slaves were property.

Early modern slavery is inseparable from the emergence of global markets and commodities that Europeans could not produce at home: Cane sugar first, then tobacco and cotton were the largest crops. Each of these crops was, moreover, labor intensive, requiring manyfold more hours of labor than wheat, for instance, or wine. While the Portuguese were the first to introduce imported African slave labor to their colonies on Madeira and the Canary Islands, the use of African slaves for the production of crops in the Caribbean followed quickly thereafter, and by the middle of the seventeenth century, all the major European commercial empires—the English, the Dutch, the Spanish, and the Portuguese—were using imported African slave labor in their colonies.

The debates that had focused on the humanity of the indigenous peoples of the Americas were not immediately taken up with regard to African slaves. With the first encounters with the indigenous peoples of the Americas, European theologians, humanists, and friars took up the questions: What is to be human? What is it to be a barbarian? Are barbarians human? Initially, those questions were driven by the desire to convert the peoples of the Americas. If they were not human, they could not be made Christian. If they could be made Christian, then, even if they were "barbarian," they still had something essential in common with Europeans—a shared human "nature." The Spanish friar Bartolomé de Las Casas (1484–1566) argued passionately for the humanity and the innocence of the indigenous peoples of the Americas and for the necessity of "gentle" conversion, conversion by education. Ultimately, the Spanish Crown and the papacy endorsed one part of Las Casas's position—that indigenous peoples indeed shared a common human nature with Europeans and thus could be converted to Christianity—but not the other: Both Crown and pope agreed to forced conversions, disregarding the friar's insistence that all conversion must be voluntary.

African slaves, however, seem to have been viewed almost exclusively in terms of the labor they provided for crops of global markets. They were essential to the shift from labor organized by corporations—primarily guilds—to wage labor, from hierarchies of skill that were self-regulating to labor as a commodity with a certain value on the market. The beneficiaries of that shift were the same men who bought and sold the slaves and who sought control over international commerce: the entrepeneurs, whether Dutch, English, French, Spanish, or Portuguese.

Many processes of abstraction can be discerned in the early modern period: as the personal rule of Renaissance monarchs was transformed into a much more abstract notion of power; as "states" and "citizens" acquired a kind of reality impossible within the dialogic relations of feudalism; and as "labor" became something distinct from the man who performs it, his particular skill, his training, his hands. Within that process of abstraction, slavery is but one efficient method for managing labor. So abstracted, the human being performing that labor disappears in the calculus of profit and productivity.

The critique of slavery belongs to the eighteenth and nineteenth centuries. From the perspective of early modern Europe, slavery would only be effectively countered when the notion of each individual's "inalienable right" to certain kinds of freedom—implicit in Thomas More's *Utopia*, articulated more fully in Thomas Hobbes's *Leviathan*, and given its modern expression in John Locke's *Treatises on Government*—became a common political conviction, and not the ideal of solitary critics of absolutism. Paradoxically, not until Europeans began to articulate, in their opposition to absolutism, a notion of the individual as an entity possessing rights and privileges that were not corporate, not dependent upon membership in a family, a lineage, a guild, an estate, but were natural to each and every human being—not until political theorists articulated a conception of individual freedom in opposition to absolutism did Europeans have the terms, the moral construct needed effectively to critique the premises of slavery.

Science and Religion

> This most beautiful system of the sun, planets, and comets, could only proceed from the counsel and dominion of an intelligent and powerful Being. . . . He is eternal and infinite, omnipotent and omniscient; that is, his duration reaches from eternity to eternity; his presence from infinity to infinity; he governs all things, and knows all things that are or can be done. . . . We know him only by his most wise and excellent contrivances of things, and final

causes; we admire him for his perfections; but we reverence and adore him on account of his dominion: for we adore him as his servants; and a god without dominion, providence, and final causes, is nothing else than Fate and Nature. Blind physical necessity, which is certainly the same always and everywhere, could produce no variety of things. All that diversity of natural things which we find suited to different times and places could arise from nothing but the ideas and will of a Being necessarily existing.   (Isaac Newton (1642–1727), from the Principia)*

The relation between religion and science in the twentieth century was largely adversarial. It was not always so. As we saw, for Galileo nature was one of the two books of revelation, wherein God's design, indeed, something of God's truth and nature, could be discerned. It was, rather, in premodern Europe, a question both of the character of nature and of God's relation to it. For the medieval scholastic Thomas Aquinas, nature demonstrated the abundance and diversity of God's creation, its multitudes a signal of God's magnificence. Galileo shared Aquinas's express delight in the abundance and diversity of nature, a sense much amplified by all the "new" flora and fauna of the "new worlds." Even Newton understood scientific inquiry in terms of revelation, but by the time Newton wrote, Europeans had come fundamentally to reconceive the character of nature and of God's relation to it.

The story of "science" in the early modern world cannot be separated from "religion." The relationship between the two was not originally adversarial: The Church often provided the education in those classical texts that served as the foundation of inquiries that we now consider "scientific." In the sixteenth century, the conflict emerged over tools for the interpretation of nature. As the Church had traditionally held and reconfirmed at the Council of Trent, Scripture was to be the hermeneutic for nature, the lens through which humankind looked in order to make sense of nature. Increasingly in the sixteenth century, men took up mathematics as that tool by which they could make sense of nature. For Galileo, God had written the "book of nature" in the language of mathematics—mathematics was a system of numbers, themselves pure symbols, with constant rules that could be applied in diverse circumstances. For Kepler, for example, mathematics offered the means to explain the elliptical movement of planets. Galileo and Kepler, in other words, saw Scripture and nature as mutually autonomous books of revelation, the one written in the living languages of Hebrew and Greek, the other in the language of mathematics, a language, moreover, Galileo understood as God's.

Galileo and the Church came to conflict not over the importance of the study of nature, or even God's hand in the creation of nature, but over a question of authority: With conflicting interpretations of optical data, which authority would decide the correct answer? The Church held that Scripture, and the long tradition of interpretation of it in the schools, was authoritative

---

*Trans. Andrew Motte, ed. Florian Cajori (Berkeley: University of California Press, 1934), pp. 544–46.

in all questions pertaining to the interpretation of nature. Galileo, Kepler, and Newton would all argue for mathematical laws—Galileo as the "language" in which the book of nature "had been written," Newton as the very laws of organization that God himself had set in motion. Galileo, one of the most combative in the entire history of "science," ridiculed the blind acceptance of ancient authorities, whether Aristotle or Ptolemy on the one hand, or Jerome or Augustine on the other, in the face of optical data that contravened their "opinions"—not truths.

Isaac Newton was born in the year Galileo died. Newton's conception of God, captured in the passage from the *Principia*, would have been utterly alien to Galileo. It was not the presence or absence of God that divided those thinkers we now call "scientific" from the Church. All held as a fundament of their investigations that God had created nature and the world as they knew it. Galileo was most certainly a Christian. As a young man, he had even considered entering a religious order. He believed in the doctrine of Incarnation, even as his experiments challenged the medieval physics that had helped to explain that doctrine "scientifically." Perhaps more revealingly, he delighted in the copiousness of God's creation and creativity: He conceived of God as essentially creative and generous.

Newton was a monotheist and, many scholars have argued, not truly Christian. His conception of God had been influenced by the writings of the great Jewish medieval scholar Moses Maimonides. As is evident in the quote from the *Principia*, Newton believed in a God, one of "dominion" more than creation, a "Being," not a Father. Newton's God ordered the universe, not out of mercy or beneficence, but out of intelligence and providence.

Experimental Science

As an increasing number of Europeans rejected Scripture as the most accurate interpretive tool, two different "methods" began to acquire definition. One, which had its origins in medieval philosophy, we now call *deduction:* One tests a hypothesis against the data of experience. The hypothesis is formulated before the experience is brought directly to test its accuracy. The other, which received its name from the English philosopher and politician Francis Bacon, *induction*, proceeds in the opposite direction: from experience to hypothesis. In *Novum Organum* (1620), Bacon argued that all things must be held possible until tested. Bacon named "the empirical faculty," which learns from experience, and argued for the superiority of a method that proceeds from the particular observed phenomenon to the general conclusion. Most modern science relies on a combination of both methods, but until the French mathematician René Descartes (1596–1650) gave deduction its current rigor, deduction suffered from the view Bacon captured: It was a method susceptible to exactly those human opinions and assumptions to which Montaigne, forty years earlier, had called attention.

"Empiricism," a modern term for a particular way of approaching the world and how one arrives at truth, has its roots in the argument for induction as a method. At center is the primary weight given to observed data. One derives constants, laws, and theorems from observations over time. Observation acquired epistemological validity in the sixteenth century. In its wake, Europeans would come to conceive of the human eye not, as it had been throughout most medieval optics, as the passive recipient of emanations from objects, but itself active. The eye did not merely receive optical information, but *processed* it first through the "lenses" of the eye—an indication of how scientific an *instrument* various thinkers came to conceive the eye as being—and then through the brain's highly complex mechanisms for the comprehension of data. They also came to develop, often through a process of trial and error, a wide range of new instruments whose function was to augment observation, from the telescope and microscope to eyeglasses.

Galileo was also one of many who contributed to the invention of new instruments that permitted the more exact measurements and more detailed observations needed by inductive science. It is probable, for example, that Dutch glassmakers first put two lenses together and discovered that they could thus obtain greater magnification. Galileo improved that initial telescope by some tenfold magnification. That improved telescope enabled him to see, for the first time in human history, the craters on the moon, some of its mountains, the texture of its surface; later improvements brought the visual knowledge of moons around Jupiter. The simple technology of two lenses, fixed at a predetermined distance from one another, so augmented the natural vision of the eye to make visible for the first time exponentially more of the heavens: more planets, moons around planets, the actual topography of the moon's surface, and, ultimately perhaps the most important, more stars than could be counted. With his observation, that the number of stars was too great to count, Galileo introduced a sense of the heavens as truly boundless. Later in the century two Dutchmen employed it in the form of a microscope—Jan Swammerdam (1637–1680) to analyze blood (he probably discovered red corpuscles), and Anthony Van Leeuwenhoek (1632–1723) to view and describe protozoa and bacteria. Thus both the telescope and the microscope made visible worlds that Europeans had never imagined: stars they had not known existed, microbes they had never conceived of. Those microbes would, eventually, provide medicine the data to develop the concept of "bacteria" that could explain a wide range of illnesses incurable until their causes were discerned. The "seen" world expanded exponentially in the sixteenth and seventeenth centuries, even as it challenged all assumptions about the world Europeans had previously held as "visible."

Working from the experiments of Galileo, other technicians developed such instruments of measurement as the thermometer and the barometer. Using the barometer, the French mathematician Blaise Pascal (1623–1662) proved that air pressure diminished with altitude; for this he went on to question the adage attributed to Rabelais, "Nature abhors a vacuum," by positing that a vacuum might be possible. The discoveries of the microscope and telescope are also inseparable from the very conceptualization of a vacuum: something that is a nothing, that the naked eye cannot see, but that can be measured using instruments developed to serve observation. It speaks to the convictions of the seventeenth century that Robert Boyle (1627–1691), son of an Irish earl, could not conclusively demonstrate the existence of a vacuum—in the twentieth century, scientists proved conclusively that it could not exist, using highly sensitive instrumentation and theories drawn from physics—but he was successful in establishing the reliability of his *method.* He sought to duplicate experience consistently as a foundation for science; that method became a standard scientific practice.

King Charles II of England roared with laughter on being told that members of his Royal Society were weighing the air. Yet the Royal Society for Improving Natural Knowledge, founded in 1662, and its French counterpart, the Académie des Sciences (1666), were important promoters of scientific investigation. An international scientific community arose through the formal exchanges of the corresponding secretaries and the publications of such academies, and also through the extensive private correspondence among members and their acquaintances. Both professionals and aristocrats joined learned societies; many a gentleman and occasionally a lady worked in a private laboratory or observatory. Robert Boyle discovered the law of physics named after him–that under compression the volume of a gas is inversely proportional to the amount of pressure. The publication of scientific discoveries helped bridge the gap between theory and practice, for it showed scientists where their work related to that of others and helped indicate which problems most needed attention.

The seventeenth can be called the century of mathematics. Many of the brightest talents, the most original minds, were captivated by mathematics in much the same way that theology captivated the brightest minds of the previous period. Galileo had called it the language in which God had written the book of nature. In the seventeenth century, mathematics was applied to many different aspects of human experience, in the process acquiring greater precision and a plethora of newly "discovered" laws. In 1585 Simon Stevin (1548–1620), a Fleming, published *The Decimal, Teaching with Unheard-of Ease How to Perform All Calculations Necessary among Men by Whole Numbers without Fractions.* Another great timesaver was devised by the Scot John Napier (1550–1617) with his *Marvelous Rule of Logarithms* (1616), which shortened the laborious processes of multiplying, dividing and finding square roots. Descartes worked out analytical geometry. The mathematical achievements of the century culminated in a method for dealing with variables and probabilities. Pascal made a beginning with studies of games of chance, and Dutch insurance actuaries devised tables to estimate the life expectancy of their clients. The Englishman Sir Isaac Newton (1642–1727) and the German baron Gottfried Wilhelm von Leibniz (1646–1716) invented calculus, apparently quite independently of each other. Without Cartesian geometry and calculus, Newton could never have made the calculations supporting his revolutionary hypotheses in astronomy and physics.

In astronomy the heliocentric theory advanced by Copernicus in the sixteenth century proved to be only a beginning. It raised many difficulties, notably when observation of planetary orbits did not confirm Copernicus's belief that the planets revolved about the sun in circular paths. The German Johannes Kepler (1571–1630) proved mathematically that the orbits were in fact elliptical. Then Galileo's telescope revealed the existence of spots on the sun, rings around Saturn, and moonlike satellites around Jupiter. All this evidence led Galileo to publish a book in 1632 defending the heliocentric concept and ridiculing supporters of the traditional geocentric (earth-centered) theory.

A celebrated story recounts Galileo's experiment of dropping balls of different weights from the Leaning Tower of Pisa to test Aristotle's theory that objects fall at velocities proportional to their weight. While the story itself may not be true, Galileo did prove Aristotle wrong. Despite the tendency toward self-promotion, Galileo's studies of projectiles, pendulums, and falling and rolling bodies helped establish modern ideas of acceleration and inertia, which Newton later formulated mathematically.

In 1687 Newton published the laws of motion together with other great discoveries in *Philosophiae Naturalis Principia Mathematica* (Mathematical Principles of Natural Philosophy). He had made many of these findings two decades earlier, when he was still an undergraduate at Cambridge; he was recognized in his later years, gaining a professorship at Cambridge, a knighthood, the presidency of the Royal Society, and the well-paid post of Master of the Mint. But Newton's greatest contribution was the law of gravitation. It followed from his laws of motion, which picture bodies moving in response to forces acting upon them. These forces are at work in the mutual attraction of the sun, the planets, and their satellites, which are thereby held in their orbits. Newton also promoted the development of optics by using a prism to separate sunlight into the colors of the spectrum. He demonstrated that color is not intrinsic to an object but the result of reflection and absorption of light. Again, in this small "discovery" was embedded a world transformed: Color was no longer the "property" of an object, but contingent upon light, existing, in other words, in the space between the observer and the object. It is how we conceive the world now, but it was yet another tiny revolution in Europeans' understanding of perception itself.

Meanwhile, the mechanistic views of the physicists were invading geology and physiology. In 1600 the English physician William Gilbert (1540–1603) suggested that the earth itself was a giant magnet. In 1628 William Harvey (1578–1657) published his demonstration that the human heart is a pump driving the blood around the body through a single circulatory system. Harvey's theory, confirmed a generation later through microscopic observation, discredited the hypothesis handed down from Galen that the blood in the arteries moved quite separately from that in the veins. And in 1679 the Italian anatomist Alphonso Borelli (1608–1679) showed that the human arm is a lever and that muscles do mechanical work.

World-Machine and Rationalism

All these investigations in the various sciences tended to undermine the older Aristotelian concept of a thing's being "perfect." Instead of perfect circles, post-Copernican astronomy posited ellipses; instead of bodies moving of themselves, Newton pictured bodies responding to forces acting upon them. All these investigations; paradoxically suggested a law of uniformity that simplified, explained, and coordinated many separate laws into one general law. Newton finally drew everything together in the grand mechanical concept that has been called the Newtonian world-machine.

The new science had obvious theological and philosophical implications. Natural science of itself does not deal with theology and philosophy; yet the rise of modern science was associated with a system of values for which the best name is probably *rationalism*. This is a broad term. It is possible to be both a rationalist and a believer in a supernatural God, like Thomas Aquinas and other medieval Schoolmen. In the early modern West, however, rationalism tended to reduce God to a First Cause that started the world-machine going but then did not interfere with its operation. The new mechanistic interpretation of the universe regarded God not as the incomprehensible Creator and Judge but as the architect of a world-machine whose operations men and women could grasp if only they could apply their reason properly.

Rationalism found its most radical spokesperson in René Descartes. Descartes took up what he considered the devastation of Montaigne's claim, that all human knowledge is subjective and contingent. He sought, as he wrote, to arrive at a foundation for certainty, for knowledge that could not be subsequently challenged as prejudiced or ill-founded. When he was a young man, as his *Discourse of Method* (1637) relates, he resolved to mistrust all authorities, theological or intellectual. His skepticism swept everything aside, until he concluded that there was only one fact that he could not doubt: his own existence. There must be reality in the self that was engaged in the process of thinking and thus of doubting: Indeed, the phrase he formulated, "Cogito ergo sum" ("I think, therefore I am"), might better have been I *doubt*, therefore I am. Building from this one fact, Descartes reconstructed the world until he arrived at God—a supreme geometer whose mathematical orderliness foreshadowed the great engineer of the Newtonian world-machine.

But where Newton would proceed inductively, at least in part, by relying on the data of scientific observations and experiments, Descartes proceeded deductively, ultimately deriving the universe and God from his initial formulation. The world that Descartes reconstructed proved to be two separate worlds—that of mind and soul, on the one hand, and that of body and matter, on the other. This was Cartesian dualism. He claimed competence to deal in detail only with the material world; yet the way in which he dealt with it intimated that it was the only world that counted—witness his boast that, if given matter and space, he could construct the universe himself.

The problem, ultimately, was that the Cartesian method could posit the existence of a perfect being, superlative in qualities of goodness, power, reason, and knowledge, but it could in no way make the case for the Christian God. Cartesianism could not account for the Incarnation, for the life of Jesus Christ, or for the qualities of divine mercy and love that had acquired such central importance in sixteenth-century theology. Descartes's God was rational and mechanical, but not loving, forgiving, or historically present in

Portrait of Descartes by Frans Hals.   *(Réunion des Musées Nationaux/Art Resource, NY)*

the lives of humankind—it was a very short step to the First Cause or, in more popular terms, the Watchmaker. Lost were God's human emotions.

In hindsight we have come to view the many different "discoveries" in the fields of optics, mathematics, physics, astronomy, botany, biology, geology, and medicine in aggregate as a "revolution." At the center were shifts in conceptualizations that would transform how Europeans understood their world and their place in it. First of those shifts was the power accorded to observation. The "discoveries" of the "new worlds" were accorded veracity, even as they contravened everything the classical and Christian traditions had taught. The human eye was granted far greater integrity, and many different Europeans sought to develop more accurate instruments for the augmentation of vision. In granting observation such epistemological weight, Europeans were confronted with opposite methods for the relation between thesis and observation: deduction and induction. In the sixteenth and seventeenth centuries, those convinced of the rightness of induction then pursued ways to regularize the gathering and interpreting of visual data. Those methods became the basis for modern scientific methods: "experimentation," elaborated by Robert Boyle, became a trusted basis for knowledge.

Psychologically, perhaps the greatest shift began with Descartes's formulation of the other method, deduction. Cartesianism severed the world of matter from the world of spirit, cutting the complex interconnections of the doctrine of Incarnation. At the same time, Descartes's insistence that human reason could be the basis of all knowledge both laid the foundation for Newton's rationalism and accepted as its *a priori* that belief could not be the basis of any true knowledge. Belief and knowledge were epistemologically discrete from one another. Cartesianism's shift in conceptualization paved the way for a sense of the world as relentlessly rational, truly *subject* to laws, whose Governor had at one time set in motion those laws, but who had now removed Himself from the realm of human affairs. The age of miracles ended with Cartesianism.

While many still considered their work to be the study of God's revelation in nature, the attention to method, the underlying conviction that nature was "governed" by "laws," altered what people conceived God's relation to nature and to humankind to be. Newton's concept of the world as a machine was tempered by his own belief that the machine depended on a nonmechanical principle, on a God. The planetary system was, he wrote, "the effect of nothing else than the Wisdom and Skill of a powerful ever living Agent." This Agent could "make Worlds of several sorts in several Parts of the Universe";* earth and humanity's activities on it were no longer the center of all existence. The relation of God to matter was reconceived, in steps, culminating in Newtons' "Agent." Capriciousness, the capacity for miracles—those moments in which God chose to overthrow his own ordering of the world—could not be accommodated in the new epistemology. "Belief" in miracles was just that, belief, an act of "faith," no longer of reason.

Together all these conceptual shifts altered how professors, doctors, and other learned elites conceptualized their world and their place in it. "Science" became a recognizable body of knowledge. It was not so much that it displaced theology or classical philosophy—those were still the subject of study—but that "science" claimed to be certain knowledge, tested by consistent methods, the product of rigorous and disciplined reason. Not until the twentieth century would "science" be trusted by the great majority of Europeans and then Americans as knowledge, but by the end of the seventeenth century, the brightest lights of Europe were drawn less to theology than to experimental science. For them, the best tools for acquiring *certain* knowledge were no longer to be found in dialectic (scholasticism), philology (humanism), or biblical hermeneutics (Reformation), but in either the inductive or deductive *method*. In that trust in the sheer power of human reason to build systems of knowledge was both the optimism of the next two centuries—the sustaining conviction that one simply needed to find the one unifying principle of the universe—and the confrontation with fragmentation,

---

*Quoted in *Main Currents of Western Thought,* ed. Franklin Le Van Baumer (New Haven: Yale University Press, 1978), pp. 323–25.

asymmetry, particularity, subjectivity, and contingency that so dominated the twentieth century.

Summary

By the sixteenth century, changes in political, social, family, and economic structure were underway that marked the beginning of what historians call the modern period. In the fifteenth and sixteenth centuries, the modern state system took shape as well-organized states competed for power in western Europe. With the emergence of Spain, France, and England came the growth of national patriotism. European states developed diplomatic services and professional armies. The first modern navies were also built. Increases in population, trade, and prices fostered conditions that led to warfare.

Some historians have called the invasion of Italy by Charles VIII of France the "first modern war." The invasion enmeshed France in a long and complex power struggle with the Habsburgs.

Philip II of Spain (r. 1556–1598), a powerful, hard-working monarch, waged a battle on many fronts: against Protestantism, against France, against the Ottoman Turks, and against his subjects in the Netherlands. The Dutch revolted against Philip's attempt to limit their autonomy and to use the Inquisition against Protestants. During a long, costly war, the northern provinces declared their independence from Spain. When Elizabeth I helped the Dutch, Philip launched an armada to invade England. The destruction of the armada marked a turning point both for Spain (a gradual international decline) and for England (an increase in international standing).

In Spain, as elsewhere, the growth of absolutism was marked by persistent struggles against local centers of power. Philip centralized administration and reduced the power of the Cortes, the representative assemblies. Yet Spain failed to establish a sound economic footing for its power. Despite the influx of New World bullion, the Spanish economy stagnated, while Philip's wars drained the treasury.

During Spain's Golden Age (1516–1659) Cervantes penned *Don Quixote*, a landmark in literature. In religion, St. Teresa of Avila and St. John of the Cross became important figures to laity everywhere. The paintings of El Greco embodied ideas of the Catholic Reformation.

In the late sixteenth century France was plunged into civil and religious strife that finally subsided after Henry of Navarre, the first Bourbon king, took the throne. By the Edict of Nantes (1598), Henry IV assured the Huguenots of some religious toleration. He tried to improve the economy but did not solve the problem of fiscal stability.

In England, Henry VIII moved cautiously in war and added to the treasury by his seizure of monastic property. Tactful in handling Parliament, which had the power to enact laws, Henry and later Elizabeth I moved against the enemies of England: Spain and the Catholic church. Elizabeth firmly established the Protestant religion in England and scored success in war with Spain.

But she had to concede rights to the House of Commons, foreshadowing the struggle between the Crown and Parliament of the next century. The Tudor period also saw the beginning of the Irish question. In literature, William Shakespeare expressed the exuberance of the Elizabethan Age, a period of significant achievement in music, architecture, and science.

The Thirty Years' War (1618–1648) began as a religious conflict but ended as a political power struggle between France and the Habsburgs. During the war, armies ravaged the land. The final settlements, negotiated at the peace conferences of Westphalia and Münster, extended the Peace of Augsburg to include Calvinists; made territorial concessions to France, Sweden, and Brandenburg; and recognized the right of individual German states to conduct their own foreign policies.

In the wake of the devastatingly conflicting claims to certainty by religious factions in the sixteenth century, Europeans worked to find a basis for certain knowledge. In the seventeenth century emerged two "methods": induction and deduction. Each of those methods had its proponents who claimed it was the basis for certain knowledge—knowledge that was not contingent, subjective, or prejudiced. Ultimately, both methods contributed to a new conceptualization of God and his relation to the universe. Both assumed that the natural world was "governed" by "laws," laws that could be mathematically determined. They shared with medieval Christianity the conviction that God could be discerned in the natural world; unlike their medieval predecessors, they approached that world not in wonder or reverence, but convinced of its inherent rationality, its subjection to mathematical—that is, purely and perfectly abstract—laws. God's humanity, his mercy and love, receded, as he was increasingly conceived as First Cause of a universe governed by mechanical laws.

Chronology

1358	Jacquerie
r. 1364–1380	King Charles V "the Wise" of France (Valois)
c. 1370–1380	Decline of Estates General
1377–1446	Filippo Brunelleschi
1378–1417	Great Schism (Western Christian Church)
1378	Revolution of the Ciompi in Florence
c. 1380–1483	Struggle in France between Burgundians and Armagnacs
1381	Peasants' Revolt in England
1386–1466	Donatello
1394–1460	Prince Henry of Portugal
1399	English first used to open Parliament

1400

15th century	Rise of trade, money economies
	First modern libraries in Italy
	Syphilis increases dramatically
	Compass and navigation charts come into general use
Early 15th century	Gunpowder first used in European wars
1405–1471	Leon Battista Alberti
c. 1412–1431	Joan of Arc
1414–1417	Council of Constance
1415	Battle of Agincourt
1420	Treaty of Troyes
r. 1422–1461	King Charles VII of France
1432	City of Angkor abandoned
1440s	Moveable type perfected in the Rhineland
c. 1444–1510	Sandro Botticelli

1450

r. 1450–1466	Francesco Sforza of Milan
1452–1498	Girolamo Savonarola
1452–1519	Leonardo da Vinci
1455–1485	Wars of the Roses in England
r. 1461–1483	King Louis XI "the Spider" of France

1462	Cosimo de' Medici founds Platonic Academy
1466–1536	Desiderius Erasmus
r. 1469–1492	Lorenzo de' Medici "the Magnificent" of Florence
1469–1527	Niccolò Machiavelli
1469	Marriage of Isabella of Castile and Ferdinand of Aragon
1471–1528	Albrecht Dürer
1472–1553	Lucas Cranach
r. 1474–1504	Queen Isabella of Castile
1474–1566	Bartolomé de Las Casas
1475–1519	Vasco Nuñez de Balboa
1475–1564	Michelangelo Buonarotti
1478	Start of Spanish Inquisition
1478–1535	Thomas More
c. 1478–1541	Francisco Pizarro
r. 1479–1516	King Ferdinand of Aragon (1504–1516, also king of Castile)
c. 1480–1547	Ferdinand Magellan
r. 1483–1498	King Charles VIII of France
r. 1483–1485	King Richard III of England (York)
1483	Russia crosses Urals into Asia
1483–1546	Martin Luther
1484–1531	Huldrych Zwingli
r. 1485–1509	King Henry VII (Tudor) of England
1485–1547	Hernan Cortés
1488	Bartholomeo Dìas rounds Cape of Good Hope
1490–1553	François Rabelais
1491–1556	Ignatius Loyola
1492	Reconquista complete: Granada, the last Muslim stronghold, surrenders to Isabel and Ferdinand; all Jews expelled from Iberian peninsula (1502, all Muslims expelled) Columbus's first voyage across the Atlantic
r. 1492–1503	Pope Alexander VI (Borgia)
r. 1493–1519	Holy Roman Emperor Maximillian I (Habsburg)
r. 1494–1525	Elector Frederick "the Wise" of Saxony
1494	Treaty of Tordesillas
1495	First Holy League

1497	Vasco da Gama reaches India
1497–1543	Hans Holbein
r. 1498–1515	King Louis XII of France

1500

16th century	Military revolutions English enclosure movement begins Serfdom virtually extinct in western Europe Decline of Hanseatic League
r. 1503–1513	Pope Julius II (della Rovere)
r. 1509–1547	King Henry VIII of England
1509–1564	John Calvin
1511	Erasmus, *Praise of Folly*
r. 1513–1521	Pope Leo X (Medici)
1513	Machiavelli, *The Prince* (published posthumously)
1515–1582	Teresa of Avila
1516	Erasmus's Greek New Testament
1516	Thomas More, *Utopia* Francis I signs the Concordat of Bologna
r. 1516–1556	King Charles I of Spain (Habsburg)
r. 1519–1556	Holy Roman Emperor Charles V (Habsburg)
1519–1522	First circumnavigation of the world
1520	Martin Luther, *To the Christian Nobility of the German Nation*
c. 1520– c. 1600	Decimation of indigenous peoples of the Americas
r. 1523–1534	Pope Clement VII (Medici)
1524–1525	The Revolution of the Common Man in the Empire
1525	Publication of *The Twelve Articles*
	Battle of Pavia
1525–1569	Pieter Brueghel
1530–1596	Jean Bodin
1533–1592	Michel Eyquem de Montaigne
r. 1534–1549	Pope Paul III (Alessandro Farnese)
1535–1540	Dissolution of the monasteries in England
1541–1614	El Greco
1542–1621	Robert Bellarmine

1543	Andreas Vesalius, *De humanis corporis fabrica* Nicolaus Copernicus, *De revolutionibus orbium coelestium*
1545	Council of Trent convened
1547	Emperor Charles V defeats League of Schmalkalden
r. 1547–1553	King Edward VI of England
1547–1616	Miguel de Cervantes

1550

c. 1552–1599	Edmund Spenser
c. 1552–1616	Richard Hakluyt
r. 1553–1558	Queen Mary of England
r. 1555–1559	Pope Paul IV (Carafa)
r. 1556–1598	King Philip II of Spain (Habsburg)
r. 1558–1603	Queen Elizabeth I of England
r. 1559–1565	Pope Pius IV (Medici)
1559	Treaty of Cateau-Cambrésis Index of Forbidden Books
1561–1626	Francis Bacon
1562–1598	Religious Wars in France
1563	Council of Trent brought to a close
1564–1616	William Shakespeare
r. 1566–1572	Pope Pius V (Ghisleri) (canonized)
1566–1648	Revolt of the Netherlands
1571	Battle of Lepanto
r. 1572–1585	Pope Gregory XIII (Ugo Buoncompagni)
1572	St. Bartholomew's Day Massacre in France
1573–1631	John Donne
1577–1640	Peter Paul Rubens
1579	Union of Utrecht
1582	Gregorian Calendar Reform
1583–1645	Hugo Grotius
1588	The Armada
1588–1679	Thomas Hobbes
r. 1589–1610	King Henry IV of France (Bourbon)
r. 1592–1605	Pope Clement VIII (Ippolito Aldobrandini)

1598	Edict of Nantes
1599–1641	Anthony van Dyck
1599–1660	Diego de Silva y Velásquez

1600

r. 1603–1625	King James I of England (James VI of Scotland) (Stuart)
r. 1605–1621	Pope Paul V (Borghese)
1606–1669	Rembrandt van Rijn
1608–1674	John Milton
r. 1623–1644	Pope Urban VIII (Maffeo Barberini)
r. 1625–1649	King Charles I of England
1632–1675	Jan Vermeer
1648	Treaties of Westphalia
1649–1660	Commonwealth of England

Suggestions for Further Reading

CHAPTER 1:   The Late Middle Ages in Eastern Europe

General Accounts

A History of the Crusades, Vol. 1: The First Hundred Years, ed. M. W. Baldwin; Vol. II: *The Later Crusades, 1189–1311,* ed. R. L. Wolff and H. W. Hazard; 2d ed., K. M. Setton, general ed. (Madison: University of Wisconsin Press, 1969). Collaborative work with authoritative contributions by many scholars; includes good bibliographies.

Cemal Kafadar, *Between Two Worlds: The Construction of the Ottoman State* (Berkeley: University of California Press, 1995). An introduction to the historiography on the Ottoman Empire, and some of the sources.

Justin McCarthy, *The Ottoman Turks: An Introductory History to 1923* (London: Longman, 1997). A survey of the Ottoman Empire from the thirteenth-century Turks to the modern day.

Steven Runciman, *A History of the Crusades,* 3 vols. (Cambridge: Cambridge University Press, 1951–1954). The fullest treatment of the subject by a single scholar; goes well beyond the Crusades.

Special Studies

Aziz A. Atiya, *The Crusade in the Later Middle Ages* (Millwood, N.Y.: Kraus, 1965). A study of the propaganda and the expeditions that marked the decline of the crusading movement.

J. W. Barker, *Manuel II Palaeologus, 1390–1425* (New Brunswick, N.J.: Rutgers University Press, 1969). Good monograph on a late Byzantine emperor.

Caroline M. Barron and Anne F. Sutton, eds., *Medieval London Widows, 1300–1500* (London: Hambledon Press, 1994). Fourteen richly detailed short biographies.

Charles M. Brand, *Byzantium Confronts the West, 1180–1204* (Cambridge, Mass.: Harvard University Press, 1968). Scholarly study of the diplomacy of an important period.

Claude Cahen, *Pre-Ottoman Turkey* (New York: Taplinger, 1968). The only extensive survey work in English on the subject; by the leading authority on the period before 1330.

Answar G. Chejne, *Muslim Spain: Its History and Culture* (Minneapolis: University of Minnesota Press, 1974). Full inquiry into Spain's political and cultural history; strong on Granada.

M. A. Cook, ed., *A History of the Ottoman Empire to 1730* (Cambridge: Cambridge University Press, 1976). Drawn from the Cambridge History of Islam and the Cambridge Modern History.

David d'Avray, *Death and the Prince: Memorial Preaching before 1350* (New York: Oxford University Press, 1995). A study of views on death and the afterlife.

J. L. I. Fennell, *Ivan the Great of Moscow* (New York: Macmillan, 1961). Valuable monograph.

Herbert A. Gibbons, *The Foundation of the Ottoman Empire* (Totowa, N.J.: Biblio Distributors, 1968). An older work whose conclusions are again finding favor.

Halil Inalcik, *The Ottoman Empire: The Classical Age, 1300–1600* (London: Weidenfeld & Nicolson, 1973). Monograph by a distinguished Turkish scholar.

Norman Itzkowitz, *Ottoman Empire and Islamic Tradition* (Chicago: University of Chicago Press, 1980). Brief introduction covering the period to the end of the eighteenth century.

Angus MacKay, *Spain in the Middle Ages: From Frontier to Empire, 1000–1500* (New York: St. Martin's, 1977). Excellent summary.

Joshua Prawer, *The Crusaders' Kingdom* (New York: Praeger, 1972). A fine study of the Crusader states as European colonies.

Donald E. Queller, *The Fourth Crusade: The Conquest of Constatinople, 1201–1204* (Philadelphia: University of Pennsylvania Press, 1977). A fine look at the reasons for the crusaders' attack on the Byzantine capital.

George Vernadsky, *The Mongols and Russia* (New Haven, Conn.: Yale University Press, 1953). Volume III of the Yale History of Russia.

Paul Wittek, *The Rise of the Ottoman Empire* (London: Royal Asiatic Society, 1938). A suggestive and still valuable essay on the elements that helped to advance the Ottoman state.

Sources

Arab Historians of the Crusades, ed. Francesco Gabrieli (Berkeley: University of California Press, 1984).

An Arab-Syrian Gentleman and Warrior in the Period of the Crusades: Memoirs of Usamah ibn-Munquidh, trans. P. K. Hitti (New York: Columbia University Press, 1929).

Anna Comnena, *The Alexiad,* trans. E. A. S. Dawes (New York: AMS Press, 1976). The life and reign of Emperor Alexius Comnenus (from 1081–1118), by his daughter.

The Crusades through Arab Eyes, ed. Amin Maalouf, trans. Jon Rothschild (New York: Schocken Books, 1987). A collection of various Arab perceptions of the crusaders and their wars.

Foucher of Chartres, *Chronicle of the First Crusade,* trans. M. E. McGinty (Philadelphia: University of Pennsylvania Press, 1941).

Turkish Letters of Ogier Ghiselin de Busbecq, Imperial Ambassador at Constantinople, 1554–1562, ed. and trans. Edward Foster (Oxford: Clarendon Press, 1927).

William, Archbishop of Tyre, *A History of Deeds Done beyond the Sea,* trans. E. A. Babcock and A. C. Krey, 2 vols. (New York: Columbia University Press, 1943). The greatest contemporary account of the crusaders' Levant.

CHAPTER 2: The Rise of the Nation

The West: General Accounts

Phillipe Ariès, *Centuries of Childhood,* trans. Robert Baldick (New York: Random House, 1965), and *Western Attitudes toward Death,* trans. Patricia M. Ranum (Baltimore: Johns Hopkins University Press, 1975). Early works to present data and speculation on two subjects previously ignored by historians.

Margaret Aston, *The Fifteenth Century: The Prospect of Europe* (New York: Norton, 1979). An overall view emphasizing social and cultural history; abundantly illustrated.

Myron P. Gilmore, *The World of Humanism, 1453–1517* (New York: Harper, 1952). Good introductory account.

Beatrice Gottlieb, *The Family in the Western World from the Black Death to the Industrial Age* (New York: Oxford University Press, 1993). A sweeping survey of family history.

Denys Hay, *Europe in the Fourteenth and Fifteenth Centuries* (New York: Holt, 1966). Excellent social, political, and economic survey with useful bibliographical footnotes.

George Holmes, *Europe: Hierarchy and Revolt, 1320–1450* (New York: Harper and Row, 1976). Clear look at the fourteenth century in particular.

Johan Huizinga, *The Waning of the Middle Ages* (New York: St. Martin's, 1924). Celebrated re-creation of the atmosphere of a whole era; emphasizes France and the Low Countries.

Frederic C. Lane, *Venice: A Maritime Republic* (Baltimore: Johns Hopkins University Press, 1973). Tough-minded account, by an economic historian, of the rise and slow decline of Venice.

M. M. Postan, *Medieval Trade and Finance* (Cambridge: Cambridge University Press, 1973). A complex inquiry into the uses of credit and the sources of capital formation.

Philip Ziegler, *The Black Death* (New York: Harper and Row, 1971). Graphic details of the havoc wrought by the plague.

National Monarchies

Christopher Allman, *Henry V* (Berkeley: University of California Press, 1993). An admirable short biography.

Stanley B. Chrimes, *English Constitutional History* (New York: AMS Press, 1975). Reliable manual.

J. H. Elliott, *Imperial Spain, 1469–1716* (New York: New American Library, 1977). Classic survey.

James C. Holt, *Robin Hood* (London: Thames and Hudson, 1982). Inquiry into the origins and meaning of a famous medieval legend.

John E. A. Joliffe, *Constitutional History of Medieval England* (New York: Norton, 1967). Good on the "new feudalism" to 1485.

P. S. Lewis, *Later Medieval France: The Polity* (New York: St. Martin's, 1968), and P. M. Kendall, *Louis XI* (New York: Norton, 1971). Stimulating studies.

Roger Lochyear and Andrew Thrush, *Henry VII* (London: Longmans, 1997). An introductory biography of the founder of the Tudor dynasty.

John Lynch, *Spain under the Hapsburgs, Vol. I* (New York: New York University Press, 1981). Begins with a good, brief evaluation of the work of Ferdinand and Isabella.

J. H. Mariejol, *The Spain of Ferdinand and Isabella,* ed. Benjamin Keen (New Brunswick, N.J.: Rutgers University Press, 1961). Celebrated older study by a French scholar; edited to bring it abreast of twentieth-century scholarship.

May McKisack, *The Fourteenth Century,* and Ernest F. Jacob, *The Fifteenth Century* (Oxford: Clarendon Press, 1959, 1961). Detailed, scholarly volumes in the Oxford History of England.

Edward Perroy, *The Hundred Years' War* (New York: Capricorn, 1965). The standard work on the subject and the best introduction to the late medieval history of France.

Richard Rex, *Henry VIII and the English Reformation* (New York: St. Martin's Press, 1993). The most recent study of the "founder" of the Anglican church.

Barbara W. Tuchman, *A Distant Mirror: The Calamitous 14th Century* (New York: Knopf, 1979). Beautifully written, rich account of the times.

Germany and Italy

Cecelia M. Ady, *Lorenzo de' Medici and Renaissance Italy* (New York: Collier, 1962). Brief, popular account.

Hans Baron, *The Crisis of the Early Italian Renaissance* (Princeton, N.J.: Princeton University Press, 1966). Monograph affording many insights into Renaissance politics.

Geoffrey Barraclough, *The Origins of Modern Germany* (Oxford: Blackwell, 1957). Still the best general treatment of late medieval Germany in English.

Jacob Burckhardt, *The Civilization of the Renaissance in Italy*, 2 vols. (New York: Harper and Row, 1958). Famous interpretation now more than a century old; its contention that the modern state originated in Renaissance Italy is no longer generally accepted.

F. L. Carsten, *Princes and Parliaments in Germany from the Fifteenth to the Eighteenth Century* (Oxford: Clarendon Press, 1959). Scholarly study of Würtemberg, Saxony, Bavaria, and other German states.

Federico Chabod, *Machiavelli and the Renaissance* (Cambridge, Mass.: Harvard University Press, 1960). Pithy, sympathetic evaluation, which may be contrasted with the more critical Herbert Butterfield, *The Statecraft of Machiavelli* (New York: Collier, 1962).

John R. Hale, *Machiavelli and Renaissance Italy* (New York: Harper and Row, n.d.). Good brief source.

J. G. A. Pocock, *The Machiavellian Moment: Florentine Political Thought and the Atlantic Republican Tradition* (Princeton, N.J.: Princeton University Press, 1975). A fine, original interpretation.

Sources

Jean Froissart, *Chronicles of England, France, Spain, etc.* (Baltimore: Penguin, 1978). A great narrative source of late medieval history.

Sam Kinser and Isabelle Cazeaux, *The Memoirs of Phillippe de Commynes* (Columbia: University of South Carolina Press, 1969). Well-edited translation. Another recent translation is by M. Jones, *Commynes: Memoirs* (Baltimore: Penguin, 1972).

Niccolò Machiavelli, *The Chief Works and Others*, 3 vols., trans. Allan Gilbert (Durham, N.C.: Duke University Press, 1965). A scholarly translation. Older translations of *The Prince* and *The Discourses* are available in many paperback editions.

CHAPTER 3: The Renaissance

General Accounts

Susan G. Bell, ed., *Women from the Greeks to the French Revolution* (Belmont, Calif.: Wadsworth, 1973). A seminal collection.

Marvin B. Becker, *Florence in Transition*, 2 vols. (Baltimore: Johns Hopkins University Press, 1967–68). Study of Florence in the fourteenth century. Consult also *Medieval Italy* (Bloomington: Indiana University Press, 1981), a study of the relationship between religious and secular thought.

Gene A. Brucker, *Renaissance Florence* (Melbourne, Fla.: Krieger, 1975). A sound introduction.

Alison Brown, *The Renaissance* (London: Longman, 1999). An elegant and brief introduction to the Renaissance.

Peter Burke, *The Italian Renaissance: Culture and Society in Italy* (Princeton: Princeton University Press, 1999). A survey by one of the leading cultural historians of the Italian Renaissance.

Peter Burke, *Culture and Society in Renaissance Italy, 1420–1540* (New York: Scribner's, 1972). Major look at how "taste" developed in Renaissance terms; by a leading inquirer into methods of popular culture studies.

Karl H. Dannenfeldt, ed., *The Renaissance: Medieval or Modern?* (Lexington, Mass.: D.C. Heath, 1973). A collection of essays directed to the question.

Elizabeth L. Eisenstein, *The Printing Press as an Agent of Change* (Cambridge: Cambridge University Press, 1979). Fundamental argument that print revolutionized the world.

Lucien Febvre, *Life in Renaissance France*, trans. Marian Rothstein (Cambridge, Mass.: Harvard University Press, 1979). Short, provocative "silhouette of a civilization."

Lucien Febvre and Henri-Jean Martin, *The Coming of the Book: The Impact of Printing, 1450–1800*, trans. David Gerard (New York: Schocken, 1976). Seminal study of the importance of printing.

Wallace K. Ferguson, *The Renaissance in Historical Thought: Five Centuries of Interpretation* (New York: AMS Press, 1977). Valuable and stimulating monograph.

J. R. Hale, *Renaissance Europe: Individual and Society, 1480–1520* (Berkeley: University of California Press, 1978). Remains one of the influential histories of the period.

J. R. Hale, ed., *A Concise Encyclopedia of the Italian Renaissance* (Oxford: Oxford University Press, 1981). Thorough, well-organized coverage by topics and persons.

Denys Hay, *The Italian Renaissance in its Historical Background* (Cambridge: Cambridge University Press, 1977). Valuable treatment of the historiography of the topic.

Denys Hay, ed., *The Renaissance Debate* (Melbourne, Fla.: Krieger, 1976). Excerpts illustrating contrasting points of view.

Lisa Jardine, *Worldly Goods: A New History of the Renaissance* (New York: Norton, 1996). Argues for the central place of material culture in our understanding of "Renaissance."

Robert S. Lopez, *The Three Ages of the Italian Renaissance* (Oxford: Oxford University Press, 1981). Fine lectures that argue for three stages of Renaissance development.

Garrett Mattingly et al., *Renaissance Profiles* (New York: Harper and Row, n.d.). Lively sketches of nine representative Italians, including Petrarch, Machiavelli, Leonardo, and Michelangelo.

The New Cambridge Modern History, Vol. I: *The Renaissance* (Cambridge: Cambridge University Press, 1957). Chapters by experts in many fields; uneven but useful for reference.

J. H. Plumb, *The Italian Renaissance* (New York: Harper and Row, 1965). Concise historical and cultural survey.

Eugene F. Rice, Jr., and Anthony Grafton, *The Foundations of Early Modern Europe, 1460–1559*, 2nd edition (New York: Norton, 1994). Good general introduction.

Ingrid Rowland, *The Culture of the High Renaissance: Ancients and Moderns in Sixteenth-Century Rome* (Cambridge: Cambridge University Press, 1998). Explores the reception of classical texts and objects in the Rome of the Renaissance papacy.

Lucette Valensi, *The Birth of the Despot: Venice and the Sublime Porte* (Ithaca, N.Y.: Cornell University Press, 1993). Crisply clear.

The Economy

Fernand Braudel, *Capitalism and Material Life, 1400–1800,* trans. Mariam Kochan (New York: Harper and Row, 1974). A rich look at fashion, housing, food, and drink.

The Cambridge Economic History of Europe, Vol. II: *Trade and Industry in the Middle Ages;* Vol. III: *Economic Organization and Policies in the Middle Ages* (Cambridge: Cambridge University Press, 1954, 1965). Advanced scholarly work and a mine of information.

Richard Ehrenberg, *Capital and Finance in the Renaissance: A Study of the Fuggers and Their Connections* (New York: Kelley, 1963). An instructive case history.

Richard W. Unger, *The Ship in the Medieval Economy, 600–1600* (London: Croom Helm, 1980). Brings together recent reinterpretations on the significance of medieval shipping.

Literature and Thought

R. R. Bolgar, *The Classical Heritage and Its Beneficiaries from the Carolingian Age to the End of the Renaissance* (Cambridge: Cambridge University Press, 1977). On the question of continuity.

Natalie Zemon Davis, *Society and Culture in Early Modern France* (Palo Alto, Calif.: Stanford University Press, 1975). Especially good on attitudes toward women.

Eugenio Garin, *Italian Humanism* (Westport, Conn.: Greenwood, 1976). Good scholarly survey.

Gilbert Highet, *The Classical Tradition: Greek and Roman Influences on Western Literature* (London: Oxford University Press, 1949). Lively, somewhat dated, general survey.

George Holmes, *The Florentine Enlightenment, 1400–1450* (New York: Pegasus, 1969). Informative monograph on humanists fascinated with classicism.

Johan Huizinga, *Erasmus and the Age of the Reformation* (New York: Harper and Row, 1957). Excellent analysis by a distinguished Dutch scholar.

Walter Kaiser, *Praisers of Folly* (Cambridge, Mass.: Harvard University Press, 1963). Folly and fools in the writings of Erasmus, Rabelais, and Shakespeare.

Paul O. Kristeller, *Renaissance Thought and Its Sources* (New York: Columbia University Press, 1981). Valuable study; stresses diversity.

N. A. Robb, *Neoplatonism of the Italian Renaissance* (New York: Octagon, 1968). Good treatment of an intellectual common denominator of the age.

Roberto Weiss, *The Spread of Italian Humanism* (New York: Hutchinson's University Library, 1964). Lucid, brief introduction.

Science

Herbert Butterfield, *The Origins of Modern Science, 1300–1800,* rev. ed. (New York: Free Press, 1965). A controversial interpretation; minizes the scientific contribution of the Renaissance.

A. C. Crombie, *Medieval and Early Modern Science,* 2d ed. (Cambridge, Mass.: Harvard University Press, 1963). Volume II of this standard survey treats the Renaissance.

Eugenio Garin, *Science and Civic Life in the Italian Renaissance* (Boston: Peter Smith, n.d.). A helpful, scholarly survey.

Emmanuel Leroy Ladurie, *The Mind and Method of the Historian,* trans. Siân and Ben Reynolds (Chicago: University of Chicago Press, 1981). Contains a fine essay on "the unification of the globe by disease" in the fourteenth to seventeenth centuries.

Mary Lindemann, *Medicine and Society in Early Modern Europe* (Cambridge: Cambridge University Press, 1999). A survey of the scholarship on early modern European medicine.

George Sarton, *Six Wings: Men of Science in the Renaissance* (Bloomington: Indiana University Press, 1957), *The Appreciation of Ancient and Medieval Science during the Renaissance* (Philadelphia: University of Pennsylvania Press, 1955), and *The History of Science and the New Humanism* (Cambridge, Mass.: Harvard University Press, 1937). Clear studies by a pioneering historian of science.

Charles Singer et al., *A History of Technology* (Oxford: Oxford University Press, 1954–1958). Volumes II and III relate to the Renaissance. Singer has also written *A Short History of Anatomy and Physiology* (New York: Dover, 1957).

Lynn Thorndike, *Science and Thought in the Fifteenth Century* (New York: Hafner, 1963). By a specialist on medieval science.

Music

Allan W. Atlas, *Renaissance Music: Music in Western Europe, 1400–1600* (New York: Norton, 1998). Introduction to Renaissance music.

Edward J. Dent, *Music of the Renaissance in Italy* (London: British Academy, 1954). Meaty lecture by a great authority.

Gustave Reese, *Music in the Renaissance* (New York: Norton, 1959). Detailed study.

Religion

Timothy Verdon and John Henderson, eds., *Christianity and the Renaissance: Image and Religious Imagination in the Quattrocento* (Syracuse, N.Y.: Syracuse University Press, 1990). A collection of articles exploring the various connections among art, literature, politics, society, and religion in fourteenth-century Italy.

Fine Arts

Frederick Antal, *Florentine Painting and Its Social Background* (New York: Harper and Row, 1975). Suggestive attempt to relate art to social and economic currents.

Otto Benesch, *The Art of the Renaissance in Northern Europe* (Cambridge, Mass.: Harvard University Press, 1945). Examines the interrelations of art, religion, and intellectual developments.

Patricia Fortini Brown, *Art and Life in Renaissance Venice* (New York: Harry N. Abrams, 1997). An elegant study of Renaissance Venetian art.

Kenneth Clark, *Leonardo da Vinci* (New York: Penguin, 1976). Lively and perceptive assessment of his art.

Walter S. Gibson, *Bruegel* (New York: Oxford University Press, 1977). Fine short work with many illustrations.

Creighton Gilbert, *History of Renaissance Art throughout Europe* (New York: Abrams, 1973). Comprehensive and profusely illustrated introduction.

Peter Humfrey, *Painting in Renaissance Venice* (New Haven, Conn.: Yale University Press, 1965). A comprehensive account from Bellini to Tintoretto.

Michael Levey, *The Early Renaissance* (New York: Penguin, 1978). Brief introduction.

Bates Lowry, *Renaissance Architecture* (New York: Braziller, 1962). Brief introduction.

Erwin Panofsky, *Renaissance and Renascences in Western Art* (New York: Harper and Row, 1972); *Studies in Iconology: Humanistic Themes in the Renaissance* (New York: Harper and Row, 1972); *The Life and Art of Albrecht Dürer* (Princeton, N.J.: Princeton University Press, 1955). Stimulating studies by an eminent scholar.

John T. Paoletti and Gary M. Radke, *Art in Renaissance Italy,* 2d ed. (New York: Harry N. Abrams, 2002). An inspired survey of the topic.

Otto von Simson, *The Gothic Cathedral* (New York: Harper and Row, 1964). A full survey.

Rudolf Wittkower, *Architectural Principles in the Age of Humanism* (New York: Norton, 1970). Important study of the links between humanism and design.

Sources

The Autobiography of Benvenuto Cellini, trans. John Addington Symonds (London: Penguin, 1956). An engrossing, inflated look into the life and ideas of the brilliant artist.

Boccaccio, *The Decameron,* ed. Peter A. Bondanella and Mark Musa (New York: Norton, 1980). One of the most popular works of the fourteenth century. The backdrop is the plague, which leads a group of men and women from Italian courts to isolate themselves and entertain themselves with stories, some fabulous, some drawn from experience.

Desiderius Erasmus, *The Praise of Folly* (London, New York: Penguin, 1993). Well annotated edition.

Samuel Putnam, ed., *The Portable Rabelais: Most of Gargantua and Pantagruel* (New York: Penguin, 1977). Well condensed.

James B. Ross and Mary M. McLaughlin, *The Portable Renaissance Reader* (New York: Penguin, 1977). Wide selection.

Giogio Vasari, *The Lives of the Artists,* trans. George Bull (Hammondsworth: Penguin, 1965). The first attempt to define which artists were "great" and "singular," through descriptions of their educations, their commissions, and their works.

CHAPTER 4: Exploration and Expansion

Background and General Accounts

J. N. L. Baker, *A History of Geographical Discovery and Exploration* (Totowa, N.J.: Cooper Square, 1972). A standard work.

The Cambridge Economic History, Vol. IV (Cambridge: Cambridge University Press, 1967). Scholarly essays on expanding Europe in the sixteenth and seventeenth centuries.

Helen Delpar, ed., *The Discoverers: An Encyclopedia of Explorers and Exploration* (New York: McGraw-Hill, 1980). Less inclusive than the title suggests, but with good short essays on the exploration of specific world regions.

Holden Furber, *Rival Empires of Trade in the Orient, 1600–1800* (Minneapolis: University of Minnesota Press, 1976). Thorough, informative look at the conflicting nature of trading empires.

Edward J. Goodman, *The Explorers of South America* (London: Macmillan, 1972). Excellent summary.

Gwyn Jones, *The Norse Atlantic Saga* (London: Oxford University Press, 1964). A summary of Viking exploration.

Samuel Eliot Morison, *The European Discovery of America: The Northern Voyages, A.D. 500–1600* (New York: Oxford University Press, 1971), and *The Southern Voyages, A.D. 1492–1616* (New York: Oxford University Press, 1974). Full, carefully argued, and beautifully written.

Charles E. Nowell, *The Great Discoveries and the First Colonial Empires* (Westport, Conn.: Greenwood, 1982). Handy, brief introduction.

John H. Parry, *The Age of Reconnaissance* (Berkeley: University of California Press, 1981), and *The Establishment of the European Hegemony, 1415–1715: Trade and Explo-*

ration in the Age of the Renaissance (New York: Harper and Row, 1963). Excellent introductions by an expert in the field.

Boies Penrose, *Travel and Discovery in the Renaissance, 1420–1620* (New York: Athaneum, 1962). Informative survey with accounts of voyages not easily available elsewhere.

Hugh Trevor-Roper, ed., *The Age of Expansion: Europe and the World, 1559–1660* (New York: McGraw-Hill, 1968). Less comprehensive in treatment than the title suggests, but with enlightening chapters on the Spaniards, the Dutch, and the Far East.

John Noble Wilford, *The Mapmakers* (New York: Knopf, 1981). A fine retelling of the story of the pioneers of cartography.

The Portuguese

Charles R. Boxer, *The Portuguese Seaborne Empire, 1415–1825* (New York: Knopf, 1969). Admirable study in the History of Human Society series. Boxer has also written a succinct survey covering the same period: *Four Centuries of Portuguese Expansion* (Berkeley: University of California Press, 1965).

Henry H. Hart, *Sea Road to the Indies* (Westport, Conn.: Greenwood, 1971). Deals with da Gama and other Portuguese explorers.

Charles M. Parr, *So Noble a Captain* (Westport, Conn.: Greenwood, 1976). A scholarly treatment of Magellan and his circumnavigation.

The Spaniards

Charles Gibson, *The Aztecs under Spanish Rule* (Palo Alto, Calif.: Stanford University Press, 1964). A case study.

Lewis B. Hanke, *The Spanish Struggle for Justice in the Conquest of America* (Boston: Little, Brown, 1965). Study of an important and often-neglected side of the Spanish record.

Samuel Eliot Morison, *Admiral of the Ocean Sea*, 2 vols. (Boston: Little, Brown, 1942). A controversial book on Columbus, by a historian who retraced Columbus's route in a small ship. Morison has also published the briefer *Christopher Columbus, Mariner* (Boston: Little, Brown, 1955).

John H. Parry, *The Spanish Seaborne Empire* (New York: Knopf, 1966). Excellent account in the useful History of Human Society series.

The Dutch

Charles R. Boxer, *The Dutch Seaborne Empire, 1600–1800* (New York: Humanities Press, 1980). Full survey; another volume in the History of Human Society series.

George Masselman, *The Cradle of Colonialism* (New Haven, Conn.: Yale University Press, 1963). Fine, balanced account of the development of the Dutch Empire in Southeast Asia.

The French and the British

John B. Brebner, *The Explorers of North America, 1492–1806* (New York: Meridian, n.d.). Good, brief survey.

Angus Calder, *Revolutionary Empire* (New York: Dutton, 1981). An ambitious, very readable effort to encompass the entire rise of the English-speaking empires from the fifteenth century to the 1780s.

Nicholas Canny, ed., *The Oxford History of the British Empire*, Vol. I: *The Origins of Empire: British Overseas Enterprise to the Close of the Seventeenth Century* (Oxford: Oxford University Press, 1998). Cutting-edge essays.

Gustave Lanctor, *History of Canada,* 2 vols. (Cambridge, Mass.: Harvard University Press, 1963–1964). Detailed study to 1713.

Anthony Pagden, *Lords of all the World: Ideologies of Empire in Spain, Britain and France c. 1500–c. 1800* (New Haven, Conn.: Yale University Press, 1995). A study of multiple conceptualizations of empire at play in the conquest of the Americas.

Marcel Trudel, *The Beginnings of New France, 1524–1663,* trans. Patricia Claxton (Toronto: McClelland and Stewart, 1973); W. J. Eccles, *Canada under Louis XIV* (Toronto: McClelland and Stewart, 1964). The best short histories of the rise of the French Empire in North America.

R. B. Wernham, *After the Armada: Elizabethan England and the Struggle for Western Europe* (Oxford: Oxford University Press, 1984). Sweeping examination of foreign policy.

Africa, Asia, and the Pacific

Arthur L. Basham, *The Wonder That Was India* (New York: Taplinger, 1968). A survey of Indian history up to the Muslim invasions.

Basil Davidson, *The African Slave Trade,* rev. ed. (Boston: Little, Brown, 1981). By a prolific writer on African history.

Henri Labouret, *Africa before the White Man* (New York: Walker, 1963); Basil Davidson, *Africa in History* (New York: Macmillan, 1974); Roland Oliver and J. D. Fage, *A Short History of Africa* (New York: New York University Press, 1962). Three helpful introductions. Fage has also written *A History of West Africa,* 4th ed. (Cambridge: Cambridge University Press, 1969), and other useful books on the continent.

William Napier et al., *Eastern Islands, Southern Seas: A History of Discovery and Exploration* (London: Aldus Books, 1973). A handsomely illustrated survey.

David Northrup, *Africa's Discovery of Europe, 1450–1850* (New York: Oxford University Press, 2002). African relations to and perceptions regarding Europe.

Edwin O. Reischauer and John K. Fairbank, *East Asia: The Great Tradition* (Boston: Houghton Mifflin, 1960). An expert survey of China, Japan, and Korea from the beginnings. Reischauer has also written *Japan: The Story of a Nation* (New York: Arno, 1974).

George B. Sansom, *A History of Japan, 1334–1615,* and *A History of Japan, 1615–1867* (Palo Alto, Calif.: Stanford University Press, 1961, 1963). Perceptive, readable accounts; a bit dated.

Schuart B. Schwartz, ed., *Implicit Understandings: Observing, Reporting, and Reflecting on the Encounters between Europeans and Other Peoples in the Early Modern Era* (Cambridge: Cambridge University Press, 1994). A collection of articles detailing specific instances of "encounter" between Europeans and people of the Americas, Asia, and Africa.

Jonathan D. Spence, *The Memory Palace of Matteo Ricci* (New York: Penguin, 1984). A brilliant study of the interaction between an Italian Jesuit and sixteenth-century Chinese scholars and courtiers in China.

The Americas

Daviel J. Boorstin, *The Americans: The Colonial Experience* (New York: Random House, 1958). A provocative briefer treatment.

Alfred W. Crosby, *The Columbia Exchange: Biological and Cultural Consequences of 1492* (Westport, Conn.: Greenwood, 1973). Provocative inquiry into the disease frontier and related matters.

Stephen Greenblatt, *Marvelous Possessions: The Wonder of the New World* (Chicago: University of Chicago Press, 1991). A Shakespearean scholar looks at the impact of "discovery" on European imaginations and the emergence of "wonder" as a value and psychological position.

Stephen Greenblatt, ed., *New World Encounters* (Berkeley: University of California Press, 1993). A collection of articles on the impact of the "encounter" between Europeans and indigenous people of the Americas on their respective cultures.

Francis Jennings, *The Invasion of America* (New York: Norton, 1976). Excellent examination of the Europeans as invaders rather than explorers or settlers.

A. P. Newton, *The European Nations in the West Indies, 1493–1688* (New York: Barnes and Noble, 1967). Still an excellent study of a great arena of colonial rivalry.

Anthony Pagden, *The Fall of Natural Man: The American Indian and the Origins of Comparative Ethnology.* (Cambridge: Cambridge University Press, 1982). A pathbreaking study of the transformation of European conceptions of culture and self through European encouters with the native cultures of the Americas.

Jacques Soustelle, *Daily Life of the Aztecs on the Eve of the Spanish Conquest* (Palo Alto, Calif.: Stanford University Press, 1961). Instructive and by an anthropologist.

Stanley J. Stein and Barbara H. Stein, *Colonial Heritage of Latin America* (London: Oxford University Press, 1970). Essays stressing its economic dependence on the parent countries.

Environmental History

Neville Brown, *History and Climate Change: A Eurocentric Perspective* (London: Routledge, 2001).

Donald J. Hughes, *An Environmental History of the World: Humankind's Changing Role in the Community of Life* (London: Routledge, 2001). An excellent, if somewhat anecdotal, general examination of the impact of humankind on the environment.

Donald J. Hughes, ed., *The Face of the Earth: Environment and World History* (Armonk, N.Y.: M.E. Sharpe, 2000). Essays by six scholars, placing specific environmental encounters in a broad context.

Sources

Juan de Betanzos, *Narrative of the Incas,* trans. and ed. Roland Hamilton and Dana Buchanan (Austin: University of Texas Press, 1996). Betanzos recorded the experiences, memories, and oral histories of his Inca wife, Doña Angelina, and other Incas in an effort to preserve Incan perceptions of the final years of the last Inca ruler. This translation is based upon the complete manuscript, discovered in the 1980s.

Pedro de Cieza de León, *The Discovery and Conquest of Peru,* trans. and ed. Alexandra Parma Cook and Noble David Cook (Durham, N.C.: Duke University Press, 1998). Based upon his interviews of other conquistadores and indigenous witnesses, the Spaniard Cieza de León wrote the earliest historical account of the conquest of Peru.

Christopher Columbus, *The Four Voyages,* trans. and ed. J. M. Cohen (Harmondsworth: Penguin, 1969). Texts of Columbus's journals from his four voyages to the Americas, primarily the Caribbean.

Hernan Cortés, *Letters from Mexico,* trans. and ed. Anthony Pagden (New Haven, Conn.: Yale University Press, 1986). Cortés's letters to the Spanish court detailing his conquest and the culture of the Aztec Empire.

Bernal Díaz, *The Conquest of New Spain*, trans. J. M. Cohen (Harmondsworth: Penguin, 1963). An acutely observant witness to Cortés's conquest of the Aztecs.

Eugene D. Genovese and Laura Foner, *Slavery in the New World* (Englewood Cliffs, N.J.: Prentice-Hall, 1969). Materials on the comparative slave policies of the imperial powers.

Richard Hakluyt, *Voyages and Discoveries*, ed. Jack Beeching (Harmondsworth: Penguin, 1972). An anthology of medieval and early modern travel accounts, including the fantastic and the factual.

George Alexander Lensen, ed., *Russia's Eastward Expansion* (New York: Spectrum, 1964). Source materials.

Joseph R. Levenson, ed., *European Expansion and the Counter Example of Asia* (Englewood Cliffs, N.J.: Prentice-Hall, 1967). Materials on technology, religion, social structure, and "spirit."

Fray Ramón Pané, *An Account of the Antiquities of the Indians*, ed. José Juan Arrom, trans. Susan C. Griswold (Durham, N.C.: Duke University Press, 1999). Pané lived among the indigenous people of Hispaniola, recording their lives and beliefs. His account is all the more important because those people and their culture disappeared by the mid-sixteenth century.

Jonathan D. Spence, ed., *The Chan's Great Continent: China in Western Minds* (New York: Norton, 1998). European, then North American perceptions of China from Marco Polo to the present day.

CHAPTER 5: The Age of Reformation

General Accounts

Euan Cameron, *The European Reformation* (Oxford: Oxford University Press, 1991). One of the most recent general surveys, focusing on the early years of the Reformation and giving greater attention to the Catholic Reformation than many other surveys.

Owen Chadwick, *The Reformation* (New York: Penguin, 1964). A comprehensive survey addressed to the general reader.

Arthur G. Dickens, *Reformation and Society in Sixteenth-Century Europe* (New York: Harcourt Brace, 1966). Informative, broad survey; includes many illustrations.

G. R. Elton, *Reformation Europe, 1517–1559* (New York: Harper and Row, 1968). A lively survey summarizing many of the findings in the more ponderous *New Cambridge Modern History: The Reformation* (Cambridge: Cambridge University Press, 1958), which Elton edited.

Robert M. Kingdon, ed., *Transition and Revolution: Problems and Issues of European Renaissance and Reformation History* (Minneapolis, Minn.: Burgess, 1974). Highly influential essays.

H. G. Koenigsburger and George L. Mosse, *Europe in the Sixteenth Century* (London: Longmans, 1971. Up-to-date, scholarly survey; includes excellent bibliographies.

Carter Lindberg, *The European Reformations* (Oxford: Blackwell, 1996). Seeks to present multiple reform movements, but gives primary focus to theologians.

Alister E. McGrath, *The Intellectual Origins of the European Reformation* (Oxford: Blackwell, 1994), and *Reformation Thought* 3d ed., 1999. Clear background studies.

E. William Monter, *Calvin's Geneva* (Melbourne, Fla.: Krieger, 1975). Examines the relationship between an environment and the development of a body of thought.

Eugene F. Rice, Jr., and Anthony Grafton, *The Foundations of Early Modern Europe, 1460–1559*, 2d edition (New York: Norton, 1994). Brief introduction.

Guy E. Swanson, *Religion and Regime* (Ann Arbor: University of Michigan Press, 1967). A challenging and controversial "sociological account of the Reformation."

Special Studies

Peter Mattheson, *The Rhetoric of the Reformation* (Edinburgh: T & T Clark, 1998). A close study of the polemics—in both print and preaching—of the Reformation.

Ulinka Rublack, *The Crimes of Women in Early Modern Germany* (Oxford: Oxford University Press, 1999). A close study of courts, the process of identification of female criminals, and the kinds of crime women were likeliest to commit.

Lee Palmer Wandel, *Voracious Idols and Violent Hands: Iconoclasm in Reformation Zurich, Strasbourg, and Basel* (Cambridge: Cambridge University Press, 1994). Iconoclasm, predominantly a lay and artisanal movement for reform, helps us to understand what was at stake in "Reformation."

Merry Wiesner-Hanks, *Women and Gender in Early Modern Europe*, 2d ed. (New York: Cambridge University Press, 2000). A survey of the scholarship.

The Lutheran Reformation

Karl Brandi, *The Emperor Charles V* (Norwood, Pa.: Telegraph, 1981). Comprehensive study of Luther's antagonist.

Arthur G. Dickens, *The German Nation and Martin Luther* (London: Arnold, 1974). A close look at the problem of the cities, printing, and nationalism.

Hartmann Grisar, *Martin Luther: His Life and Works* (New York: AMS Press, 1971). From the Catholic point of view.

Heiko A. Oberman, *Luther: Man between God and the Devil* (New York: Image Books, 1992). A magisterial study of the reformer.

Ernest G. Schwiebert, *Luther and His Times* (St. Louis: Concordia, 1952). From the Lutheran point of view; particularly useful for the setting and the effects of Luther's revolt.

Gerald Strauss, *Luther's House of Learning* (Baltimiore: Johns Hopkins University Press, 1979). On Luther's educational ideas and the indoctrination of the young.

Protestant Founders: Zwingli, Calvin, and Others

William Bouwsma, *John Calvin: A Sixteenth-Century Portrait* (Oxford: Oxford University Press, 1988). An original biography of Calvin as a Renaissance figure.

Jacques Courvoisier, *Zwingli: A Reformed Theologian* (Atlanta, Ga.: John Knox, 1963). Good study of an important and often-neglected figure.

David Daniell, *William Tyndale* (New Haven, Conn. Yale University Press, 1994). Portrait of an underappreciated genius.

A. G. Dickens, *The English Reformation* (New York: Schocken, 1968). Detailed study through 1559; includes a useful biography.

John D. Mackie, *The Early Tudors, 1485–1558* (Oxford: Clarendon Press, 1972). Authoritative and thorough, especially good on Henry VIII.

Bernd Moeller, *Imperial Cities and the Reformation* (Durham, N.C.: Labyrinth Press, 1982). Translation of three complex, highly influential essays on the cities' role in the Reformation.

Steven E. Ozment, *The Reformation in the Cities* (New Haven, Conn. Yale University Press, 1980). Fresh emphasis on the role of German and Swiss municipalities in furthering the social ethic of Protestantism.

T. H. L. Parker, *Calvin: An Introduction to His Thought* (Louisville: Westminister Press,

1995); and *Calvin's Preaching* (1992): two fine introductions to dimensions of Calvin.

W. P. Stephens, *Zwingli: An Introduction to His Thought* (Oxford: Clarendon Press, 1992). An introduction to Zwingli's theology, quite apart from his activity as a reformer.

François Wendel, *Calvin: The Origins and Development of His Religious Thought* (New York: Harper and Row, 1963). Translation of a solid study of Philip Mainer.

The other Protestant Reformation

Hans-Jürgen Goertz, *The Anabaptists* (London: Routledge, 1996). An introduction by one of the leading scholars of Anabaptists.

T. M. Parker, *The English Reformation to 1558*, 2d ed. (New York: Oxford University Press, 1966). Excellent short account.

George H. Williams, *The Radical Reformation* (London: Westminster, 1977). Encyclopedic study of the Anabaptists and other left-wing reformers.

The Catholic Reformation

Arthur G. Dickens, *The Counter-Reformation* (New York: Norton, 1979). Comprehensive survey by an English Protestant scholar.

James R. Farr, *Authority and Sexuality in Early Modern Burgundy (1550–1730)* (New York: Oxford University Press, 1995). Explores religion, law, and sexual morality during the Catholic Reformation.

Beresford J. Kidd, *The Counter-Reformation* (Westport, Conn.: Greenwood, 1980). Scholarly account by an Anglican.

David M. Luebke, ed., *The Counter-Reformation: The Essential Readings* (Malden, Mass.: Blackwell, 1999). A collection of seminal articles on the topic.

Michael A. Mullett, *The Catholic Reformation* (London: Routledge, 1999). A survey of the new orders, Council of Trent, and lay responses of Catholics.

John O'Malley, S.J., *The First Jesuits* (Cambridge, Mass.: Harvard University Press, 1993). After a quick summary of the founding, this study focuses on the first decades of the order and on specific personalities who shaped the order as they were establishing it.

John O'Malley, S.J., *Trent and All That: Renaming Catholicism in the Early Modern Era* (Cambridge, Mass.: Harvard University Press, 2000). A review of the historiographical debate about what to call the Catholic movements of the sixteenth century.

Protestantism and Progress

Steven Ozment, *Protestants: The Birth of a Revolution* (New York: Doubleday, 1992).

Richard H. Tawney, *Religion and the Rise of Capitalism* (Boston: Peter Smith, 1963). Turns the Weber thesis around to emphasize economic motivation.

Keith Thomas, *Religion and the Decline of Magic* (New York: Charles Scribner's Sons, 1971). Influential study arguing for progress from medieval superstition through Protestant Reformation to science and the Enlightenment.

Ernst Toeltsch, *Protestantism and Progress* (Boston: Beacon, 1958). By a leading church historian.

Max Weber, *The Protestant Ethic and the Spirit of Capitalism* (New York: Scribner's, 1958). Advances the famous thesis on the interrelationships of religion and economics.

Sources

Henry S. Bettenson, ed., *Documents of the Christian Church*, 2d ed. (New York: Oxford University Press, 1963). Admirable compilation; particularly valuable for the Reformation.

John Calvin, *Institutes of the Christian Religion*, 2 vols., ed. John T. McNeill, trans. Ford Lewis Battles (Philadelphia: Westminster Press, 1960). Calvin's most widely read work, which he saw as an instrument for teaching the faithful.

John Dillenberger, ed., *John Calvin, Selections from His Writings* (Missoula, Mont.: Scholars Press, 1975). A range of Calvin's texts, from letters through sermons and ordinances to selections from the *Institutes*.

H. J. Hillerbrand, ed., *The Reformation in Its Own Words* (New York: Harper and Row, n.d.). Another useful compilation of primary material.

Ignatius Loyola, *St. Ignatius' Own Story. As Told to Luis Gonzalez de Camara*, trans. William J. Young, S. J. (Chicago: Loyola University Press, 1980). The autobiography of the founder of the Society of Jesus, or the Jesuits.

Ignatius Loyola, *The Spiritual Exercises of St. Ignatius*, trans. Anthony Mottola (Garden City, N.Y.: Image Books, 1964). The central text of the Jesuits.

E. G. Rupp and Benjamin Drewery, eds., *Martin Luther* (New York: St. Martin's, 1970). An anthology of his significant writings; includes helpful editorial comment.

Lewis W. Spitz, ed., *The Protestant Reformation* (Englewood Cliffs, N.J.: Prentice-Hall, 1966). Good, quite short collection.

Teresa of Avila, *The Life of Teresa of Jesus*, trans. and ed. E. Allison Peers (New York: Image Books, 1991). The autobiography of the most influential female saint of the Counter-Reformation.

Juan Luis Vives, *The Education of a Christian Woman*, trans. and ed. Charles Fantazzi (Chicago: University of Chicago Press, 2000). The handbook for educating women in Christian virtue and morality.

CHAPTER 6: The Great Powers in Conflict

General Accounts

Trevor Aston, ed., *Crisis in Europe, 1560–1600: Essays from Past and Present* (London: Routledge and Kegan Paul, 1965). Essays from one of the best journals.

Lacey Baldwin Smith, *The Elizabethan World* (Boston: Houghton Mifflin, 1967). Balanced look at the Elizabethans in the context of European history generally.

J. H. Ball, *Merchants and Merchandise: The Expansion of Trade in Europe: 1500–1630* (New York: St. Martin's, 1977). Excellent short survey of sixteenth-century trade.

Fernand Braudel, *Capitalism and Material Life, 1400–1800* (New York: Harper and Row, 1974). Fine, debatable examination of trends in population, climate, and daily life.

The Cambridge Economic History of Europe, Vol. IV: *The Economy of Expanding Europe in the Sixteenth and Seventeenth Centuries* (Cambridge: Cambridge University Press, 1967). Scholarly chapters by experts on selected aspects of the economy.

J. H. Elliott, *Europe Divided, 1559–1598* (Ithaca, N.Y.: Cornell University Press, 1982). Useful introduction to the times of Philip II.

Henry Kamen, *European Society, 1500–1700* (London: Hutchinson, 1985). Revealing social history.

H. G. Koenigsberger and George L. Mosse, *Europe in the Sixteenth Century* (London: Longmans, 1971). An excellent survey with useful bibliographical footnotes.

Marvin R. O'Connell, *The Counter Reformation, 1559–1610* (New York: Harper and Row, 1952), and Carl J. Friedrich, *The Age of the Baroque* (New York: Harper and

Row, 1952). Comprehensive volumes with full biographies; in the Rise of Modern Europe series.

Theodore K. Rabb, *The Struggle for Stability in Early Modern Europe* (New York: Oxford University Press, 1975). A brief, thoughtful inquiry into the use of "crisis" terminology and analysis as the unifying principle for the seventeenth century.

Eugene F. Rice, Jr., and Anthony Grafton, *The Foundations of Early Modern Europe, 1460–1559,* 2d edition (New York: Norton, 1994); and Richard S. Dunn, *The Age of Religious Wars, 1559–1689* (New York: Norton, 1979). Enlightening surveys in a justifiably famous series.

War and Diplomacy

Charles H. Carter, *The Secret Diplomacy of the Habsburgs, 1598–1625* (New York: Columbia University Press, 1964). An instructive case study in diplomatic history.

Ludwig Dehio, *The Precarious Balance: Four Centuries of the European Power Struggle* (New York: Knopf, 1962). A German historian interprets the shifting balance of power beginning with the sixteenth century.

Henry Kamen, *The Rise of Toleration* (London: World University Library, 1972). A short, clear account of changing attitudes toward religious toleration.

Garrett Mattingly, *Renaissance Diplomacy* (Boston: Houghton Mifflin, 1972). A stimulating and indispensable look at the invention of diplomacy, through resident ambassadors.

Charles W. Oman, *A History of the Art of War in the Sixteenth Century* (New York: AMS Press, 1975). Highly interesting examination of a less-studied aspect of history.

Geoffrey Parker, *The Military Revolution: Military Innovation and the Rise of the West, 1500–1800,* 2d ed. (Cambridge: Cambridge University Press, 1996). A pathbreaking study of military technology and strategy in the early modern world.

Spain

Fernand Braudel, *The Mediterranean and the Mediterranean World in the Age of Philip II,* 2d ed. (New York: Harper and Row, 1976). An important geographical and socioeconomic study of Spain's involvement with Italy and the Ottoman Empire.

Cecil John Cadoux, *Philip of Spain and the Netherlands* (Hamden, Conn.: Shoe String, 1969). A sharp attack on Philip II and a defense of William of Orange.

R. T. Davies, *The Golden Century of Spain* (London: Macmillan, 1937), and *Spain in Decline, 1621–1700* (New York: St. Martin's, 1957). Popular accounts addressed to the general reader.

J. H. Elliot, *The Old World and the New, 1492–1650* (Cambridge: Cambridge University Press, 1970). A thoughtful reevaluation of arguments about the impact of bullion on the European and especially the Spanish economy.

John Lynch, *Spain under the Habsburgs,* 2 vols. (New York: New York University Press, 1981). A thorough and up-to-date scholarly study; the first volume treats the sixteenth century; the second, the seventeenth.

Colin Martin and Geoffrey Parker, *The Spanish Armada* (London: Penguin, 1992). A readable and dramatic account.

Antonio Dominguez Ortiz, *The Golden Age of Spain, 1516–1659,* trans. James Casey (New York: Basic Books, 1971). Balanced account with excellent sections on the economy, religious life, and cultural developments.

Geoffrey Parker, *Philip II* (Boston: Little, Brown, 1978). Perhaps the best short biography. *The Army of Flanders and the Spanish Road, 1567–1659* (Cambridge: Cambridge University Press, 1972). Close study of the disastrous consequences for the

Spanish economy of keeping a vast army in the field. *The Dutch Revolt* (Ithaca, N.Y.: Cornell University Press, 1977). Fresh interpretation based on wide-ranging sources. See also Colin Martin.

R. A. Stradling, *Europe and the Decline of Spain* (London: Allen and Unwin, 1981). Up-to-date, methodologically fashionable look at "the Spanish system" from 1580 to 1720.

France

Natalie Zemon Davis, *Society and Culture in Early Modern France* (Stanford, Calif.: Stanford University Press, 1975). Path-breaking studies of apprentices, women, and "rites of violence."

Mark Greengrass, *France in the Age of Henri IV and the Struggle for Stability*, 2d ed. (London: Longmans, 1995). A survey of France after the Wars of Religion.

Albert L. Guerard, *France in the Classical Age: The Life and Death of an Ideal* (New York: Brazillier, 1956). Lively, provocative, and highly personal interpretation of French history from the Renaissance to Napoleon.

Alexandra D. Lublinskaya, *French Absolutism: The Crucial Phase, 1629–1690* (Cambridge: Cambridge University Press, 1969). Good on Richelieu.

J. E. Neale, *The Age of Catherine de' Medici* (Lawrence, Mass.: Merrimack, 1978). Excellent short introduction to French civil and religious change.

W. J. Stankiewicz, *Politics and Religion in Seventeenth-Century France* (Westport, Conn.: Greenwood, 1976). Goes back to the *politiques* of the late sixteenth century.

G. R. R. Treasure, *Seventeenth-Century France* (London: John Murray, 1981). Balanced, full survey.

England

Stanley T. Bindoff, *Tudor England* (Baltimore: Penguin, 1967). Sound, short introduction.

Linda Colley, *Britons: Forging the Nation, 1707–1837* (New Haven, Conn.: Yale University Press, 1992). On how a distinctive sense of nationhood grew.

Antonio Fraser, *Mary, Queen of Scots* (New York: Delacorte, 1978). Popular biography of Elizabeth's impulsive antagonist.

W. P. Haugaard, *Elizabeth and the English Reformation* (Cambridge: Cambridge University Press, 1968). Excellent scholarly assessment.

Christopher Hibbert, *The English: A Social History, 1066–1945* (New York: Norton, 1987). A rich, long, popular history, especially good for this period.

Elizabeth Jenkins, *Elizabeth the Great* (New York: Coward, 1959). Sound biography focused more on the person than on the office.

Wallace T. MacCaffrey, *Queen Elizabeth and the Making of Policy, 1572–1588* (Princeton, N.J.: Princeton University Press, 1981). Intricate analysis of Elizabeth's policy, focusing (as she did) on the Netherlands. *The Shaping of the Elizabethan Regime* (Princeton, N.J.: Princeton University Press, 1971). Able study of Elizabeth's early years in power.

John D. Mackie, *The Earlier Tudors, 1485–1558;* and J. B. Black, *The Reign of Elizabeth, 1558–1603* (London: Clarendon Press, 1952, 1960). Comprehensive, scholarly volumes in the Oxford History of England.

Garrett Mattingly, *The Armada* (Boston: Houghton Mifflin, n.d.). A beautifully written work of history.

Conyers Read, *The Tudors* (New York: Norton, 1969). Excellent introduction to the interrelations of personalities and politics. Also *The Government of England under Elizabeth* (Cranbury, N.J.: Folger Books, 1979).

J. J. Scarisbrick, *Henry VIII* (Berkeley: University of California Press, 1968). A fine scholarly biography; may be supplemented with a psychological study by Lacey Baldwin-Smith, *Henry VIII: The Mask of Royalty* (Lawrence, Mass.: Merrimack, 1980).

The Dutch Republic

Violet Barbour, *Capitalism in Amsterdam in the Seventeenth Century* (New York: AMS Press, 1978). Illuminating study of an important factor in Dutch success.

Jan De Vries, *The First Modern Economy: Success, Failure, and Perseverance in the Dutch Economy, 1500–1815* (Cambridge: Cambridge University Press, 1997). Striking reinterpretation.

Pieter Geyl, *The Revolt of the Netherlands, 1555–1609* (New York: Barnes and Noble, 1980), and *The Netherlands in the Seventeenth Century* (New York: Barnes and Noble, 1964). Detailed studies by a Dutch historian. A briefer statement may be found in his *History of the Low Countries* (New York: St. Martin's, 1964).

Johan Huizinga, *Dutch Civilization in the Seventeenth Century and Other Essays* (New York: Harper and Row, n.d.). The title essay is a thoughtful evaluation by another distinguished Dutch historian.

Jonathan Israel, *The Dutch Republic: Its, Rise, Greatness, and Fall, 1477–1806* (Oxford: Oxford University Press, 1995). A magisterial survey of the politics and society of the provinces which became the Netherlands.

C. V. Wedgewood, *William the Silent* (New York: Norton, 1968). Sound biography of the Dutch national hero.

Germany and the Thirty Years' War

Erich Kahler, *The Germans*, trans. Robert and Rita Kimbler (Princeton, N.J.: Princeton University Press, 1982). Good on the problem of German particularism; strong on the Reformation issues.

Geoffrey Parker, ed. *The Thirty Years' War* (London: Routledge, 1997). A substantial and thoughtful collectively written narrative of the war.

Theodore K. Rabb, ed., *The Thirty Years' War: Problems of Motive, Extent, and Effect* (New York: University Press of America, 1981). Sampler of differing views of these controversial questions.

Michael Roberts, *Gustavus Adolphus: A History of Sweden, 1611–1632*, 2 vols. (New York: Longmans, 1953–1958). Sympathetic, detailed biography.

Sigfrid H. Steinberg, *The "Thirty Years' War" and the Conflict for European Hegemony, 1600–1660* (New York: Norton, 1967). Brief account.

C. V. Wedgewood, *The Thirty Years' War* (New York: Methuen, 1981). Full and generally well-balanced narrative.

Science

Fulton H. Anderson, *Francis Bacon: His Career and His Thought* (Westport, Conn.: Greenwood, 1977). Good appraisal of an important figure.

Floris H. Cohen, *The Scientific Revolution: A Historiographical Inquiry* (Chicago: University of Chicago Press, 1994). Explores the different conceptualizations of (and oppositions to) the "scientific revolution" in the scholarship.

E. J. Dijksterhuis, *The Mechanization of the World Picture* (Cambridge: Cambridge University Press, 1961). Able study of the intellectual impact of science.

Stillman Drake, *Galileo Studies: Personality, Tradition, and Revolution* (Ann Arbor: University of Michigan Press, 1970). Excellent set of essays on the range of Galileo's interests.

Alfred R. Hall, *The Scientific Revolution, 1500–1800* (Boston: Beacon, 1966). A solid account, somewhat dense with detail.

Lisa Jardine, *Ingenious Pursuits: Building the Scientific Revolution* (New York: Anchor Books, 1999). Explores the emergence of "science" among a diverse group of thinkers.

Hugh Kearney, *Science and Change, 1500–1700* (New York: McGraw-Hill, 1971). Succinct, wide-ranging introduction to a still much-debated subject.

Thomas S. Kuhn, *The Copernican Revolution: Planetary Astronomy in the Development of Western Thought* (Cambridge, Mass.: Harvard University Press, 1957). Complex, path-breaking study.

Franklin Le Van Baumer, *Religion and the Rise of Skepticism* (New York: Harcourt, n.d.). Assesses the spiritual impact of science.

David C. Lindberg and Ronald L. Numbers, eds., *God and Nature: Historical Essays on the Encounter between Christianity and Science* (Berkeley: University of California Press, 1986). Essays on the encounter from earliest Christianity to the present.

David B. Ruderman. *Jewish Thought and Scientific Discovery in Early Modern Europe* (New Haven, Conn.: Yale University Press, 1995). On *converso* physicians.

Giorgio de Santillana, *The Crime of Galileo* (Chicago: University of Chicago Press, 1955). Stimulating examination of how Galileo's thought constituted a heresy for the church.

Steven Shapin and Simon Schaffer, *Leviathan and the Air-Pump: Hobbes, Boyle, and the Experimental Life* (Princeton, N.J.: Princeton University Press, 1985). An important study of the political and intellectual context for the "scientific revolution."

Slavery

Robin Blackburn, *The Making of New World Slavery: From the Baroque to the Modern, 1492–1800* (London: Verso, 1997). A survey of the importation and maintenance of all forms of slavery in the Americas.

David Eltis, *The Rise of African Slavery in the Americas* (Cambridge: Cambridge University Press, 2000). More narrowly concerned with slaves imported from Africa and their significance for the political claims of the Americas.

Sources

G. R. Elton, *The Tudor Constitution: Documents and Commentary* (Cambridge: Cambridge University Press, 1972). Fine selection of the key documents.

Hiram Hayden, ed., *The Portable Elizabethan Reader* (New York: Penguin, 1980). A good anthology.

Samuel Putnam, ed., *The Portable Cervantes* (New York: Putnam, 1977). Selections from the editor's admirable translation of Don Quixote.

Nancy Roelker, ed., *The Paris of Henry of Navarre* (Cambridge, Mass.: Harvard University Press, 1958). Selections from the informative *Memoires-journaux of Pierre de L'Etoile*, a rich source of social history.

Hans J. C. Von Grimmelshausen, *Simplicius Simplicissimus* (Indianapolis: Bobbs Merril, 1965). Picaresque but realistic novel written in the seventeenth century and set against the background of war-ravaged Germany.

Charles Wilson and Geoffrey Parker, eds., *An introduction to the Sources of European Economic History, 1500–1800* (Ithaca, N.Y.: Cornell University Press, 1977). Valuable compilation of contemporary data on economic developments.

Index

9 780195 154481